TAX AND EXPENDITURE LIMITATIONS: HOW TO IMPLEMENT AND LIVE WITHIN THEM

TAX AND EXPENDITURE LIMITATIONS: HOW TO IMPLEMENT AND LIVE WITHIN THEM

Edited by Jerome G. Rose

Center for Urban Policy Research
Rutgers, the State University of New Jersey
P. O. Box 489
Piscataway, New Jersey 08854

Published in the United States of America
by the Center for Urban Policy Research
Building 4051–Kilmer Campus
New Brunswick, New Jersey 08903

Library of Congress Cataloging in Publication Data

Main entry under title:

Tax and expenditure limitations.

1. Tax and expenditure limitations–United States–Addresses, essays, lectures. I. Rose, Jerome G. II. Rutgers University. Center for Urban Policy Research.
HJ2051.T283 336.73 82-1251
ISBN 0-88285-078-4 AACR2

Contents

III. THE NEW JERSEY SYSTEM

IV. THE TEXAS SYSTEM

V. THE MASSACHUSETTS SYSTEM

VI. THE VARIETY OF CONSEQUENCES OF TAX AND EXPENDITURE LIMITATIONS

ABOUT THE EDITOR

Jerome G. Rose has a J.D. from Harvard Law School and is a member of the New York Bar. He is professor of urban planning at Rutgers University and editor-in-chief of *Real Estate Law Journal.* He is author of *The Legal Advisor on Home Ownership* (1967); *Landlords and Tenants: A Complete Guide to the Residential Rental Relationship* (1973); *Legal Foundations of Environmental Planning: Cases and Materials on Environmental Law* (1974); *New Approaches to State Land Use Policies,* with Melvin R. Levin and Joseph S. Slavett (1974); *The Transfer of Development Rights* (1976); *After Mount Laurel: The New Suburban Zoning,* with Robert E. Rothman (1977); and *Legal Foundations of Land Use Planning* (1979).

Acknowledgments

This collection of essays was made possible by the interest and support of two persons: Professor Donald G. Hagman and Dr. George Sternlieb. Professor Hagman conceived of the idea, organized a symposium on tax and expenditure limitations, and helped to persuade the participants to put their ideas into written form. Dr. Sternlieb recognized the potential value of such a collection and made the editorial facilities of the Rutgers Center for Urban Policy Research available for its publication.

Barbara Tieger of the Center for Urban Policy Research and Barry Jones converted the manuscript into a book. Carole Baker assisted in the preparation of two of the essays on the New Jersey "cap" law.

The following authors contributed the articles of which this collection is comprised:

Angiolillo-Bent, Laurie, J.D., Harvard Law School

Chernick, Howard, Office of Income Security Policy, U.S. Department of Health and Human Services

Freilich, Robert, Hulen Professor of Law in Urban Affairs, University of Missouri-Kansas City School of Law

Hagman, Donald G., Professor of Law, U.C.L.A. School of Law

Hanson, Royce, Chairman, The Maryland-National Capital Park and Planning Commission

Kramer, Bruce M., Professor of Law, Texas Tech University School of Law

Mikels, Marjorie, J.D., U.C.L.A. School of Law

Netter, Edith, Staff Attorney, American Planning Association and Editor, *Land Use Law and Zoning Digest*

Perry, Steven M., J.D., University of Missouri-Kansas City School of Law

Peterson, George, Director of the Public Finance Program, The Urban Institute

Reschovsky, Andrew, Assistant Professor of Economics, Tufts University

Reock, Ernest C., Jr., Director, Bureau of Government Research, Rutgers University

Rose, Jerome G., Professor of Urban Planning, Rutgers University

Strauss, Betsy, Legal Counsel, League of California Cities

Wolman, Harold, Senior Research Associate, Public Finance Program, Urban Institute

We wish to express our appreciation to the following publications for their permission to reprint material published therein:

The Real Estate Law Journal

Rose, "Limitations on State Taxation and Spending: The Impact on Future Land Use and Development," 9 *Real Estate Law Journal* 91 (1980)

Kramer, "Development Agreements: To What Extent Are They Enforceable?" 10 *Real Estate Law Journal* 29 (1981)

Rose, "How Will Real Estate Development be Affected by State Tax and Spending Limitations?—Predictions by Some Land Use Experts," 10 *Real Estate Journal* (1982)

The Urban Interest

Wolman & Peterson, "Policy Consequences of Local Expenditure Constraint," 2 *The Urban Interest* 75 (1980)

I. INTRODUCTION TO TAX AND EXPENDITURE LIMITATIONS (TELS)

1

Exploration of the Concepts and Summary of the Articles

JEROME G. ROSE

A New Era in Public Finance

Limitations on the power of state and local governments to tax and spend public funds are not new. However, until the beginning of the recent "Era of Proposition 13" these limitations have been more covert, indirect, and subtle. For example, forty eight states have had, for many decades, constitutional and statutory limits on the ability of state and local governments to incur debts. Debt limitations, a common constitutional provision, provide an indirect limitation on the ability of governments to spend because if a government cannot borrow to spend it must increase taxes, and political forces usually limit the ability to obtain increased revenue by increasing taxes.

One of the earlier forms of spending limitations, adopted by several states, is the constitutional requirement for a larger than majority vote for revenue and appropriation bills. Many states have instituted, long before the "Era of Proposition 13," restrictions on the power of local governments to tax and expend local revenue.

It was not until the mid 1970s that tax and expenditure limitations (hereafter referred to as TELS) began to attract national attention. New Jersey adopted its spending limitations, known as the "cap" law, in 1976. Tennessee adopted a constitutional limitation on spending in 1978 and California adopted Proposition 13 that same year. These new limitations on state and local taxation and spending have created a new era of state and local finance and have a direct effect on the public policy and planning programs that depend on the availability of public funds.

Limitations on the ability of state and local governments to raise revenue through taxation and spend that revenue can have a dramatic effect on the delivery of governmental services, the nature, location and extent of future growth and development, and the interrelationship among federal, state, and local governments.

In an effort to explore the implications of the new forms of fiscal restraints on state and local governments, the American Law Institute-American Bar Association (ALI-ABA) scheduled a symposium in Arlington, Virginia in March 1980 under the direction of Professor Donald Hagman, U.C.L.A. School of Law. Professor Hagman invited a group of experts in state and local finance and land use controls to participate in a discussion and analysis of the recently adopted forms of fiscal constraints. Most of the essays in this compendium are based on papers presented at that symposium. In addition, the contribution of several other experts not present at the symposium are included to cover additional important components of the issue.

The California System

The first section presents an analysis of the California system. The paper written by Betsy Strauss, Marjorie Mikels, and Donald Hagman describes the major provisions of Propositions 13 and 4 and suggests some of the effects of those programs on land use policies. Proposition 13 limits the power to *tax.* It has four major provisions: It (1) limits the property tax to one percent of 1975 market value, (2) limits increases in assessments to 2 percent a year except for changes of ownership or new construction; (3) requires a two-thirds vote of the state legislature to increase states taxes; and (4) requires approval of two-thirds of the voters for certain nonproperty taxes imposed by local government.

Proposition 4 limits the power to *spend.* It limits increases in state and local government appropriations to a formula based on increases in population, changes in the national cost of living or changes in statewide per capita personal income, whichever is less.

The authors observe that local governments have adopted four alternative methods to maintain governmental services and still comply with the tax and spending limitations: (1) user fees, (2) private sector capital, (3) special assessments, and (4) long term bonded debt.

Proposition 13 has reduced the revenue available to local government. To maintain the services provided before this reduction in revenue some governments have imposed user charges for such services as police protection, firefighting, and garbage disposal. In addition, some local governments have increased the fees charged to provide services to new developments, such as fees for sewer, water and drainage connections, and building permits.

Privatization of public services is the phrase used by the authors to describe a device by which developers are required to pay for the costs of infrastructure and other service costs for the development. *Development agreements* between subdividers and local governments are authorized by California's Development Agreement Law and will probably become one of the means by which developers will finance a greater amount of public facilities in return for an assurance of stability in land use regulations.

The authors discuss the effect of Proposition 13 on *special assessments* for such development improvements as sewer and water extension, and street and sidewalk paving. Reduced property tax revenue and developer reluctance to finance public facilities has caused local governments to turn to the special assessment to finance public improvements.

The authors discuss the effect of Proposition 13 on the ability of local government to finance infrastructure improvements through the sale of long term bonds. In general, since Proposition 13, debt financing by local governments has been more difficult and expensive. Debts incurred before January 1, 1979 are exempt from otherwise applicable limitations. However, all debts incurred after that date and funded by general obligation bonds must be repaid out of revenue limited to the one percent property tax assessment of Proposition 13. Consequently, municipalities must reduce public services to finance long term capital improvements. Although *revenue bonds* are not secured by the general funds of the issuing local government, the diminished ability to raise revenue for the general fund has resulted in higher interest rates for revenue bonds.

The authors suggest that Propositions 13 and 4 have had a detrimental effect on the ability of local governments in California to finance the redevelopment of blighted areas. Such redevelopment is financed in California by the sale of *tax allocation bonds,* also known as *tax increment bonds.* Under the California constitution, redevelopment agencies are able to sell bonds secured by that portion of property tax revenue in the redevelopment area derived from the increase in assessed value of the project area. This method of financing redevelopment projects is jeopardized by the Proposition 13 limitation of one percent of assessed value and the Proposition 4 limitation of appropriations of revenue derived therefrom.

In the second article in this section, Strauss, Mikels, and Hagman analyze the impact of the California TELS on land use policies. The effect of Proposition 13 on residential growth is subject to controversy. There is an ongoing debate in California about whether, after Proposition 13, new residential development produces enough revenue to pay for the cost of services it requires. In either event it had been predicted that Proposition 13 will cause developers to foresake suburban areas, in which the cost of development improvements is high, and build instead on urban land where municipal facilities are already in place. It still remains to be seen whether this prediction will come true.

However, it does seem clear that municipalities will continue to respond to reduced revenues by increasing front-end development fees. Professor Hagman has suggested that not all of these costs will be passed on to new residents: Some of these costs could be *passed back* to owners of undeveloped land in the form of lower land prices. Nevertheless, it also seems clear that Proposition 13 aggravates the problem of exclusionary zoning. The limited ability of local government to raise and spend the money necessary to service new developments will tend to encourage municipalities to use land use regulations to discourage new developments.

The article then points to an interesting paradox resulting from the interrelation of Propositions 13 and 4. It is suggested that Proposition 4 will limit the commercial and industrial growth encouraged by Proposition 13 because the tax revenue produced by new commercial and industrial ratables cannot be appropriated without a reduction in other tax revenue. In addition, communities will no longer be able to compete with each other in attracting industrial ratables by reducing taxes. Under Proposition 13 the tax rate will be substantially the same statewide.

In conclusion, the authors point up the interplay between Propositions 13 and 4 in determining land use effects. For example, Proposition 13 will encourage commercial and industrial development that produces sales tax revenue and requires minimal costly services; but Proposition 4 will limit the ability of the host municipality to spend that sales tax revenue. Another illustration of the interplay is the prediction that Proposition 13 will encourage development in urban areas where capital infrastructure is in place. However,

Proposition 4 has an adverse effect on urban areas with a declining population because the appropriation limitation is measured in part by changes in population. Propositions 13 and 4 both encourage the use of development fees to pay for the costs of services required by the development. These fees tend to increase the cost of housing to the extent that moderate-income families may be excluded. This then is the dilemma of Propositions 13 and 4: how to finance the infrastructure costs of development without the use of development fees and other nontax revenues to avoid raising the costs of housing to the point of its being exclusionary.

The third article in this section on the California system is written by Robert Freilich and Steven M. Perry and describes the effect of the California tax and expenditure limitations on housing, growth management, and development mix. Freilich and Perry emphasize the detrimental effect of Proposition 13 on the ability of local governments to finance capital facilities through the use of general obligation bonds. The property tax limitation prevents local government from raising sufficient revenue to meet operational costs and also pay debt service on the bonds. It is thought that this limitation will therefore cause governments to defer capital construction.

Proposition 13 can have an especially serious effect on the ability of municipalities to finance redevelopment in blighted areas of central cities. The authors describe the system of tax-increment financing, by which the increment in property tax revenue resulting from the redevelopment is used to retire the bonds issued to finance that redevelopment. Proposition 13 limits the amount of revenue available from the redevelopment area and could prevent the generation of sufficient revenue to repay the bonds.

The second half of the Freilich-Perry article discusses alternatives available to California municipalities to raise the money for municipal services cut off by property tax limitations. Subdivision exactions and impact fees are the most likely techniques of requiring developers and subdividers to bear the cost of the burden of new development on municipal facilities. Public utility law may be used to control the timing and location of development into areas where capital facilities are already in existence. Growth management systems may be adopted to control the timing and sequence of development in a way that may ease the fiscal strains on local government. And, when possible, local governments will be encouraged to use the special assessment as a method of imposing the cost of capital facilities directly on adjacent properties that benefit from that improvement.

Authors Freilich and Perry conclude with a caveat that all of the above methods of raising revenue may not be satisfactory alternatives of providing the facilities for growth and development into new areas. Limited revenue for new facilities may encourage the development of housing in bypassed areas where capital facilities already exist.

The clear consensus of the land use and finance experts is that, to the extent that new subdivision and other housing development take place in California, local government will attempt to pass on to the developer the costs of capital improvements and other municipal infrastructure. Developers can be put into a situation where they are required to make substantial front-end investments in capital improvements without any real assurance that their right to proceed with the development has "vested" so that the local government cannot change land use regulations and other conditions of approval. In response to this serious situation the California Legislature adopted a statute that authorizes local governments to enter into "development agreements" limiting their ability to change the conditions of the proposed development.

In the next article in this section Bruce M. Kramer, Texas Tech. University School of Law, raises the troublesome question of whether such development agreements are enforceable. The California Development Agreements Law provides that a municipality may enter into an agreement with a developer for a limited duration in which the proposed development is described in terms of permitted uses, density, bulk regulations on the size and height of the buildings, dedications or reservations of land, etc. Such an agreement is entered into after a public hearing and is adopted as a legislative act. Once adopted it cannot be amended or canceled except by mutual agreement of the parties, noncompliance with the terms by the developer, or, if necessary, to comply with subsequently adopted federal or state laws. Professor Kramer's article is concerned with the question of whether such agreements are valid. Two legal issues are raised by the statutory scheme authorizing such agreements: (1) Does it violate the "contracts clause" of the United States Constitution? (2) Does it violate the "reserved powers" doctrine that limits a government's ability to contract away its police power? Professor Kramer examines both issues in great detail and concludes that the validity of the California Development Agreements Law is in doubt because of cases holding that agreements contracting away a government's police power are enforceable. To the extent that there is uncertainty about the enforceability of development agreements, their use and effectiveness will be limited.

The New Jersey System

The first two articles in Section III are based on material prepared for the ALI-ABA symposium on TELS concerning the limitations on spending adopted by the state of New Jersey. The first article discusses the political and judicial events that made it necessary and politically possible for the New Jersey legislature to put a limit or "cap" on spending by state and local governments. Unlike the state of California, where tax and expenditure limitations were the result of a taxpayers' and homeowners' revolt against government spending, the "cap" law was precipitated by a constitutional crisis created when the New Jersey Supreme Court decided that the state system of financing public education violated the state constitution.

In response to the judicial requirement for more equitable funding of public education, the legislature adopted a tax reform program that included a state gross income tax and new forms of state aid to municipalities. The limitations on spending became necessary to prevent municipal governments from spending excess funds that would result from the new state aid programs. Thus the New Jersey limitation on government spending was only one part of a tax reform program that included a more equitable method of funding of public education, a state income tax and programs to reduce property taxes.

The second article in this section offers some speculation on the impact of the New Jersey limitations on government spending on future state growth and development. The increased state aid to cities would reduce the disparities in municipal services between cities and some of the wealthier suburbs. However, this article suggests that improvement of fiscal problems is not enough to improve the future of central cities.

In the suburbs, exclusionary zoning may be encouraged by limitations on spending in that spending limitations cause local officials to become very concerned with the fiscal consequences of new development. Where new development aggravates an already tight budgetary problem, land use restrictions may be used to discourage such development. The article also suggests that the limitations on state expenditures will encourage increased leadership by the executive branch of state government in planning how land is to be developed in the state. Limited funds for capital expenditures for new highways, water supply, and sewerage facilities will encourage state officials to plan for compact development that conserves energy, open space, and state funds. The limited funds for capital improvements will tend to encourage more intensive development in existing urban areas. As local governments become more dependent on state programs of financial assistance, there will be a greater tendency for local governments to respond to the planning leadership of the state.

The article concludes with the observation that the New Jersey limitations on spending and the allocation of state assistance will probably provide the greatest benefits to developing municipalities, outside of, but in close proximity to, the cities and older built-up areas. These are the areas of the state where the population and land values will increase the most.

The last article in the section, written by Ernest C. Reock, Jr., Director of the Bureau of Government Research, Rutgers University, analyses the effects of limitations on spending by local school districts in New Jersey. The spending limits, known as the "school budget caps," are calculated in accordance with two statutory formulas: one for school districts that have been spending at a level *below* the state average per pupil, and the other for districts that have been spending *at or above* the state average per pupil.

Professor Reock calls attention to the four major purposes for which the school budget caps were adopted: (1) to avoid annual school budget increases, particularly where state aid is to be increased; (2) limit the need for continuing state financial aid in the future; (3) ensure that a substantial part of the new state aid to school districts is passed on to the taxpayers in the form of reduced property taxation; and (4) to help low-budget school districts of the state move toward more equal expenditures per pupil.

After an analysis of the expenditures of New Jersey school districts during the past ten years, Professor Reock has concluded that the school budget caps in New Jersey have achieved the first three objectives, namely that they (1) have prevented large and inefficient annual increases in school budgets; (2) have limited the need for future state financial aid; (3) have ensured that there will be some property tax relief. However, Professor Reock contends that the New Jersey school budget cap law has failed to achieve its fourth objective, to help equalize per-pupil expenditures among school districts.

The reason for this unintended result is that student enrollment in the wealthier districts has declined to a greater extent than student enrollment in the poorer districts. When enrollment declines, the limited amount of dollar increases permitted under the statutory cap formula may be spread over a smaller number of students. Thus, the greater the rate of decline in student enrollment, the larger the amount of expenditure *per pupil* in the school district. Professor Reock concludes with the observation that because of the varying rates of enrollment decline among wealthy and poorer school districts, the statutory limitation on school district expenditures has become an obstacle that prevents the low budget districts from increasing their expenditures to bring them up toward the level of the higher-budget districts. Unless this obstacle is removed by amendment of the statutory formula, the constitutional validity of the New Jersey School Budget Cap law will be brought into question.

The Texas System

Professor Kramer's second article analyzes the Texas Tax Relief Amendment of 1978. The limitation on state taxation in Texas was part of a seven-part program of tax reform adopted by amendment of the Texas Constitution in 1978. The other parts of the tax reform program provided for (1) exemption of intangible personal property from the property tax; (2) exemption of household goods and personal effects; (3) preferential treatment of agricultural land; (4) homestead exemptions; (5) disclosure by local governments of the amount by which the property tax revenue exceeds revenue in the preceding year; and (6) measures to reduce unequal and unfair assessment practices.

The most significant component of the Texas Tax Reform Amendment is the provision that state appropriations in any period may not exceed the appropriation of the prior period at a rate greater than the state's economic growth. The methodology for determining the levels of economic growth for current and prior periods is left to the state legislature and so far the legislature has not responded to this problem. By not defining "economic growth," the state legislature cannot implement the spending limitation in the state constitution. Furthermore, even when this phrase is defined, a simple majority of the state legislature may declare an "emergency" and thereby override the limits on state spending.

Professor Kramer suggests that the Texas Tax Reform Amendment may have been used to defuse the "Proposition 13" fever that was spreading throughout the country at that time. He also notes that the Texas program focuses its attention on state *spending* rather than on *tax* limitations. As a result, it has had the greatest impact to date on school districts rather than on municipalities that regulate land use and development. Unlike the situation in California, Texas municipalities have not had to turn to development fees and exactions for revenue and there has been no need to do so. Texas municipalities are enjoying substantial growth and prosperity and increases in tax revenue. However, Professor Kramer suggests that there is evidence of growing taxpayer resistence to increases in property taxation and this attitude may lead to further attempts to impose tax limitations in the future.

The Massachusetts System

Laurie Angiolillo-Bent has made an extensive analysis of Proposition 2½ in Massachusetts. This statute was adopted by the Massachusetts voters by a three to two margin in an initiative bill that had been voted down by the Massachusetts House of Representatives by a vote of 146 to 5. The law contains thirteen sections providing sundry reforms of the state property tax. The most far reaching provisions of the statute are those sections that (1) set a *rate limit* of 25 dollars of tax for every 1,000 dollars of property value and (2) a *levy limit* of 102.5 percent of the previous year's levy.

Ms. Angiolillo-Bent's analysis focuses on the problems of administration of these forms of tax limitation. For example, the article analyzes the question of how Proposition 2½, which requires assessment at "fair cash value," can be implemented when many Massachusetts communities have not yet achieved "full value" assessment. This discussion directs attention to a problem that exists in most states, namely that in spite of constitutional requirements of "equal and uniform" assessments, there is a wide disparity between assessed value and "full value" of property subject to the property tax. Thus, a TELS provision that seeks to limit property taxation by a formula based on assessed value will be subject to all the inequities and problems of administration of the assessment procedure of the property tax.

This problem is further complicated in Massachusetts and other states that permit municipalities to classify property according to use. Ms. Angiolillo-Bent suggests that the two laws are not necessarily in conflict. The classification law permits, without requiring, a municipality to allocate the property tax among the four different categories of property: residential, commercial, industrial and open space. That is, the classification law deals with the issue of the *allocation* of a property tax levy, and not to its size or rate of growth. Proposition 2½, on the other hand, limits the size and growth of the property tax levy but not its allocation.

A similar issue arises with respect to property tax exemptions. More specifically, the question arises whether exempted property is to be included in the tax base for the purpose of calculating the tax limit. Under the Massachusetts statute there is some ambiguity but it is suggested that the tax base, for purposes of calculating the rate and levy limits of Proposition 2½, does not include exempt property.

The adoption of Proposition 2½ by the people of Massachusetts will focus attention on the role of the property tax as the primary source of municipal revenue. It may also direct attention to the inequities and problems in property tax administration. However, the effects of the law are also more immediate. Proposition 2½ will result in a reduction in tax revenue of about $332 million in 1982. This loss of revenue has caused municipalities throughout the state to cut expenses and find alternate sources of revenue. Municipalities have begun to cut back on services and lay off employees. In Cambridge, where the city has had to cut its budget by twenty-five percent, the city council has asked for legislative approval of a one percent payroll tax on the employees of the city's largest tax-exempt institutions, Harvard University and Massachusetts Institute of Technology. It is expected that municipalities may seek to create new taxing districts and adopt user charges and fees as an alternative to the property tax.

Effect on Metropolitan Growth

The remaining articles analyze some of the effects of tax and expenditure limitations. Royce Hanson, Chairman of the Maryland National Capital Park and Planning Commission, proposes the skeptical view that TELS are the result of a distrust by the electorate of elected government. This distrust is based on the observation that elected officials are unable to resist powerful interest groups and require a statute or constitutional provision as the excuse for saying "no" to influential constituents.

Hanson believes that TELS undermine representative government by substituting plebescitary budgeting for the bargaining, accommodation, and compromise that usually take place in the budgetary process. TELS represent one interest group's ideas of what is important. Once adopted, the demands of other interest groups will have to be met by more costly, less responsible techniques such as special districts and authorities to administer user charges and exactions and fees that shift, at least temporarily, the fiscal burden.

Hanson observes that the adoption of TELS comes at a time when there is a need for *increases,* rather than decreases in expenditures by metropolitan governments. The infrastructure in the older metropolitan areas is deteriorating. The extensive leakages in water and sewerage systems are notorious examples. Educational costs are expected to rise in spite of declining enrollment because of a greater proportion of older teachers at the top of pay grades. Vested municipal retirement systems with generous retirement benefits will be a substantial drain on many local treasuries. Bonding costs to finance long-term capital improvements have increased.

TELS will also have an adverse effect upon socially equitable growth management and planning programs. For example, in Maryland and Virginia, county-wide services have prevented exclusionary practices that exist in many other areas. These programs could be impeded by the increased use of special service districts, increased development costs, special assessments, and development fees.

TELS will tend to undermine general purpose local government. To the extent that the spending or tax restrictions can be avoided by special tax districts or authorities, these forms of limited and invisible government will substitute for general purpose government where elected officials must make decisions based on a comparative or competitive claim to limited municipal resources.

In Hanson's view the most pernicious effect of TELS is to divert attention from the disparity between the local economic base and the tax base, which he believes to be the fundamental problem of local government finance. Within a metropolitan area the local governments with the greatest need for tax revenue frequently are not the governments that generate the wealth and the revenue. That some of these governments generate more revenue than they need for their own use has in fact fueled the demand for tax and expenditure limitations. A more equitable system of redistribution of revenue potential within a metropolitan area rather than limitations on taxation and spending is the kind of program that would be more responsive to the needs of metropolitan areas.

The article written by Howard Chernick and Andrew Reschovsky contains an analysis of the question whether Proposition 13 provides greater benefits to higher- or lower-income taxpayers in California. One basic question of this analysis is: compared to what? If the impact of Proposition 13 is compared with a situation in which there is no tax limitation, the authors conclude that the overall impact of Proposition 13 has been to favor *slightly* high-income households in California. However, the authors concede that when the combined effect on both property taxation and income taxation is considered, the net impact of Proposition 13 is to favor *slightly* lower-income households.

On the other hand, when compared with an alternative tax reform program that would cut sales and excise taxes, Proposition 13 is considerably more advantageous to lower-income households. Thus the authors conclude that in isolation Proposition 13 would appear to favor higher-income persons. However, by reducing the importance of the property tax relative to more broad-based state taxes, it is in fact highly favorable to the lower-income persons in California.

Harold Wolman and George Peterson draw upon a series of studies by the Urban Institute to determine how local governments respond to the fiscal restraints imposed by tax and expenditure limitations. In general, governments have three policy choices when facing fiscal constraints: they can seek increased intergovernmental revenues, increase their own source of revenue, reduce expenditures, or pursue a combination of the above.

When possible, local governments may substitute funds from the state or federal government for local funds. For example, the city of Trenton, New Jersey, uses its entire general revenue sharing payment to support its fire department. In 1979 Buffalo used CETA funds for approximately twenty-five percent of its workforce. Of course this policy option assumes the continuation of funding from the federal and state governments, funding that was sharply curtailed by the federal government in spring 1981.

The second option that may be available to local governments is to increase its own local revenues by increasing tax rates or adding new taxes. In some states tax and expenditure limitations may prevent any increases in taxes. Under these circumstances the local government is more apt to turn to user charges and fees.

The third option available to local governments is the one that is frequently the intended consequence of tax and expenditure limitations; namely, to reduce expenditures. It may be possible to maintain the former level of service by reducing waste and improving efficiency. For example, Trenton dropped expensive insurance policies and adopted a system of self-insurance. Some local governments have made greater use of automatic data processing to increase productivity. Another technique of reducing local expenditures is to shift the costs to other levels of government. For example, the city of Cincinnati persuaded the state of Ohio to take over the responsibility of operating the University of Cincinnati. Frequently administrators try to absorb reductions in expenditures at the expense of ancillary and support functions, such as reduction in travel, overtime, and the purchase of equipment. The health department of the city of Trenton, for example, responded to a reduction in state funds by cutting expenditures for supplies and travel rather than reducing personnel. One of the recurring issues involved in reducing expenditures is whether to make across-the-board reductions among departments and functions or to make targeted and selected cuts. The political forces within the bureaucracy will exert strong force to adopt across-the-board reductions with discretion to department heads to determine how to allocate the cuts within the department. In either case expenditure reductions will be made first in areas with the least public visibility and the smallest constituencies.

After a description of the above and other techniques and strategies to reduce expenditures, the authors conclude with the observation that if tax and expenditure limitations continue for any period of time it remains to be seen whether local officials will be able to avoid a more formal system of setting priorities to determine reductions in expenditures in the future.

The last article, by Edith Netter, staff attorney, American Planning Association and editor of the *Land Use Law and Zoning Digest*, discusses the effects of TELS on planning staffs and municipal provision of public services. Ms. Netter's investigation indicates that to date there has not been a substantial decrease in the number of planners employed by local governments in California. Long-range planning services seem to be the most vulnerable to budget cuts. Many California cities have avoided a substantial cutback in planning staffs by charging higher planning and development fees.

One of the potentially serious consequences of tax and expenditure limitations is the temptation for municipalities to attempt to save money by limiting services in neighborhoods occupied by poor and minority groups. There are several suits currently pending that allege that the municipality has failed to provide equality in such municipal services as street paving; lighting, sewage, and drainage facilities; fire protection; and parks. Ms. Netter concludes that equalization-of-service suits can be successfully prosecuted where a municipality fails to provide comparable services to white and black communities. She suggests in conclusion that tax and expenditure limitations will probably have an adverse effect on planning staffs and on public services but she believes that the need for regulatory simplification will improve the development process.

II. THE CALIFORNIA SYSTEM

2

Description of Propositions 13 and 4

BETSY STRAUSS
MARJORIE MIKELS
DONALD G. HAGMAN

On November 7, 1978, the people of the State of California by initiative[1] added Article XIIIA to the State Constitution. Proposition 13 has four tax limiting provisions:

1. Ad valorem taxes are limited to one percent of the "full cash value;" an exception to repay indebtedness voter-approved prior to July 1, 1978, is provided;
2. Property tax assessments are "rolled back" to the 1975-76 fiscal year; reassessment to current market values occurs on "change of ownership" and "new construction;" the full cash value base "may reflect an annual inflation rate not to exceed 2 percent per year;"[2]
3. Any change in state taxes must receive approval by two-thirds vote of the State Legislature; no new property taxes or taxes on sales of real property are allowed;
4. Cities, counties and special districts may impose "special taxes"[3] by a two-thirds vote of those persons voting on the proposed "special tax."[4]

The first year (1978-79) tax reduction was estimated to be $6.4 billion based upon an estimated $7 billion reduction in property tax revenue offset by an estimated $600 million "bailout" of local governments from state reserves.[5]

Ms. Strauss is Legal Counsel, League of California Cities.
Ms. Mikels is a third year student, U.C.L.A. School of Law
Mr. Hagman is Professor of Law, U.C.L.A. School of Law.

On November 6, 1979, the people of the State of California by initiative[6] added Article XIIIB to the California Constitution. Proposition 4 is a limitation on the growth of state and local governments' annual appropriations. Beginning with the 1980-81 fiscal year, the state and each local government's appropriations of "proceeds of taxes"[7] must come within its appropriations limit. That limit is the appropriations of proceeds of taxes in 1978-79 adjusted annually by the jurisdiction's change in population and United States change in cost of living (or change in statewide per capita personal income, whichever is less).[8] Because Proposition 4 did not take effect until July 1, 1980, its definitive effect is not yet apparent.[9]

When California voters overwhelmingly approved both Proposition 13 in 1978 and Proposition 4 in 1979, few analysts considered the impact each of these initiatives would have on local land use policies and restrictions. That each would have a significant impact is predictable once it is noted that (1) cities and counties are the primary determinators of land use in California; (2) the development of *urban* land use is primarily under the auspices of cities; (3) cities are responsible both for raising revenue from and providing services to these land uses; (4) certain land uses produce more revenue and require less service than other land uses; (5) the historical source of unrestricted revenue from which to finance services is the property tax, a source which was reduced by 60 percent for cities statewide;[10] and (6) to the extent alternative sources of revenue may be raised to finance the provision of urban services if the source is determined to be a "special tax" a two-thirds vote is required and the appropriation of the special tax revenue is subject to the city's appropriations limit.[11] Prior to Proposition 13, only the locally levied sales tax was beyond local influence. A city determined its property tax rate, user fees and charges and matched up these revenue sources with the city-determined mix of land uses. Land use control was exercised through fiscal management and zoning. Zoning remains, but the parameters of fiscal management have been severely restricted by Propositions 13 and 4.[12]

More specifically, California's tax and expenditure limitations have impacted the following land use policies:

1. Residential growth management
2. Economic growth management
3. Urban renewal and redevelopment
4. Capital improvement financing,
5. Reorganization of local government jurisdictions: boundary changes and the supply of services

The impact of each of these land use policies will be discussed following an explanation of alternative fiscal responses to the tax and expenditure limitations.

Fiscal Response to Propositions 13 and 4: Spreading the Loss

Since the adoption of Propositions 13 and 4, it has become clear that the California voter wants lower taxes and less government spending with no decrease in the quality of local services. Local government jurisdictions have looked to four alternatives to respond to the voters' demand: (1) user fees and charges; (2) private sector capital; (3) benefit assessments; and (4) long-term bonded debt.

USER FEES AND CHARGES

Historically, local government services have been financed primarily from property tax revenues. Communities desiring additional public services or a higher level of existing services could tax themselves at a higher rate.[14] Services for new development were financed by imposing the jurisdiction's property tax rate on the new residents. Proposition 13 not only decreased the amount of property tax revenue received, it also destroyed the fiscal flexibility enjoyed by local legislators and local residents. Local legislators have been faced with the choice of decreasing municipal expenditures, utilizing the few remaining revenue tools available under Proposition 13, or both. The substantial local costs of new residential development, particularly, have stressed local budgets. With a 60 percent reduction in revenue, how does a city continue to provide its current residents with continued high quality municipal services and finance the provision of services to new residents? Local legislators have responded with local development fees and exactions as a potential source of additional revenue.[15] As a percentage of general city revenue, local development fees and exactions accounted for 8.23 percent of cities' general revenue in the 1977-78 fiscal year and 9.15 percent of cities' general revenue in the 1978-79 fiscal year. Put in perspective, the property tax accounted for 21.9 percent of cities' general revenue in the 1977-78 fiscal year and 10.55 percent of cities' general revenue in the 1978-79 fiscal year.[16] These figures, of course, do not include exactions in kind.

A California city derives its authority to levy fees and user charges from two distinct enabling powers. Fees levied for regulatory activities—such as building permit fees, Subdivision Map Act processing fees and conditional use permit and variance fees—are levied pursuant to the police power.[17] User charges imposed for the provision of public services—such as police protection, firefighting or garbage disposal—are levied pursuant to a city's corporate and statutory powers (Government Code Sections 37103, 38600, 38630, 38900, 38730). Pursuant to the police power, a city regulates behavior to promote the public health, safety and general welfare. Pursuant to the corporate power, a city provides public services for the special benefit and advantage of the community embraced within the corporate boundaries.

Regulatory Fees. A city's regulatory actions are subject to the general qualification that they be reasonably related and calculated to promote the public health, safety and general welfare. Fees levied to regulate conduct (such as building permit or Subdivision Map Act processing fees) are limited to the city's incurred costs (including the salaries and fringe benefits of the city employee processing the permit or inspecting the plans and specifications) to take those actions required to ensure a healthy and safe environment.[19]

User Charges. User charges levied to provide public services on a volitional basis are subject only to the restriction that they not be confiscatory and may be in an amount sufficient to establish reserves to be used to meet unforeseen emergencies. A city may provide, among other services, fire protection (Government Code Section 38600), police protection (Government Code Section 38630), water service (Government Code Section 38730), sewer service (Government Code Section 38900), and may operate transportation facilities, public libraries and parks (Government Code Section 39732[a]). A city's ability to charge for these services derives from several sources and differs depending upon the city's status as a general law or charter city.

1. *Impact Fees:* Impact fees are charges on new development that straddle the line between a fee and a tax. In fact, in these instances in which such a fee was upheld, the city had characterized the fee as a "business license tax."[20] These fees are different from subdivision exactions in that exactions are usually limited to construction of physical facilities reasonably related to the subdivision project. Services (such as police and fire protection), maintenance of existing facilities, and construction of major off-site facilties are the primary recipients of impact fees. A city may treat these funds as unrestricted general revenues, without demonstrating their benefit to the development from which they are derived.
2. *User Charges–Charter Cities:* A charter city has authority to impose a user charge for those services which are municipal affairs (sewer service, furnishing water, garbage collection and disposal, parks, operation of

transportation systems, etc.). These charges may be imposed whether or not the resident actually is receiving the service if that service promotes the public health or safety.[21]

3. *User Charges–General Law Cities:* Government Code Section 37112 codifies "Dillon's Rule" to provide that a city may take any action "necessary or proper" to carry out the services it is authorized to provide. Arguably, this statute is sufficient authority to allow a general law city to levy a user charge to provide authorized services. There is little precedent for such a procedure, primarily because of the historic use of the property tax to fund municipal services.

   There is specific statutory authority for both general law and charter cities to impose a charge for services financed by revenue bonds including furnishing of water, garbage disposal and sewer treatment (Government Code Section 54344, 54309, and 54514), for the cost of installing and maintaining fire hydrants (Government Code Section 53069.9), and for the use of park facilities (Government Code Section 50402).
4. *Subdivision Map Act Charges for Capital Improvements.* It must be noted that exaction from subdividers to fund bridges and major thoroughfares (Government Code Section 66484), to construct and maintain parks and recreational facilities (Government Code Section 66477) and to construct and maintain a sanitary sewer system (Government Code Section 66483) are limited to costs of providing those facilities. Therefore, although such facilities are provided as a corporate rather than regulatory fuction, these statutes limit charges levied to the costs of constructing the facilities. Government Code Section (66483.1 does provide that any surplus remaining after completion of drainage and sewer facilities may be transferred to the general fund or refunded.

Two significant surveys of local fee increases since Proposition 13 have been undertaken.

The Association of Bay Area Governments surveyed local officials in the nine-county San Francisco Bay Area region.[22] For purposes of analysis, four hypothetical, but typical, structures were created. The buildings and their characteristics were selected specifically to represent a broad spectrum of types, so as to encompass the widest possible range of development fees. The hypothetical buildings are: (1) a three-bedroom, single-family home within a new subdivision of 100 such homes; (2) a seven-unit multifamily dwelling; (3) a restaurant seating 48 people; and (4) a print shop.

In an attempt to increase comparability across the Bay Area, it was assumed that these identical four structures would be built in each of the cities and counties in the region. It was further assumed that each building would have the same valuation or construction cost throughout the Bay Area. Although this may have artifically inflated development fees in outlying areas (where valuation is lower), the majority of fees which are based on valuation are those for building permits and plan checks, which show only minor differences within the region.

The following development fees were studied: (1) planning fees, such as those assessed for rezoning, environmental studies, and map approval; (2) building department fees for building, plumbing, mechanical, and electrical permits; (3) "growth-impact" fees, such as those assessed for parks and schools; and (4) utility charges for storm drain, sewer, and water connections.

The ABAG survey found that many cities have increased their fees in an attempt to compenstate for the loss of property tax revenues or General Fund revenues that occurred after the passage of Proposition 13. Prior to the reduction of property taxes, fees for planning, utilities, and other services did not cover the cost of these services to local governments. Governments and existing residents, in effect, subsidized new developments via the property tax. With this source of income drastically reduced, it has become prohibitively expensive for localities to support large-scale development unless these developments go further towards paying for themselves—thus the increase in fees.

Some fees have been doubled, or even tripled, and new fees (such as "bedroom taxes" and school impact fees) have been adopted. School impact fees in particular are being considered by a number of cities facing the prospect of overcrowded classrooms. Many cities have adopted some form of pay-as-you-go policy to cover the cost of development-related services. A typical example of the direction cities are headed occurred in a city which raised its fees in 1979 to cover 50 percent of the costs associated with planning services. This same city is now considering raising its fees to cover all of its planning costs. Other cities have already raised their fees to cover total current operating costs. One city has been able to pay for some advance planning out of its new fees, which have been designed primarily to affect large developers.[23]

In 1976, the regional mean fee was $1,121 per standard single-family home. In 1979, the figure had risen $384 to $1,505 per home, or an increase of approximately 34 percent. Whereas in 1976 only four communities, or six percent of these jurisdictions surveyed, imposed fees of $2,100 or more on the construction of the standard home, 18 communities, or approximately 28 percent, imposed fees calculated at or above this level in 1979. These changes encompass increases in previously existing fees as well as imposition of new fees.[24]

The second study was undertaken by the Governor's Office of Planning and Research.[25] Both impact fees and planning fees were surveyed to determine fee increases since Proposition 13.

Eighty-three (of 421) cities were questioned about changes in fees imposed to finance services, parks, schools, drainage, water systems, and other capital facilities required by new development. On an average, the following increases were found in the following fees:

	Percent
Sewer connection	93
Water & drainage connection	72
Sewer capacity surchage	403
Building permits	40
Bedroom tax	63

The office of Planning and Research received responses from 286 cities to its survey of planning fees: fees charged to offset, partially, the government's cost of analyzing an application and issuing a permit. Of the 286 cities, 136 raised fees after Proposition 13—48 percent of those responding. The average fee increase of those jurisdictions increasing fees was 255 percent.

In evaluating this response of local governments to Proposition 13, five points must be noted:

1. In the performance of a government function, a city may not charge a fee which produces revenues in excess of its costs. When the cost line is crossed, a tax has been imposed.[26]
2. Fee increases since Proposition 13 have occurred for reasons in addition to the most obvious one: a response to Proposition 13 revenue reductions. In the Association of Bay Area Governments Survey,[27] local attitudes towards growth, quality of local amenities, and increasing sophistication of local governments with respect to ascertaining the fiscal impacts of development, in the wake of unprecedented demand for housing, were also cited by localities as the force behind fee increases.[28]
3. Proposition 4 imposes two different limitations on local government fee increases. Article XIIIB, Section 8(c) provides that to the extent the proceeds of regulatory licenses, user charges and user fees exceed the costs of reasonably borne by the entity providing the service, such proceeds are the "proceeds of taxes." The appropriation of proceeds of taxes is subject to the historically based appropriations limit. Article XIIIB, Section 3(b) provides that if an entity levies or increases regulatory licenses, user charges or user fees to finance a service previously financed wholly or partially from some other source, the appropriations

limit of the entity is reduced.[29] New or additional services can be provided and paid for by user fees without an impact on the appropriations limit.[30]

4. Fees charged to provide services to new development which are provided by property taxes to existing development may be subject to challenge as in violation of the equal protection clause if the old development and the new development are both burdened by the same taxes and receive the same services.[31]
5. Litigation is pending in the lower and appellate courts in California relating to whether a variety of different types of fees and charges constitute "special taxes" which require two-thirds voter approval to impose. As of May 1981, two appellate court decisions had been rendered in this area. *Mills v. County of Trinity*[32] reviewed the imposition of both fee increases and new fees following the adoption of Proposition 13 for county services in processing subdivision, zoning and other land-use applications. *Trent-Meredith, Inc. v. City of Oxnard* determined that a fee levied to relieve temporary school overcrowding, as long as it related to the benefits received or burdens created, was not a tax.[33]

The appellate court in the *Mills* case held that

> the 'special tax' referred to in Section 4 of Article XIIIA does not embrace fees charged in connection with regulatory activities which do not exceed the reasonable cost of providing services necessary to the activity for which the fee is charged and which are not levied for unrelated revenue purposes.[34]

Pending on appeal are several significant Superior Court decisions relative to whether the following fees constitute "special taxes": (1) school impact fee authorized by Government Code Section 65970;[35] (2) fire service fee;[36] (3) drainage permit fee.[37] In addition, the Attorney General of the State of California has opined that:

1. School impact fees are special taxes,[38]
2. Subdivision Map Act fees (Government Code Section 66484) are not special taxes,[39]
3. An in-lieu fee imposed as part of the building permit fee to provide housing for low and moderate income families is a special tax,[40]
4. County Service Area charges imposed pursuant to Government Code Section 25210.77a constitute special taxes if levied for revenue-raising purposes.[41]

PRIVATIZATION OF PUBLIC SERVICES

As has been noted,[42] a number of studies conducted since the imposition of California Constitution Articles XIIIA demonstrate the dramatic effect Proposition 13 has had on fees and exactions imposed on developers to defray infrastructure and other service costs.[43] The adoption of Proposition 4 and development agreement legislation seem to continue this trend.

Proposition 4. There is evidence to support the premise that the addition of Article XIIIB to the California Constitution will continue this trend toward the privatization of public services. Section 8(d) of Article XIIIB provides that an appropriations limit be established for each "local government." Questions arise as to whether some governmental entities are "local governments" the appropriations of which are subject to an appropriation limit. The Legislative Counsel has opined about a variety of entities: some are clearly not local governments, others are clearly local governments and still others are questionable and could be defined either way by the Legislature. In the first category, included are a nonprofit corporation and a joint powers authority.[44] Since tax and expenditure limitations apply only to local governments, there may be a tendency to furnish services through nonprofit organizations, such as homeowner associations.[45] Likewise, to the extent a quasipublic agency like a joint powers authority[46] is not a local government, its utilization is likely to increase.

Two provisions of Proposition 4 argue against this trend: (1) Article XIIIB, Section 3(b) provides that if a government entity transfers responsibility of providing a program or service to a private entity, its appropriations limit must be decreased accordingly. This provision may discourage moves toward more efficient production of services. (2) The source of seed money for nonprofit organizations and joint powers authorities often is an appropriation by a city or the cities affected by the private provider's activities. To the extent the appropriation by the city is an appropriation of proceeds of taxes, the appropriation is subject to the city's appropriations limit.

Development Agreements. The increase in fees and exactions imposed upon developer since Proposition 13 requires a developer to commit money to finance the public improvements required for the development prior to beginning construction on the development itself. Under California's "vested rights" rule,[47] the developer could commit money to public improvements and if substantail construction had not been undertaken, the local jurisdiction could change the rules under which the development would proceed. This expenditure of developer capital prior to certainty of development heightens the risk under which the developer operates. Although California's Development Agreement law[48] was enacted in response to developer frustration with the increasing uncertainty of subdividing in California, it may provide an interesting effect on land use development after Proposition 13.

California Government Code Sections 65864-65869.5 propose to allow governments to enter into "development agreements" with developers which will freeze the local governmental land use regulations on the property in question. The development must in "good faith" prosecute the development of the parcel; otherwise, the agreement may be unilaterally terminated or modified. The agreement must be of a delimited duration, specify the permitted uses, density and intensity of such uses, maximum height and size of proposed buildings along with the reservation or dedication of land. The agreement is to be periodically reviewed to determine the good faith compliance by the developer, and can only be entered into after a public hearing is held and cannot be amended or cancled unless by mutual agreement of the parties. The agreement is considered to be a legislative act subjecting it to the referendum provisions of the California Constitution.[49] The agreement does not protect against subsequently changed state or federal laws affecting the development. The stated purpose of this article is to maximize the efficient utilization of land resources with least economic cost to the public. If this purpose is to be achieved, then remedies available upon an alleged breach must be identified. Possible remedies include actions for damages, specific performance and other contractual remedies.[50]

One possible response to the increasing fees and exactions by a developer is to request the local jurisdiction to enter into a development agreement. Although nothing in the statute would require a local government to enter into such an agreement, the local government may be willing to give up some of its flexibility to assure developer financing of public facilities, perhaps beyond what could be exacted. This use of the development agreement legislation has been discussed in Sacramento, California, wherein a development agreement has been proposed pursuant to which the county would approve a 3,000 acre subdivision to be developed over ten years, and the developer would agree to pay $1,000 per dwelling unit to the school district to finance a new school plus undetermined amounts to be fire district to finance a new fire station and to the regional transit district to finance bus stop shelters.

BENEFIT ASSESSMENTS

Assessments to finance the benefits conferred upon real or personal property have been an historically significant method of financing capital improvements in California. Special assessment bonds issued by an assessment district and paid back by benefit assessments levied on the benefited property owners provide less expensive financing through their tax-exempt status. Sewer and water line extensions, street lighting and paving, and sidewalks are often constructed with special assessment financing.

Assessment bonds issued under the 1911 Improvement Act[51] are secured only by the property owned by those assessed and are unaffected by Proposition 13.[52] Under legislation signed into law in July, 1980, neither the appropriation of bond proceeds nor the appropriation of nontax levies imposed to pay back debt is an appropriation subject to limitation for purposes of Proposition 4.[53] However, the climate of uncertainty has had an effect on the municipal securities market. It was reported in December 1978 that the City of Los Angeles, California, failed to receive bids on six projects financed by 1911 Act bonds.[54]

The other significant type of special assessment bonds are authorized by the 1915 Improvement Bond Act.[55] This financing source has been weakened considerably by elimination of the added security provided by the issuing agency. Before Proposition 13, if a property owner failed to pay an installment, the issuing agency paid the delinquency from its existing funds or raised the money from a special property tax levy of up to 10 cents. The added security of 1915 Act bonds made them more attractive to bond buyers and reduced their cost to the issuing agency.

Proposition 13 and implementing legislation (SB 154, Chapter 1292, 1978 Statutes) eliminated the assurance of the 10-cent levy behind these bonds. Municipalities can no longer impose new property taxes.

An agency unable to use 1915 Act bonds is still free to turn to financing under the 1911 Act. But the cost will be greater—if willing investors can be found.

Urgency legislation (SB 973; Chapter 149, Statutes of 1979) signed by Governor Brown on June 27 attempts to restore some marketability to 1915 Act bonds. The bill permits building a revenue bond feature into 1915 Act bonds by establishing a special reserve fund to cover delinquencies. The new law also permits 1915 Act bond issuers to promise to seek judicial foreclosure when unable to collect delinquent assessment installments. The ability to pledge quick foreclosure and the special security reserve fund are expected to make these bonds a viable financing alternative.

Even if the current uncertainty surrounding the viability of special assessment financing is reduced, this form of borrowing in its traditional application is useful only when the improvements made are of direct benefit to the property assessed.[56]

Reduced property tax revenues, landowner/developer reluctance to finance public facilities and concern over increasing housing prices have led cities and counties to look toward the expanded use of benefit assessment financing of public improvements. The due process clause implications of assessing a property owner for public improvements which provide a benefit through the service provided but are not of direct benefit to the real or personal property have not been fully explored. However, in response to the generalized concern that the costs of more public improvements should be financed at lower interest rates and amortized over thirty years, the Legislature adopted Chapter 397 in the 1979 session.

Chapter 397 added Sections 53970-53980 to the Government Code to authorize governmental providers of police or fire services to levy a standby or availability charge for police protection or fire suppression services directly related to the benefits of such services subject to the affirmative vote of two-thirds of the voters on the proposal.[57] The public provider of these services must hold a noticed public hearing on the proposal and its annual adjustment and a majority protest procedure is provided, subject to its overruling by four-fifths vote of the legislative body. The charges may be imposed "for the purpose of obtaining, furnishing, operating and maintaining fire suppression or police protection equipment or apparatus or for the purpose of paying the salaries and benefits to firefighting or police protection personnel . . . whether or not such fire suppression service or police protection is actually used by or upon such parcel, improvement, or use of property."[58] Several questions arise relative to the viability of this authorization, including (1) due process limitations on "assessing" (not *taxing*) property which is not "benefited;" (2) equal protection limitations on assessing one group of homeowners in an area of the city who are paying property taxes and receiving the same level of service as another group of homeowners who are paying property taxes but not assessed; (3) Proposition 13 limitations precluding additional ad valorem taxes; and (4) statutory limitations precluding the use of this financing device for capital improvements.[59]

Within two years of its adoption, some thirty-nine special districts and cities levied benefit assessments or special taxes pursuant to this authorization, having received the affirmative two-thirds of the voters on the proposal.

DEBT FINANCING

Borrowing Generally. Prior to the adoption of the California tax and expenditure limitation measures, California bond ratings were Aas—among the highest in the nation. A study of the effects of Proposition 13 on state and municipal debt in California during three periods—1977; the first five months of 1978 (time between the qualification of Proposition 13 for the ballot and its enactment); and June, 1978, to March, 1979—reaches the following conclusions:

In mid-1977 California local government bonds were about at the national average in interest rates for Moody's Aaa rated bonds. The local bonds, whether general obligation, revenue, tax allocation or lease purchase, all bore substantially the same interest rate. Beginning in August of 1977, tax allocation (increment) bond interest rates began to rise (perhaps due to supply effects, i.e., many issuers tried to get under the Proposition 13 wire) and by the time of the last issuance, shortly before the vote on Proposition 13, tax allocation bond interest in California was almost 3 percent over what it was in August of 1977 and over what Moody's Aaa bond interest was at that time. Lease purchase bond interest rose to almost 1.5 percent higher than Moody's Aaa bonds and revenue and general obligation bonds rose to almost .5 percent higher. As of March 1979, local general obligation bonds carried about .5 percent rates, revenue bonds almost 1 percent and lease purchase bonds over 1 percent. State general obligation bonds in the earlier period were .37 percent below the Aaa interest rate and continued in the final period to be lower, although only .11 percent lower.[60]

Standard and Poor Corporation lowered California's credit rating from Aaa to Aa plus, increasing the cost of borrowing by about .1 percent (10 basis points) or $100,000 a year on a $100,000,000 borrowing.[61]

Also since the adoption of California's TELS, California underwriters have become more frequent bidders on Oregon bond sales.[62]

The general effect of the measures on borrowing has been to make local government debt financing more difficult and expensive to obtain. Since this is the case, infrastructure costs are being imposed on developers and, thus, new home buyers through fees, charges and special assessments. The interest costs on mortgage financing are approximately 5 percent higher than on tax-exempt borrowing, thus increasing the total costs involved.[63]

Both Propositions 13 and 4 exempt voter-approved bonds from their provisions. Article XIIIA, Section 1(b) excludes taxes for pre-existing voter-approved indebtedness from Proposition 13's 1 percent tax rate limit. Article XIIIB, Section 7, states, "Nothing in this article shall be construed to impair the ability of the state or of any local government to meet its obligations with respect to existing or future bonded indebtedness." And Section 9 (a) exempts the appropriation of proceeds of taxes for debt service on obligations existing on January 1, 1979, from the appropriations limit imposed. It still remains possible therefore for tax levies to exceed the 1 percent limit, or for spending appropriations to exceed the given appropriation limits if it is to repay past indebtedness which was voter approved. These provisions have been court-tested with the following results:

> Where a local water agency, with voter approval, had contracted with a state agency for water and the state agency financed the water bonds it had issued through property taxes levied by the local agency, the court held that such taxes were "ad valorem taxes . . . to pay . . . indebtedness approved by the voters" and were excluded from the Proposition 13 tax limit.[64]
>
> Article XIIIA, Section 1 (b), which excludes taxes for pre-existing indebtedness from Proposition 13's 1 percent limit applies to property annexed to a water district. Thus, a water district's statute, which provides that annexed property will be subject to levy for a district's pre-existing indebtedness, was valid under Proposition 13 and not impliedly repealed by it.[65]

General Obligation Bonds. "Public capital is in many ways complementary to private capital."[66] Certain types of public improvements —roads, schools and sewers—attract private capital. Professor Shulman opines that "if there is any single overriding defect in Proposition 13, it is the de facto limitation on the sale of general obligation bonds and the resulting hindrance to the development of public works."[67]

General obligation bonds issued by local governments were secured historically by the ability of the issuing entity to levy an unlimited property tax. It has been this ability and the basic security inherent in real property which has made these bonds particularly attractive to municipal bond investors. Lower interest rates and the subsequent savings to issuing agencies resulted. Historically, the general obligation bond has been the lowest cost financing mechanism for public capital improvements.[68]

All post-Proposition 13 general obligation bonds, however, must be funded out of the 1 percent tax limit. Voters can no longer commit a jurisdiction's taxing authority as collateral for loans. As a result, public entities cannot issue general obligation bonds unless the bonds were voter-approved before July 1, 1978.[69] This means that voters will have to cut current public services in order to fund long-term capital improvements. Professor Shulman points out that developing areas thus face a nearly insurmountable bottleneck to their growth; they are unable to finance the public improvements necessary to attract private capital.[70]

Proposition 4 on the general election ballot in November, 1980, would amend Article XIIIA to provide for an additional exemption to the 1 percent property tax limitation to finance the improvement or acquisition of real or personal property approved by an affirmative vote of two-thirds of those voting on the proposal.[71]

Revenue Bonds. Revenue bonds are commonly secured and repaid by revenue-producing facilities either through user fees and charges or lease payments. Typical users of revenue bonds are parking authorities and water districts. The parking authority issues revenue bonds to finance the construction of a parking facility. The bonds are repaid by the revenues collected from the users of the facility. Likewise, the water district issues revenue bonds to finance the construction of a water treatment facility. The bonds are repaid by the user charges levied on the water users.

A revenue bond is not secured by the "general obligation" of the issuing agency. However, if default on revenue bonds was imminent, presumably the general funds of the issuing agency could be tapped. California's tax limitation has diminished the issuing agency's ability to raise revenue for its general fund, thus rendering the general fund a substantially weakened source of ultimate security. "It would not be unusual for an issuer to pay an interest rate for revenue bonds which is one and one-half percentage points higher than would be required for general obligation bonds to finance the same facility. This difference in interest rate for a 20-year, $1,000,000 level debt service bond issue amounts to a total interest increase of $218,152, or 21.8 percent of the principal amount borrowed with the bonds.[72]

California's expenditure limitation provides an exemption for "debt service." An appropriation to repay indebtedness existing on January 1, 1979, or to repay bonded indebtedness thereafter approved by a vote of the electors of the issuing entity is not subject to an appropriations limit. The California Legislature enacted Senate Bill 1389 (Craven) during the 1979-80 legislative session as Chapter 516, 1980 Stats., to provide that the appropriation of nontax levies to repay bonded indebtedness incurred on or after January 1, 1979, is not an appropriation subject to limitation. Revenue bonds are repaid by nontax levies; their issuance and repayment are unaffected by California's Proposition 4.[73]

Lease-Revenue Bonds. Lease-revenue bonds are a particular type of revenue bonds repaid by lease payments on the facility constructed by the facility user to the issuing agency. Most commonly, a nonprofit corporation or joint powers authority will issue revenue bonds to finance the construction of a public facility. A city or county will lease the facility from the issuing entity. The bonds are repaid from the lease payments. If lease payments are funded from the lessee's general fund revenues, Proposition 13 affects the amount of revenue available to make the payments and, assuming sufficient revenue exists, Proposition 4 affects the amount of revenue available to be appropriated. However, if lease payments are funded from the facility's users, the source of revenue and its appropriations are secure and unaffected by the tax and expenditure limitation.[74]

Tax Allocation Bonds. Second in impact to general obligation bond financing is the impact of Proposition 13 and 4 on tax allocation (also called tax increment) bond financing. Although Propositions 13 and 4 did not completely preclude tax-allocation financing as they did general obligation bond finance, they cut into its viability and effectiveness substantially.[75]

The California Constitution provides the authority to establish redevelopment agencies to acquire property and finance the redevelopment of blighted areas. Such an agency's funding is constitutionally secured through obtaining that portion of the property tax in the redevelopment project area derived by multiplying the property tax rate by the increase in assessed value of the project area. This allocation of property taxes to the agency (which has no statutory authority to levy a property tax) may be irrevocably pledged to the payment of principal and interest on bonded or contractual indebtedness.[76]

When a redevelopment project area is established, the assessed valuation of the taxable property within the designated area is frozen at the value shown on the assessment rolls when the redevelopment plan is adopted. As the assessed valuation of the area thereafter increases, property tax revenues attributable to the incremental increase in valuation are allocated entirely to the redevelopment agency to repay its incurred indebtedness; the other taxing jurisdictions whose boundaries encompass all or a portion of the redevelopment area receive none of the revenues attributable to the incremental assessed valuation increase during the term of the agency's indebtedness. A 1976 study found that of California's 229 redevelopment projects, 214 were utilizing tax-allocation financing, which accounted for 56 percent of redevelopment agency revenues.[77]

Three impacts of Proposition 13 on tax-increment financing can be cited:

1. The tax rate limitation of 1 percent of full cash value (rather than a typical 2 to 3 percent) reduces revenues available for tax-increment financing considerably;[78]

2. The rollback of property tax assessments to the 1975-76 fiscal year with a 2 percent annual growth limit thereafter and with adjustments permitted to current valuation only for new construction and change of ownership removed inflation and appreciation from projects which in the past enhanced project feasibility and allowed for faster debt retirement;
3. The allowance for an adjustment of assessed valuation to current valuation for change of ownership provides a disincentive to cooperate to the redevelopment project area resident who would be forced to relocate as a result of the agency's activities.

Two impacts of Proposition 13 on tax-allocation bonds can be cited:

1. By authorizing a tax levy in excess of the 1 percent limitation only for prior "voter-approved" indebtedness, non-voter-approved tax allocation debt was not protected;
2. In 1978-79 only one tax-allocation bond issue was in danger of default, out of 114 redevelopment tax-allocation bond issues outstanding. However, there were seventeen bond issues in "technical default" (failure to maintain reserves for bond issues as specified by convenant in the bond resolution). Most defaults, it has been estimated, would begin in the 1979-80 fiscal year with as many as nineteen estimated by 1983.[79]

Not only are revenues available to redevelopment agencies limited by Article XIIIA, but the appropriation of those revenues by the agency are limited by Article XIIIB. Article XIIIB, Section 8(e), defines a "local government" impacted by the Article to mean "any city, county, city and county, school district, *special district, authority or other political subdivision of the state.*" (Emphasis added.) Although an argument can be made that a redevelopment agency's legal status is neither a special district nor an authority nor some other political subdivision of the state,[80] Chapter 1205 of the 1980 California Statutes determined that a redevelopment agency is subject to the Constitutional Amendment. More significantly, however, Chapter 1205, based on the argument that Article XIIIB is in constitutional conflict with Article XVI, Section 16, authorizing the allocation to and expenditure of tax increments by redevelopment agencies,[81] enacted amendments to existing law providing that the appropriations of tax increments are not subject to the appropriations limit.

If a redevelopment agency's appropriations were limited by an appropriations limit, that appropriations limit, in most cases, would be $0, thereby precluding appropriations for future redevelopment projects. A redevelopment agency's appropriations limit would be calculated by determining the agency's appropriations subject to limitation in the 1978-79 fiscal year as adopted annually as provided by

Article XIIB, Section I. The three other primary sources of an agency's appropriations in 1978-79 are all exempt revenues: federal funds, developer contributions and the costs of debt service.

Notes

1. Proposition 13: the Jarvis-Gann Initiative.
2. For a discussion of Proposition 4 on the November 1980 ballot amending Article XIIIA, see, text accompanying notes, 116-117, *infra.*
3. For a discussion of the way in which "special tax" has been interpreted, see, text accompanying notes, 31-40, *infra.*
4. California Government Code Section 50027. See Appendix I for copy of Proposition 13.
5. Cal. Legislative Analyst, An Analysis of Proposition 13: The Jarvis-Gann Property Tax Initiative, S-5 (1978).
6. Proposition 4: The Gann Initiative.
7. California Constitution, Article XIII B, Section 8(c) provides: "(c) 'Proceeds of taxes' shall include, but not be restricted to, all tax revenues and the proceeds to an entity of government, from (i) regulatory licenses, user charges, and user fees to the extent that such proceeds exceed the costs reasonably borne by such entity in providing the regulation, product, or service, and (ii) the investment of tax revenues. With respect to any local government, 'proceeds of taxes' shall include subventions received from the state, other than pursuant to Section 6 of this Article, and, with respect to the state, proceeds of taxes shall exclude such subventions."
8. California Constitution, Article XIIIB, Section 9 provides for certain exemptions to the general rule limiting the appropriation of proceeds of taxes. The appropriation of proceeds of taxes for debt service, to comply with mandates of the courts or federal government or by an special district which existed on January 1, 1978, and which did not as of the 1977-78 fiscal year levy a property tax in excess of 12½ cents per $100 of assessed value is not an appropriation subject to limitation.
9. See, generally, D. Misczynski, Office of Planning and Research, Gann Survey, March, 1980.
10. See, generally, Cal. State Controller, Annual Report of Financial Transactions Concerning Cities of California Fiscal Year 1978-79; Cal. State Controller, Annual Report of Financial Transactions Concerning Counties of California Fiscal Year 1978-79; Cal. State Controller, Annual Report of Financial Transactions Concerning Special Districts in California Fiscal Year 1978-79. Property tax loss due to Proposition 13 has been deceptive in fiscal year 1979-80 because of skyrocketing new home prices. Most analysts agree that the full impact of Proposition 13 will not be quantified accurately until fiscal year 1981-82 in which property tax revenues will reflect the downturn in the housing market experienced in 1980-81.
11. Cal. Constitution Article XIIIB, Section 4 provides that a jurisdiction's appropriations limit may be changed by a vote of the electors for a period not to exceed four years. Therefore, if the jurisdiction submitted a "special tax" for

voter approval, a voter-approved increase in the appropriations limit to allow for the appropriation of the special tax revenues could be a concurrent proposal.

12. J. Chapman, J. Kirlin, "Land Use Consequences of Proposition 13," 53 USC L. Rev. 95 (1979).

13. As noted in the text accompanying notes 2-4 *supra*, cities, counties and districts are authorized to levy a special tax subject to the approval of two-thirds of those voting on such a tax. As of August, 1980, only two jurisdictions, the Town of Hillsborough and the City of Rancho Palos Verdes, have submitted special taxes to the electors. Of the two, only the Town of Hillsborough, with an estimated June 1979 population of 8,753 and 1978-79 total revenue receipts of $2,558,190, has received the necessary two-thirds vote. Although levying a special tax may become a practical alternative when the full impact of Proposition 13 is felt by the voters, i.e., as municipal service levels continue to decrease, in the 1980-81 fiscal year, the special tax is not a politically acceptable alternative for California local jurisdictions.

14. See, generally, Cal. Rev. & Tax Code Sections 2201 et seq. (1973).

15. For a discussion of the effect of increasing fees and exactions on housing prices, see text accompanying notes 83-88, *infra.*

16. Cal. State Controller, Annual Report of Financial Transactions Concerning Cities of California Fiscal Year 1978-79.

17. Cal. Const. Art. XI, Sec. 7.

18. Vilas v. Manila, 220 U.S. 345 (1910), 55 L.Ed. 491, 315 C. 416.

19. Ayres v. City of Los Angeles, 34 Cal. 2d 31 (1949) 207 P. 2d 1; Associated Home Builders v. City of Walnut Creek, 4 Cal. 3d 633 (1971) 484 P. 2d 606, 94 Cal. Rptr. 630; Scrutton v. County of Sacramento, 275 Cal. App. 2d 421 (1969), 74 Cal. Rptr. 872.

20. Associated Home Builders v. Newark, 18 Cal. App. 3d 107 (1971): Westfield-Palos Verdes Co. v. City of Rancho Palos Verdes, 13 Cal. App. 3d 486 (1977). But see, City and County of San Francisco v. Farrell, _Cal. App. 3d _, 172 Cal. Rptr. 116 (1981) (hearing granted) in which the district court of appeal held that the business tax levied by the chartered city and county of San Francisco was a "special tax" for purposes of Article XIIIA, Section 4 of the California Constitution.

21. City of Glendale v. Trondsen, 48 C. 2d 93 (1957), 308 P. 2d 1.

22. Association of Bay Area Governments, *Development Fees in the San Francisco Bay Area: A Survey,* (Feb. 1980).

23. *Id.* at 2-4, 34-36.

24. S. Gabriel, L. Katz, J. Wolch, "Local Land-Use Regulation and Proposition 13," Taxing and Spending (Spring 1980).

25. Cal. Office of Planning and Research, Housing After Proposition 13: Why Housing Construction May Stop (August 3, 1979).

26. Trent-Meredith, Inc. v. City of Oxnard, _Cal. App. 3d_, 170 Cal. Rptr. 685 (1981); Steiner, Legal Limits on Imposing Exactions, Fees, New Taxes and Assessments, Office of Planning and Research, Nov. 1, 1978.

27. Association of Bay Area Governments, *Development Fees in the San Francisco Bay Area: A Survey* (Feb. 1980).

28. S. Gabriel, L. Katz, J. Wolch, "Local Land-Use Regulation and Proposition 13," Taxing and Spending (Spring 1980).

29. Chapter 1205 of the California 1980 Statutes added Section 7913 to the Revenue and Taxation Code to provide that a transfer, and consequent reduction in appropriations limit, does not occur unless the dollar amount of "other source" revenue contributed to provide the service is reduced. Under Section 7913, if a city were contributing $1,000,000 to finance a transit system and was collecting $1,000,000 from a $.25 toll at the fare box, the city's appropriations limit would not be reduced by a toll increase to $.35. A reduction would occur by a toll increase to $.35 and a general fund subsidy decrease to $750,000.

30. Legislative Counsel of California, Opinion No. 5581, June 16, 1979.

31. Legislative Counsel of California, Opinion No. 5581, June 16, 1979. In response to this perceived problem, AB 2068 has been introduced into the 1981 legislative session to prohibit a city or county from imposing a "special tax" to finance city services or public improvements on new residental development if existing residential development is not subject to the same tax.

32. Mills v. County of Trinity, 108 Cal. App. 3d 656 (1980).

33. Trent-Meredith, Inc. v. City of Oxnard, _Cal. App. 3d_; 170 Cal. Rptr. 685 (1981).

34. Mills v. County of Trinity, 108 Cal. App. 3d 656, 663 (1980).

35. Winberry Development Co., Inc. v. County of Shasta, Shasta Superior Court No. 62705. Appeal pending in Third District Count of Appeal following a trial court ruling on plantiff's motion for summary judgment that school impact fees authorized by Government Code, Section 65970 et seq. are "special taxes" and, therefore, had been levied invalidly by the County without having obtained prior voter approval.

36. Brown, et al. v. City of Inglewood, et al., Los Angeles Superior Court No. CA 000534. Complaint for declaratory relief, injunction and mandate challenging an urgency ordinance enacted by the City Council on June 13, 1978, imposing a fire service fee is either an invalid ad valorem property tax or an invalid "special tax."

37. Berg v. City of Dixon, Solano County Superior Court No. 70270. Action challenging building permit, drainage permit and other regulatory permit fee increases (and a bedroom tax increase) passed on an urgency basis on June 26, 1978. Parties have agreed to drop the case form the trial calendar because of the decision on appeal in Kehrlein v. City of Oakland, _Cal. App. 3d_; 1972 Cal. Rptr. 111 (1981) in which the district court of appeal held that California Constitution Article XIIIA, Section 4, requiring a two-thirds vote for special taxes took effect July 1, 1978. Therefore, a tax adopted prior to that date, but after the election enacting Article XIIIA, Section 4, (June 6, 1978) was not subject to the limitation.

38. No. CV 78/123, May 18, 1979. 62 Ops. Cal. Atty. Gen. 253. This opinion was held in error by the district court of appeal in Trent-Meredith, Inc., v. City of Oxnard, _Cal. App. 3d_; 170 Cal. Rptr. 685 (1981).

39. No. 79-712, Nov. 1, 1979. 62 Ops. Cal. Atty. Gen. 663.

40. No. 79-724, Nov. 1, 1979. 62 Ops. Cal. Atty. Gen. 673.

41. No. 79-1003, Dec. 28, 1979. 62 Ops. Cal. Atty. Gen. 83.

42. See, text accompanying notes 15-30 *supra.*

43. Besides fees and exactions imposed on development, according to the Cal-Tax Conference on Construction Activity Post-Proposition 13, held on November 8, 1979, cities are also attempting to limit future maintenance costs by demanding higher standards. For example, one city required streets to be constructed to twenty rather than ten-year maintenance-free standards. In other instances, cities are forming business partnerships with developers. The City of Fairfield, California, recently approved the Hahn Company's project of construct a $60 million, two-story shopping mall, only after Hahn agreed to pay the city $350,000 annually to finance off-site improvements, 10 percent of all profits exceeding $250,000 per year and 15 percent of all profits exceeding $500, 000 per year.

44. Legislative Counsel of California Opinion No. 8276, Aug. 14, 1979.

45. California Department of Finance, The Gann Initiative, Oct. 1979, p. 80.

46. Cal. Govt. Code Sections 6500 et seq.

47. D. Hagman, "Estoppel and Vesting in the Age of Multi-Land Use Permits," 11 Southwestern U.L. Rev. 545 (1979); D. Hagman, "The Vesting Issue: The Right of Fetal Development Vis a Vis the Abortion of Public Whimsy," 7 Env. L. 519 (1977); B. Kramer, "A Review of the 'Thou Shalt Not Contract Away the Police Powers' Doctrine in the Light of TELS." ALI-ABA Course of Study, State and Local Tax Expenditure Limitations: Impact on Land Use and Development. March 1980.

48. Cal. Govt. Code Sections 65864-65869.5 (1979).

49. Cal. Const. Art. IV, Section 1.

50. D. Hagman, *Development Agreements,* Zoning and Planning Law Reports (Oct. 1980), League of California Cities, Development Agreements, Draft (Sept. 5, 1980). Professor Kramer has identified three "interesting issues" (and possible legal hurdles) raised by the development agreement scheme. The major legal issue involving the validity of a development agreement is whether such an agreement "contracts away" the police power of the contracting city or county and is thus invalid, or whether such an agreement is a valid contract suhject to the protection of the federal contract clause prohibiting the impairment of obligation (United States Constitution, Article I, Section 10, Chapter 1). Other issues raised and discussed by Professor Kramer include the reserved powers doctrine as a limit on a government's ability to bind itself and the legality of contract zoning. B. Kramer at. p. 223.

51. Cal. Streets & Highways Code Sections 5000 et seq.

52. The Court in County of Fresno v. Malmstrom, 94 Cal. App. 3d 974 (1979), 156 Cal. Rptr. 777, held that the benefit assessment levied under the 1911 Improvement Act was neither a prohibited ad valorem tax nor a "special tax" requiring two-thirds voter approval. See, also, Solvang Municipal Improvement District v. Board of Supervisors of Santa Barbara County, 112 Cal. App. 3d 545; 169 Cal. Rptr. 291 (1980) in which the court held that where a special assessment was levied annually to pay principal and interest bonds issued to acquire lots for parking, and the yearly levy varied according to assessed value, the amount of traffic to each establishment, and the amount of private parking, the assessment was not an ad valorem property tax subject to the one percent

limit of Proposition 13. The court admonished local agencies to be sure that special assessments are used for local public improvements of direct benefit to particular property rather than of general benefit to the jurisdiction as a whole in which case the line between an assessment and a tax may be crossed.

53. Ch. 516, 1980, Cal. Stats. This statute has been validated by the Fourth District Court of Appeal in County of Placer v. Corin, _Cal. App. 3d_ (1980): 170 Cal. Rptr. 232.

54. "Municipal Financing Letter," Stone and Youngberg Municipal Financing Consultants, Inc.; No. 61, May 18, 1979, p. 3.

55. Cal. Streets & Highways Code Sections 8500 et seq.

56. Solvang Municipal Improvement District v. Board of Supervisors of Santa Barbara County, 112 Cal. App. 3d 545; 169 Cal. Rptr. 391 (1980); John Sullivan, "When It's Time to Build," Cal-Tax Research Bulletin, August 1979.

57. Benefit assessments levied under the 1911 Improvement Act and the 1913 Improvement Act are subject to a majority protest, but no affirmative vote requirement. The "directness" of the benefit may be liberally interpreted. See, e.g., Dawson v. Town of Los Altos Hills, 16 Cal. 3d 676, 129 Cal. Rptr. 97, 547 P. 2d 1277 (1976), allowing special assessments for sewer capacity rights.

58. Cal. Govt. Code Section 53973.

59. The equipment and facilities which local governments would like to finance through assessment districts are, under traditional thinking, of general benefit rather than of special benefit to the land to be assessed. Proposition 13 prompts the concern that an assessment for certain public facilities where there may not be any special benefit could be construed as a "special tax" requiring the affirmative vote of two-thirds of the electors. See, e.g., Solvang Municipal Improvement District v. Board of Supervisors of Santa Barbara County, 112 Cal. App. 3d 545, 169 Cal. Rptr. 391 (1980).

60. Beebe, "Proposition 13 and the Cost of California Debt," 32 National Tax J. 243 (June 1979).

61. Bry, "S&P Lowers State Bond Rating," The Los Angeles Times, Jan. 23, 1980, Pt. 3, at 1, Col. 1.

62. Rankin, Osburn & Rogers, "Municipal Bonds and Property Tax Limitations," 9 Env. L. 454, note 77 (1979).

63. Recht, "California's Fiscal Dilemma Affects New Development," APA California Planner, Jan. 1980, at 1.

64. Kern County Water Agency v. Board of Supervisors of Kern County, 96 Cal. App. 3d 874 (1979), 158 Cal. Rptr. 430.

65. Metro W. D. v. Dorff, 98 Cal. App. 3d 874 (1979), 159 Cal. Rptr. 775.

66. D. Shulman, "Proposition 13 and the Spatial Allocation of Economic Activities," 53 U.S.C.L. Rev. 125, 131 (1979).

67. *Id.*

68. See, e.g., H. Groves, Financing Government, 568-70 (1954).

69. Cal. Const. Art. XIIIA, Section 1(a).

70. Shulman, at p. 132.

71. See, text accompanying notes 116-117, *infra.*

72. Rankin, Osburn & Rogers, "Municipal Bonds and Property Tax Limitations," 9 Env. L. 454, 467 (1979).

73. County of Placer v. Corin, _Cal. App. 3d_, 170 Cal. Rptr. 232 (1980).

74. Drexel Burnham Lambert, Inc., "The Effect of Proposition 13 on California Municipal Securities," Investors Services, October 13, 1978.

75. Both Standard and Poor's Corporation and Moody's Investor's Service suspended rating on all tax allocation bond issues after January 1, 1979. See, generally, Bry, "Proposition 13 and 4 Add Up to Trouble for Municipal Bonds in State," Los Angeles Times, Dec. 2, 1979, Outlook at 1, Col. 1.

76. Cal. Consti. Art. XVI, Section 16 (Nov. 4, 1952).

77. In 1977-78, 51 percent of the revenue of the 126 active redevelopment agencies in California came from tax-increments–a total of $179,140,830. Coomes, Tax Allocation Bonds, Seminar: California Municipal Finance After Jarvis-Gann, San Francisco, Jan. 10-12, 1979. Although there has been widespread acceptance of this financing device, there is a challenge pending to its constitutionality in the Los Angeles Superior Court–McNutt, et al. v. City of Los Angeles, et al.

78. Because of Proposition 13, tax revenues for eighty-two project areas declined over 50 percent, on the average, despite an increase in assessed valuation of 33 percent. In some projects there was no decrease; in other projects, the revenues decreased by as much as 74.1 percent.

79. Coomes, Tax Allocation Bonds, Seminar: California Municipal Finance After Jarvis-Gann, San Francisco, Jan. 10-12, 1979. For a discussion of what measures have been adopted to delay or eliminate default, see, text accompanying notes 105-115, *infra.* Of the eighty-nine projects studied in 1979, twenty were able to cover current and maximum debt service with tax increments, thirteen were able to cover current but not maximum annual debt service and fifty-six could cover neither. Of the latter, twenty-five projects issued bonds in the first six months of 1978, just prior to the adoption of Proposition 13. Merrill Lynch, Pierce, Fenner and Smith, Inc., "California's Tax Allocation Bonds: Victims of Proposition 13, Municipal Bond Research, Oct., 1979.

80. Coomes, The Impact of Proposition 4 on Redevelopment, testimony before a Joint Hearing of the Senate and Assembly Local Government Committees, November, 1979.

81. In County of San Diego v Lonergan, _Cal. 3d_ (1980), 80 Daily Journal D.A.R. 2305 (Cal. Sup. Ct., Aug. 14, 1980), the California Supreme Court was asked to harmonize two apparently conflicting constitutional provisions: Article XIIIA, Section 1, and Article XIII, Section 12. Article XIIIA, Section 1, limits the ad valorem tax on real property to one percent of full cash value. Article XIIIA, Section 12 provides that taxes on unsecured property are levied at the rate fixed for the secured roll in the prior tax year. The issue before the court was the appropriate tax rate for the unsecured roll in fiscal year 1978-79 (the first fiscal year Article XIIIA was in effect). Under Article XIIIA, Section 1, arguably the rate is one percent of full cash value. Under Article XIII, Section 12, arguably, the rate is the prior year's (pre-Article XIIIA) secured roll rate. In concluding that the rate on the unsecured roll for the 1978-79 fiscal year was the rate on the secured roll for the prior year, the court stated "It is well settled that a constitutional amendment is to be construed in harmony with the existing framework of which it forms a part, so as to avoid a conflict in Serrano v. Priest

(1971), 5 Cal. 3d 584, 596, 96 Cal. Rptr. 601, 487 P. 2d 1241." Cal. 3d. (1980), *id.* at 2306. The court further stated that nothing in Article XIIIA suggests it was intended to apply to unsecured taxes–there was no express repeal. And, "the law shuns repeals by implication . . . ." Cal. 3d. (1980), *Id.* at 2306.

3

Effect of Propositions 13 and 4 on Land Use and Development

BETSY STRAUSS
MARJORIE MIKELS
DONALD G. HAGMAN

"It is the irony of ironies that the man who is the savior of cities or the father of planning is not myself or Alfred Heller (founder of the anti-sprawl *California Tomorrow*)–but rather Howard Jarvis."[1]

Residential Growth Management

Professor Shulman states that Proposition 13 "promises to be the most sweeping land-use control law in the country" based upon the following "predictable effects:"

1. Local governments, strapped to meet the cost of serving existing neighborhoods, will bring to a halt new developments on the suburban fringe by refusing zoning permits;
2. California residents will be reluctant to purchase new housing because, as new buyers, they will face a higher tax burden than that borne by established residents;
3. Mortgage payments will be raised by an amount approximate to that saved by lower tax rates;
4. Those few new developments completed in the years to come will face imposing "front-end" facilities charges imposed by local governments that will virtually eliminate the construction of new moderate-cost single family housing.[2]

This section will discuss the first and fourth of these "predictable effects."

THE FISCAL IMPACT OF NEW RESIDENTIAL DEVELOPMENT

Two years after the passage of Proposition 13, builders and public agencies still speculate regarding its ultimate impacts on new development. Contrary to some predictions, the measure has not brought local government to a halt, nor has new residential development been denied state-wide. One reaction to Proposition 13 is apparent and whether accurate or not, this local government perception will certainly influence the course of new residential development: new housing developments represent fiscal liabilities which can only be countered by severe growth limitations. Based upon the assumption that servicing residential development, prior to Proposition 13, required a substantial subsidy from revenues not generated from the residential development itself, the post-Proposition 13 fear is that substantially diminished property tax coffers render new residential development a sure fiscal loser. In-place residents fear that the dramatic lowering of property tax revenues obtained from residential uses that demand a high level of local public services will dilute the quality of services to an unacceptably low level.[3] Development would thus be welcome only in areas where the marginal cost of providing public services is low. These areas are generally in cities and older suburban communities rather than the new suburbs.[4]

In 1978, the California's Governor's Office of Planning and Research surveyed ten California cities to determine whether new housing paid its own way in post-Proposition 13 California.[5] This study concluded "that new residential development does not pay its own way in the post-Proposition 13 world" and suggested that the only type of new residential development that would not represent a net fiscal drain on local government resources is infilling–developing areas that are already urbanized.[6]

In August 1979 the California Council for Environmental and Economic Balance (CCEEB), a nonprofit organization primarily of labor leaders and business and industry leaders, published "The Fiscal Impact of New Residential Development After Proposition 13–An Evaluation of the Governor's Office of Planning and Research Study –'New Housing: Paying Its Way?'." Taking strong exception not only to OPR's conclusions but to its methodology, the CCEEB study concluded:

1. Based upon differing statistical data, new housing can pay its own way in the post-Proposition 13 era;

2. The total burden of financing municipal services to residential development cannot be placed on the homeowner. If housing is to be constructed at an affordable price, a mix of land uses for cross-subsidization must be encouraged;
3. The property tax is not the sole source of funding for residential municipal sources. With increased population comes increased state subventions distributed on a per capita basis plus other revenues such as Federal Revenue Sharing Funds and Community Development Block Grants.[7]

Although analysts continue to argue about whether or not new residential development pays its way after Proposition 13 and some continue to assert that developers will be forced to use urban lots to keep housing costs down, new developments will be linked whenever possible to existing services and facilities, the supply of land for new development will shrink, land shortages will boost the value of urban lots and, the demand for housing remaining unsatiated, it will simply turn inward, displacing low-income families who cannot afford to purchase homes and who may be forced out of their city-center units to make room for new development. Two years after the passage of Proposition 13,[8] this scenario has not yet come to pass. Three reasons can be found for the delay in this particular impact of Proposition 13:

1. In July 1978, the California Legislature passed the one-year "bailout bill," SB 154 (Chapter 292, 1978 Stats.) providing each unit of local government with a state grant (from the state general fund) which compensated for approximately 40 percent of the loss in revenue resulting from Proposition 13;
2. The 1978-79 fiscal year in California was characterized by significant residential growth pushing assessed valuation upward, on the average statewide at a level of approximately 10 percent.[9] Local governments did not have to make the expected hard fiscal choices.
3. The 1978-79 and 1979-80 fiscal years in California were characterized by a dramatic downturn in housing starts due to soaring interest rates and uncertainty over local rent control policies.[10] Local governments did not have to impose growth moratoria, the market imposed a moratorium on itself.

It is safe to speculate that the 1981-82 fiscal year will be characterized as the first year that the impact of Proposition 13 will be noted. The housing construction recession is expected to continue through the end of 1980 and the beginning of 1981. In addition, twenty-two of California's fifty-eight counties will receive a "windfall" of some $500 million from a court decision determining that the appropriate tax rate on the unsecured property tax roll in 1978-79 was the tax rate in 1977-78, not the 1 percent ($4.00 tax rate) limit imposed by Proposition 13.[11] Until such time as local government must face a significant increase in residential development proposals with a significant decrease in revenues, fiscal zoning will not become a reality. The surplus with which the government has operated for several years has been eliminated through increased aid to local governments, indexing the state income tax and higher levels of state expenditures. To balance the deficit in the 1981-82 fiscal year, the governor has proposed a cut of $420 million to local governments in state aid; a cut of approximately 80 percent of the original "bail-out" aid.

HIGHER FEES MEAN HIGHER HOUSING PRICES

As has been discussed, the most common response to reduced revenues has been to increase front-end development fees.[12] Not only do increased fees provide increased revenues for operating budgets, increased exactions provide perhaps the best alternative to general obligation bond financing for capital improvement budgets.

The rapid increase in fees has sparked considerable controversy with some commentators voicing that higher fees are pricing moderate income families out of the housing market and blackmailing developers into providing extra services for the community at large,[13] other speculating that the fees are either borne by the homebuyer or landowner and in either case, lower building activity is the result,[14] while still others argue that higher fees have a minimal, if any, effect on the ultimate cost of the housing unit.[15]

Co-author Hagman not only sees the increase in fees and exactions as necessary after Proposition 13 but also believes that "even if construction fees or other similar exactions for financing infrastructure are passed on to new residents the existing community probably has both a financial and moral justification for setting them as high as the market will bear." By precluding new competitive development, existing residents increase the value of their own homes. It is not unfair that the community should do so in that it is the existing community through its taxes which made the community a desirable place to live and which already provided its own infrastructure. New development should pay its full infrastructure costs as well as a buy-in fee to the existing community infrastructure costs.[16]

The fees are not necessarily passed on to new residents, however, in Hagman's opinion. The increases could be passed back to the owners of undeveloped land in the form of lower land prices. Land prices may be set by what builders will pay for land after their other costs and profits are covered. If housing costs cannot be increased because the market won't bear it an increase in construction costs on builders leads to lower prices being offered by builders to invest in land. It is fair that this should be the case in that "land owners do little to make an existing community desirable." Why should land owners profit for merely holding land when it is the existing community which pays for the infrastructure which gives the land development potential and thus its value? After Proposition 13, taxpayers will no longer be able to subsidize landowners in this manner. Further, if fees are shifted back to landowners it will merely recapture the windfall gained by landowners as a result of Proposition 13 in that the decrease in property taxes made holding costs on land much lower. Hagman concludes that construction fees on builders merely recapture the Proposition 13 windfall of landowners.[17] While the dispute continues between academic theorists, fees continue to increase, new exactions continue to be created and developers continue to abide by the new rules as the demand for an estimated 280,000 housing units annually remains unsatisfied. Housing continues to be constructed; the question is, at what price?

The conclusions of the study undertaken by the Association of Bay Area Governments[18] demonstrate the complexity of evaluating local government's residential growth control response to Proposition 13. Sample localities were grouped with regard to fee level and local regulatory response to Proposition 13. The classifications were utilized to illuminate those community characteristics important in the determination of local regulatory shifts stemming from Proposition 13.

> Group I: Inner-Ring Suburb. The city of Burlingame, located south of San Francisco in San Mateo County, is illustrative of a class of communities within the Bay Area not typified by the general trend of fee increases. These communities are characterized by low development fees, few changes in fee levels subsequent to Proposition 13, and no moratoria on growth management plans affecting residential development. City council representatives are generally neutral in their attitudes toward growth and carrying costs imposed by these municipalities on developers are low. The jurisdictions are also characterized by almost no remaining developable land, nor land yet suitable for redevelopment. For example, of the approximately 12,000 housing units in Burlingame, only about 20 percent have been built since 1960. Fee revenue generated by new residential development thus has negligible impact on these cities' decision-making with regard to expenditures on urban services. Further, the often perceived dangers of changing community composition due to large population influx are of little consequence here. In Burlingame, the city council has

become more aware of the fiscal benefits of commercial as opposed to residential development in the aftermath of Proposition 13 and has blocked a major planned rezoning of commercial to residential development in the city's bayfront district.

Group II: Fringe Suburbs. Another class of communities can be characterized as similar to Benecia, California, located at the northern end of the San Francisco Bay. These communities contain a high proportion of land available for residential development. Over the decade of the seventies, a high regional demand for housing has translated into increased development pressure for these outlying localities. Despite these pressures, these communities have imposed no moratoria or growth management plans, and city council members have consistently favored growth.

However, development fees have risen dramatically. For example, in Benica fees in real terms have risen from a total of approximately $590 per single-family dwelling unit in 1976 to about $24,000 per unit in 1979—a 375 percent increase. Not only have existing fees risen, but new developer exactions have been instituted such as a new school impact fee in Benecia of $1,600 per unit. This fee was levied two weeks before the Proposition 13 vote, attesting to community concern over diminished ability of finance services with the advent of Proposition 13. Apart from fee increases resulting from Proposition 13, local planners typically attribute the rise in development fees to the fact that these growng communities have not yet acquired a level of capital infrastructure (public facilities and equipment) sufficient to support projected population growth. Thus, fee increases have been viewed as necessary for the community to cover the high marginal costs of new residential growth.

Group III: No Growth Suburbs. A further group of cities, similar to Mill Valley, an affluent bedroom suburb located in Marin County, have maintained long-standing, restrictive policies concerning growth. While jurisdictions in this group imposed moderately high development and planning fees in 1976, they exhibited only moderate fee changes in the wake of Proposition 13. Residential construction in communities of this type has been curtailed by other means, including moratoria, large lot zoning, municipal approval delays and infrastructure capacity limitations. In fact, the Marin Municipal Water District, which covers most jurisdictions in Marin County, had a water connection moratorium from June, 1973, to March, 1978. In addition, powerful environmental groups have successfully pressured for large chunks of potentially developable land to be designated as open space, sharply limiting the supply of land available for residential development. Municipal policies and citizen lobbies have thus effectively promoted no-growth and exclusion; due to the virtual prohibition of growth, changes in development fee levels offer little in potential revenue.

Group IV: In-Growth Suburbs. Milpitas, located in northeastern Santa Clara County, typifies a group of middle income communities which encourage residential growth. Large-scale residential development is a relatively new phenomenon in most of these communities. This is evident in Milpitas, where approximately 80 percent of the dwelling units located there were constructed after 1960, whereas less than 2 percent existed prior to 1940. The communities in this group are characterized by abundant supplies of developable land, the absence of growth management plans, and a low level of municipally induced carrying costs. Further, this set of localities levies lower than average development and planning fees, which have in general exhibited only minor change in the aftermath of Proposition 13. Despite the fact that residential development is a fiscal loss in these cities, Milpitas looks at residential development as a necessary tool for attracting commercial development and accompanying sales tax revenues. In Milpitas, new capital infrastructure required for remaining residential development was completed prior to the property tax limitation. This factor in conjunction with the city's positive view of growth serves to explain the minimal level of fee change subsequent to Proposition 13.[19]

Attitudes towards residential growth by local jurisdictions since Proposition 13 is decidedly mixed. Some cities seek to halt the influx of newcomers, others encourage growth and still others have little room for new housing and thus little motivation for regulation. It is certainly safe to say that Proposition 13 has aggravated the trend toward exclusionary housing policies. Both uncertainty concerning the ability to support new development and increasing pressure from the building community to stop fee increases have forced communities to resort to increasingly strict land-use regulation to discourage development. To conclude that such policies are common statewide, however, is incorrect. The high costs of construction and money certainly have contributed their share to a housing supply which is not keeping up with demand. These costs, over which local government exercises no control, along with changes in household formation rates and increasing fuel prices, may impact more significantly than Propositions 13 and 4 on residential growth in the coming years in California.

Economic Growth Management

In the economic development area, the debate over whether new housing pays its way shifts its focus to whether industrial and commercial development pay their way.[20] Proposition 4 quickly put a damper on the boon to increased commercial and industrial growth created by Proposition 13. After the adoption of Proposition 13, the analysis went something like this: Since some development results in higher costs than others, and since the amount of property taxes are limited, as well as the ability to freely increase other taxes, development which results in higher service costs should be resisted. Whatever sorts of development did not "pay" before in terms of the governmental "profit and loss" statement, will even more clearly not pay now. Such development will tend, therefore to be excluded. Commercial and industrial development still "paid their way" by increasing property and sales tax revenues (distributed by situs of sale) and requiring minimal municipal services. However, since the adoption of Proposition 4, the analysis has changed dramatically: Proposition 4 imposes a limitation on the growth in a city's appropriations of proceeds of taxes based upon the city's appropriations in the 1978-79 fiscal year. New commercial or industrial development will produce a significant increase in sales tax revenue; but under Proposition 4, this new tax revenue may not be able to be appropriated without a reduction in other tax revenues.

Four other factors contributing to the disincentive to encourage industrial and commercial development should be noted:

1. To the extent housing is a fiscal drain on the city and commercial and industrial development requires in-city housing for workers, commercial and industrial development will not be encouraged.
2. California law[21] provides that if a city or county collects sales tax or property tax in excess of what it may appropriate under its appropriations limit, one-half of the excess sales tax and one-quarter of the excess property tax is "returned" to the state in the form of reduced subventions. The state uses the subventions instead for a school construction facilities fund to finance new school construction statewide. A city or county, in anticipation of these provisions, could reduce its implicit property tax rate, although there is some debate over whether a subsequent increase in its property tax rate to its previous share of the $4.00 countywide rate would require a two-thirds vote of the electors.
3. The competition among local governments to lure business is reduced by Proposition 13. The tax-rate, except for marginal differences to pay past indebtedness, is the same statewide. From a tax-rate standpoint, it makes no difference where an industrial firm locates in California. There is little incentive to relocate and acquire new property because the "change in ownership" or "new construction" will increase the tax. This may mean less migration of industrial firms from central cities to suburbs.[22]
4. Proposition 4 provides that a jurisdiction's appropriations limit is adjusted annually by the change in cost of living (or per capita personal income) and change in population. Many urban centers in California are experiencing a resident population decline while experiencing a commuter population increase as the household formation rate decreases

> and suburban flight continues. The decline in resident population negatively affects the appropriations limit, disallowing the appropriation of taxes generated by flourishing economic development to pay the costs of servicing the increasing commuter population.[23]

A positive attitude towards economic growth was encouraged by Proposition 13 and discouraged by Proposition 4. However, a study completed in the fall of 1979 indicated that only forty-five cities of the one hundred and twenty-three cities with populations over 50,000 would reach their appropriations limit in the 1980-81 fiscal year. Until the gap narrows between a city's appropriations and its appropriations limit, the amount of tax revenue received is the more restrictive determinant of a city's appropriations. If this is the case, there is room in many jurisdictions for the increased tax revenues produced by economic growth. The concomitant housing responsibility may be the most influential factor in influencing future economic growth.[24]

Redevelopment

The severity of the impact of both Propositions 13 and 4[25] on redevelopment financing required immediate, albeit ultimately, short-term legislative solutions.

The tax-allocation system of property tax distribution as authorized by Article XVI, Section 16, of the California Constitution provides that if a redevelopment agency has incurred debt (bonded or otherwise), the agency can receive tax increments to repay that debt.[26] Proposition 13 allows for a property tax levy in excess of 1 percent of full cash value to repay indebtedness voter approved prior to Proposition 13. After the adoption of Proposition 13, redevelopment agencies in some areas received their allocations of revenues on the basis of the maximum rate ($4.00 per $100) plus the rate for past indebtedness. Other agencies received their allocation of tax increments solely on the basis of the maximum rate. In the 1978-79 legislative session, Revenue and Taxation Code Section 2237 was adopted to allow redevelopment agencies to receive tax increments on the basis of the maximum rate plus a rate sufficient to repay past indebtedness.[27]

The average 60 percent reduction in property tax revenues after Proposition 13 put one agency in danger of imminent default on its bonds and several other agencies in technical default.[28] The Legislature responded in July, 1978, by establishing a thirty million dollar loan fund—the Local Agency Indebtedness Fund—for local agencies in imminent danger of default because of Proposition 13. The term of loans was three years. The fund was extended for an additional year in 1979. In 1980, the State Treasurer, who, as chair of the Pooled Money Investment Board, determines the appropriateness of loans made from the Local Agency Indebtedness Fund, refused to approve an application by the Redevelopment agency of Pasadena, California, because Pasadena was allegedly unable to repay the loan within three years. In response to this refusal, the Legislature, in July, 1980, amended the terms of the Local Agency Indebtedness Fund to provide for loans with a term of twenty years and to terminate the fund on December 31, 1980. With predictions of increasing numbers of defaults by 1982-83, either the Legislature will have to recreate the loan fund or the issue of whether Proposition 13 unlawfully impairs obligations of tax allocation bonds will be brought to the courts. In *Amador Valley Joint Union High School District vs. State Board of Equalization,* the California Supreme Court said that this issue was raised prematurely—there had been no direct impairment yet because the Legislature filled the gap with the Local Agency Indebtedness Fund. When eventually challenged, only municipal obligees, bondholders, or creditors alleging actual or potential impairment of their rights will have standing.[29]

A second legislative response to replace the funds flowing to redevelopment agencies from tax increments was the enactment in 1978 of a statutory scheme which authorizes a redevelopment agency to repay indebtedness incurred prior to Proposition 13 for which tax increments are insufficient, through benefit assessments.[30] Property owners within the project area could be subject to an assessment based upon their benefit from the redevelopment agency project activity. This device has not been widely utilized—only the redevelopment agencies of the cities of Brea, Corona, and Hawthrone, California, have utilized this authority—primarily because the assessments can only be calculated on the basis of properties as they existed on July 1, 1978, and must be calculated in proportion to the benefits such properties received from agency-initiated improvements constructed prior to that date. In many areas, not much development had taken place by that time although indebtedness had been incurred. Hardest hit were those redevelopment projects where development was really complete and those where it had not yet begun.[31] A final damper on the enthusiasm with which this solution has been accepted was provided by a lawsuit initiated in early 1980 by the property owners within the Corona, California, Redevelopment Agency Project area, challenging the benefit assessment district drawn by the Agency as unconstitutional on its face (as invalidly levied "special tax" in violation of Proposition 13) and as applied to the property owners.

A partial alternative to tax-increment financing was proposed to the California Legislature by Senator Watson (D-Los Angeles) as Senate Bill 1352 in the 1981 legislative session. Senate Bill 1352 would have authorized a redevelopment agency to levy a sales tax within its project area on the conditions that (1) the city provide a credit against the city sales tax collected within the project area for any retailer subject to the redevelopment agency's sales tax; and (2) the agency commit 20 percent of the sales tax collected to increasing the supply of housing for low and moderate income families. The prime use of this device would most likely be by a redevelopment agency located within a city in which the economic development of the city occurs within the redevelopment agency.[32] Senate Bill 1980 was defeated.

The most significant legislative response to the dramatic effect of Propositions 13 and 4 on the continued redevelopment of California's cities was provided by Senator Campbell's (R-Hacienda Heights) Senate Bill 1972, enacted as Chapter 1342 of the 1980 Statutes. Chapter 1342 provides that tax increments are not "proceeds of taxes" and that the appropriation of tax increments is not an appropriation subject to the agency's appropriations limit. This statute strengthens existing law by reiterating that the use of tax increments is limited to redevelopment purposes, and precludes the use of redevelopment agency's exempt appropriations for traditional municipal services.

The exemption from Proposition 4 for tax-increment financing is based on (1) an interpretation of Proposition 4, (2) the constitutional conflict between Article XIIIB and Article XVI, Section 16, and (3) a philosophical commitment to continued redevelopment. Article XIIIB, Section 8(b) defines "appropriations subject to limitation" as "any authorization to expend . . . the proceeds of taxes *levied by or for that entity* . . . ." (emphasis added). A redevelopment agency neither levies a tax nor are taxes levied on its behalf.[33] Restructuring the appropriation of proceeds of taxes under Article XIIIB conflicts with the authorization to expend tax-increments provided by Article XVI, Section 16. There is nothing in Article XIIIB which can be construed as a repeal of the existing authority provided by Article XVI, Section 6. In discussing the effect of Article XIIIA (the 1 percent of full cash value limitation) on Article XIII, Section 12 (the unsecured roll is taxed at the previous year's secured roll rate), the California Supreme Court stated that an effort must be made to harmonize apparently conflicting constitutional provisions. There was no indication provided by Article XIIIA that it was intended to repeal the provisions of Article XIII, Section 12. The court is reluctant to construe implied repeal of a constitutional provision.[34]

Finally, the absence of Chapter 1342 would have made continuing redevelopment virtually impossible because, in most instances, an agency's appropriations limit, based upon its appropriations for debt service, federal funds and developer contributions (all exempt appropriations) will be $0. Therefore, with the exception of an appropriation for debt service to repay indebtedness before January 1, 1979, no other appropriation of tax increments would be possible. This result comes at a time when the financing mechanism authorized for redevelopment agencies provide perhaps the most effective means of providing housing and economic development within California cities.[35]

Capital Improvement Financing

Proposition 4 on the November 1980 California general ballot would have amended Article XIIIA to provide an additional exemption from the 1 percent of full cash value limitation on ad valorem taxes for indebtedness approved by a two-thirds affirmative vote of those persons voting for the purpose of acquiring or improving real property. Although the problem was detected immediately, response to the virtual elimination of general obligation debts[36] has taken nearly two years. Proposition 4 on the November 1980 general election ballot was a legislatively initiated constitutional amendment (SCA 26 [Craven]) sponsored by the California Taxpayers Association and supported by a wide variety of interest groups, including builders, cities, counties and water districts. The importance of restoring general obligation bonds is primarily the lower costs incurred by this type of debt financing.[37] However, the biggest question surrounding restoration was: How much will they be used? SCA 26 requires a two-thirds voter approval of the added tax to repay the bonds. Whether the difficulty of getting a two-thirds vote would preclude their use is difficult to predict. Voters, however, were not apparently convinced that local officials are managing a lean operation and that capital improvement is needed, since the amendment failed by a margin of 25 percent in favor and 75 percent against.

Even with general obligation bonds, local governments will use a variety of methods to fund capital improvements. At the time of Proposition 13's passage, 40 percent of local government's bonded debt was in general obligation bonds, the rest was in revenue, improvement district, special assessment and similar kinds of obligations. The City of San Diego, California, to implement its system of timed and sequential growth management, is pioneering an expanded use of benefit assessments to finance not only the traditional streets and sidewalks, but also a wide variety of capital facility construction including police stations, firehouses, schools and park acquisition. Described as a "compromise" between the City of San Diego and a developer wishing to construct several thousand units, the "public facilities implementation program" provides for "facilities benefits assessments" spread on a benefit basis throughout an "area of benefit" which it can demonstrate specially benefits from the construction of the improvements. The system is based upon the assumptions that new development burdens the existing community and the fact that if the general fun is tapped to finance the improvements required by new development, the increased costs will require a reduction in service levels. Because the city intends to finance public facilities not currently authorized to be financed by benefit assessment under state law, the bonds issued under this plan will have to be validated in court.[38] If validated, this extension of the traditional use of benefit assessment financing could be a model for other charter cities (which, in the area of "municipal affairs" may exercise their home rule powers without the need for state enabling legislation) as well as a legislative proposal for general law cities.

Benefit assessment financing does permit construction to move ahead, but poses some questions about the equity of sharing the costs of facilities. The new homeowner whose housing costs may be increased by assessments or developer agreements may also be paying part of the property tax to repay outstanding bonds which financed facilities in existing neighborhoods. At the same time established homeowners are getting some general benefit from the facilities paid for by special assessments on others, they are spared added property taxes to help finance facilities for the newcomers.

In a state with so much new growth, it is easy to forget that public facilities construction includes replacement as well as original improvements for new developments. When the times comes to replace sewers and water mains in older neighborhoods, the shoe will be on the other foot. This is an argument for retaining some degree of broad local tax financing of capital improvements.

Reorganization of Local Governments

In the wake of Proposition 13, the Governor of the State of California established the Commission for Government Reform, chaired by Alan Post, former Legislative Analyst for the State of California, to study the effects of Proposition 13 on a wide variety of subject areas. One subject area was how to reorganize the 6,502 local governments in California. The generally accepted view at the time of this study was that the reduced revenues resulting from Proposition 13 would require more efficiency in the deliverance of local government services to lower costs through either reducing the number of local providers or consolidating the way in which services were provided. Based upon this assumption, the "Post Commission" recommended:

1. That the Governor and the Legislature review existing legal and fiscal barriers to local government boundary reform and simplification, with the goal of rationalizing the distribution of local governmental functions and costs, promoting citizen accountability, and providing for the effective delivery of governmental services and functions
2. That state legislation be enacted encouraging the establishment of local government review and evaluation commissions in each county to study matters which could improve the efficiency and effectiveness of the delivery of services by all elements of government at the local level[39]

Neither of these recommendations has been acted upon in the two years since Proposition 13.

In fact, in the two years since Proposition 13, five new cities have incorporated (with three additional proposals on the November 1980 general election ballot) and there has not been a single disincorporation of a city or dissolution of an independent special-purpose district, although changes in organization have been studied. Several reasons can be cited for this unexpected trend:

1. Although Proposition 13 originally provided a disincentive to form new governments because the original implementing legislation[40] provided for the allocation of property tax revenues based on the ratio that a local agency's property taxes in prior years bore to the total amount of property taxes collected by all taxing jurisdictions in the county, the "clean-up" to the original legislation provided for the allocation of property tax revenues on a "situs basis" and for an adjustment in allocation for annexations, detachments and new formations.[41] The formula for allocating taxes to new governments is based on the ratio of property tax revenues to total generated revenues of the jurisdiction which will no longer be rendering the service.
2. Prior to Proposition 13, some disincentive existed to the formation of new governments by the property tax rate system which allowed for the imposition of a tax rate by the new jurisdiction which was in addition to that imposed upon the same taxpayers by their former tax-levying jurisdictions. Proposition 13 eliminated this disincentive by the imposition of the 1 percent of full cash value limitation. New governments can be formed without increasing property tax burdens. However, property tax revenues must be allocated from the shares of existing

property tax revenues must be allocated from the shares of existing governments.

3. According to the California State Board of Equalization, the assessed value of property subject to ad valorem taxes increased in California by 18 percent average statewide in the 1979-80 fiscal year. This 18 percent increase in revenues blunts the impact of Proposition 13 and decreases the likelihood of a reduction in the numbers of local governments. Generally, if revenues continue to be available, services will continue to be provided, and little incentive will exist for consolidation or other reform. This is not to indicate that consolidation of services has not occurred on an intra-agency basis.
4. Special districts which existed on January 1, 1978, and levied a property tax rate of less than $.12 per $100 of assessed value are exempted from the Gann Initiative by Article XIIIB, Section 9(c). The appropriations of these special districts are limited only by available revenues.
5. Many special districts financed by property taxes historically were formed by developers or landowners to provide the public works—water, sewer—necessary for development and urbanization. Governed by an independently elected Board of Directors, these special districts enjoy a longevity and loyalty from their residents which makes reorganization difficult.

Based upon the premise that growth should occur within the urbanized areas of the state,[42] annexation of developed or developing territory to a city has been the normal growth pattern in California. However, Proposition 13 has provided a disincentive to annex territory and the result has been anti-growth.

Proposition 13 eliminated the way in which a city traditionally financed the provision of municipal services to newly annexed territory: a city would impose (usually higher) property tax rate on the new territory to finance its (usually higher quality) municipal services. The uniform 1 percent ($4.00 county-wide rate) eliminated this practice. Secondly, the first year's legislative implementation of Proposition 13 allocated property tax revenues on the basis of previous year's tax effort. There was no provision for a reallocation of revenues upon a boundary change. The second year's legislative implementation of Proposition 13 did provide for a change in the allocation system when boundaries were altered by annexations and detachments. Since July 24, 1979, California Revenue and Taxation Code Section 99 provides the amount of property tax revenues to be exchanged between and among affected agencies must be negotiated by those affected agencies. Since July 24, 1979, some twenty counties and the cities within those counties have agreed upon a system of property tax exchange. In the remaining twenty-eight counties, no agreement has been reached, all annexations initiated since July 24, 1979, are pending and development proposals are stalled. The failure to reach a negotiated compromise is primarily due to the fact that any revenues transferred to the annexing agency necessarily is a loss to the agency giving up service responsibility.

On the one hand a city will in most cases be expected by its new residents to provide a higher and more costly level of services than was provided by the county; on the other hand, the county must continue to receive a portion of the property tax revenues generated by the subject territory because of its continuing service responsibility in the areas of health, welfare and the courts. During 1979-80, the Legislature considered and rejected a partial solution to this impasse–Assembly Bill 2376 (Lancaster and Knox)–which would have imposed a formula to determine property tax exchange for those jurisdictional changes pending on May 21, 1980. Prospectively, all jurisdictional changes would have continued to be subject to the negotiations process.[43] The impasse in negotiations experienced relative to property tax transfer would seem to be a preview of things to come under the Gann Initiative. Article XIIIB, Section 3(a) provides that when one entity of government gives up service responsibility which is assumed by a separate entity of government, "the appropriations limit of the transferee entity shall be increased by such reasonable amount as the said entities *shall mutually agree* and the appropriations limit of the transferrer entity shall be decreased by the same amount." (emphasis added).[44]

Conclusion

Perhaps the most difficult part of assessing the impact of California's tax and expenditure limitations is isolating the respective effects of the use of massive state subventions to ameliorate Proposition 13's reduction in property tax revenue, inflationary price increases, the cost of construction and the cost of money in California, generally, from the land use effects of Propositions 13 and 4. Presumably when several years of the effects of these limitations have been quantified, the answers will become more apparent. In the meantime, what remains for discussion is what has happened for whatever cause, and what might happen in the future.

In analyzing the land use implications of coping with limited revenues under Proposition 13 and of coping with limited appropriations under Proposition 4, it becomes apparent that the interplay between the two constitutional provisions may provide more significant landuse effects than either Proposition viewed separately. For example:

1. Proposition 13 seemed to signal a boom for commercial and industrial development which provided increased sales tax and required minimal costly city services. But Proposition 4 will not all the appropriation of these sales tax revenues to the extent that their growth is dramatic relative to base-year appropriations.
2. Proposition 13 was applauded by urban strategists who argued that it forced a policy of urban containment onto cities which would lose money on housing development on the urban fringes where costly services did not exist and which would encourage new housing in built-up areas where services are already available. But Proposition 4 adversely affects California's urban centers whose populations generally are declining. Such a city's appropriations limit will decline as well, thereby making it more difficult to service the new housing which is constructed.
3. Proposition 13 eliminated general obligation bonds, the primary source of capital improvement financing. Proposition 4 would encourage the restoration of general obligation bonds to finance capital improvements since under Proposition 4 the appropriation of debt service to repay the voter-approved bonds is exempted from the appropriations limit.
4. Most cities perceive Proposition 13 as providing the final argument in favor of the statement that housing development does not pay for itself. However, Proposition 13 provides for reassessment for "new construction". In the 1979-80 fiscal year, assessed value growth reached 18 percent. But, on the average, a city's appropriations limit could only be adjusted by 12 percent in the 1979-80 fiscal year (change in per capita personal income and change in population).
5. The incentive to offset the reduction of property tax revenues under the tax limitation by an increase in the revenues, generally, is offset by the inability to appropriate those tax revenues under the expenditure limitations. Sources of nontax revenues must be tapped in order to fund the local services required by new growth. Both Proposition 13 and Proposition 4 encourage the use of fees which do not exceed the costs of providing the service for which the fee is charged.

The costs of the search for nontax revenues may be more expensive than the services which must be provided to new and existing residents. Before Proposition 13 was enacted, California was experiencing unprecedented escalation of housing costs. With an increase in amount of regulatory fees and in assessments for services based upon benefit, those who purchase homes in new subdivisions are required to purchase community facilities as well. New charges and assessments may push the moderate income family out of the homebuying market. Secondly, to the extent that the urban centers become more attractive and infill lots are developed to take advantage of existing services, urban land values will rise accordingly, thereby displacing low and moderate income residents and increase the burden on local services at a time when social services are being cut back in response to the reduction of available revenues.

The dilemma of Proposition 13 and Proposition 4 is how to finance local government services with nontax revenues without adversely impacting low and moderate income residents. Until this dilemma is resolved through a new system of indebtedness or through taxpayer frustration with decreasing local services, land use decisions will continue to be made by balancing the effects of the tax limitation and the expenditure limitation on each other and by balancing both against the unsatiated demand for continued residential and economic development.

Notes

1. Inan, "Savior of the Cities–Would You Believe, Howard Jarvis," 10 Cal. J. 138, 139 (1979) (quoting Bill Press, former Director of the Governor of California's Office of Planning and Research).

2. Shulman, "For Land's Sake, What's Prop. 13 Done?" Los Angeles Times, July 23, 1978, Section 4, at 5, Col. 1.

3. Shulman, "Proposition 13 and the Spatial Allocation of Economic Activities," 3 U.S.C. L. Rev. 125, 130 (1979).

4. *Id.*

5. Cal. Office of Planning and Research, *New Housing: Paying Its Way* (1978).

6. *Id.* It must be noted that a significant change in the law has occurred since this study was completed. In 1978, the California Legislature passed its Proposition 13 "bailout bill," Chapter 292, 1978 Stats., which provided a one-time state grant to each unit of local government based upon previous property tax effort (Cal. Govt. Code Sec. 16499.5). In addition, the property tax was allocated on the basis of prior tax effort based on a local jurisdiction's percentage of the countywide tax effort. Tax revenues derived from new construction were shared countywide while the costs associated with the new development were incurred by the local jurisdiction. An individual local jurisdiction thus had no incentive to have new tax producing development within its boundaries.

In 1979, the Legislature passed AB 8 (Chapter 282, 1979 Statutes) which corrected this defect. Under AB 8, tax revenues are distributed on a "situs basis"–only those taking jurisdictions covering the area which provides the tax revenues receive a portion of the revenues attributable to the area.

7. California Council for Environmental and Economic Balance. The Fiscal Impact of New Residential Development after Proposition 13. An Evaluation of the OPR Report, "New Housing: Paying Its Way?" (August 1979).

8. Inan, "Savior of the Cities–Would You Believe, Howard Jarvis?" 10 Cal. J. 138, 139 (1979).

9. California State Controller, 1978-79 Annual Report Financial Transactions Concerning Cities of California, VII.

10. Omit.

11. County of San Diego v. Lonergan, Cal. 3d. (1980), 80 Daily Journal 2305 (Cal. Sup. Ct., Aug. 14, 1980). However, there are proposals in the 1981 legislative session which would provide for a reduction of state subvention revenues to any agency otherwise receiving revenues as a result of this court decision.

12. See, text accompanying notes, 22-25, *supra.* preceding article.

13. Kinchen, "MIT Professor Enters Excessive Fees Fray," Los Angeles Times, Oct. 21, 1979, Pt. VI, at 12, col. 5.

14. D. Shulman, "Propositions 13 and the Spatial Allocation of Economic Activities," 53 U.S.C. L. Rev. 125, 131 (1979).

15. Hagman, "Reliance on Infrastructure Fees Indicates Resurgent Interest in Growth Control," Los Angeles Times, July 29, 1979, Part VIII at 29.

16. It can also be argued that the message of both Propositions 13 and 4 was for local government to increase its reliance on fees as a means of funding municipal service and decrease its reliance on the property tax. This message is clearly received from the voters who overwhelmingly adopted Proposition 13, wanting lower property taxes with the same level of municipal services. Written into Proposition 4, the limitation on the growth in appropriations of taxes, is a provision delimiting fees which do not exceed the costs of providing the service for which the fee is charged as nontaxes—an implicit endorsement of fees for services.

17. A response to Professor Hagman's reasoning is given by C. V. Holden in "Builder Spokesman Offers Argument Against Excessive Infrastructure Fees," Los Angeles Times, Sept. 9, 1979, Pt. VIII.

18. Association of Bay Area Governments, "Development Fees in the San Francisco Bay Area: A Survey," (Feb. 1980).

19. Gabriel, Katz and Wolch, "Local Land Use Regulations and Proposition 13," Taxing and Spending, pp. 73-81 (Spring 1980).

20. Construction Activity Post-Proposition 13, Cal-Tax Conference, November 8, 1979, p. 47.

21. Cal. Revenue & Tax Code, Section 100.1 (1979).

22. Van Ness and Shoup, "State and Local Tax Incentives to Attract Business: Will They Work After Proposition 13?" Conference, Lincoln Institute for Land Policy, February 9, 1979. California was one of three states nationwide in which there was no authority for the state or local government to issue industrial development bonds to finance industrial and commercial development. During the 1979-80 Legislative Session, Chapter was enacted to provide local governments with this authority.

23. The City of San Francisco, California, has experienced a resident population decline annually from 1973-1980. The city's response was the introduction of *SB 960* (Marks) in the 1979-80 Legislative Session which would provide that San Francisco's population change for purposes of Proposition 4 is to be identical to the change in population for the region encompassed by the Association of Bay Area Governments. *SB 960* was enacted as Chapter . The most recent response by the City of San Francisco to this problem was the enactment of an ordinance imposing an assessment on commercial establishments in the downtown area to help finance the city's transit system which primarily is used by downtown office workers.

24. The County of Santa Clara, California, has experienced significant industrial growth during the past decade. However, the firms associated with the Santa Clara Manufacturing Group are concerned about their continuing ability to attract employees because of the high cost and shortage of housing units. The County of Santa Clara and the Santa Clara Manufacturing Group are studying the adverse effects of the jobs/no housing phenomenon on an already burdened transit system.

25. See, text accompanying notes 74-80, *supra.* preceding article.

26. See, text accompanying notes 75-76, *supra.* preceding article.

27. Co-author Hagman worries that the levy authorized by Revenue and Taxation Code Section 2237 is a tax for redevelopment agency past indebtedness, which was *not* voter-approved and therefore unconstitutional as it is in conflict with California Constitution Article XIIIA, Section 1. However, Joe Coomes, redevelopment agency attorney with the firm of McDonough, Holland, Schwartz & Allen in Sacramento, California, argues that agencies should be able to collect additional tax levies for "voter approved indebtedness prior to the effective date of Proposition 13, in that the votes did approve the mechanics or act on which the allocation financing is based when the California Constitution was amended by the voters to add Article XVI, Section 16. In support of his position, Mr. Coomes cites Redevelopment Agency v. County of San Bernardino, 21 Cal. 3d 255, 267 (1978), 145 Cal. Rptr. 886, 578 P. 2d 133; 61 Ops. Cal. Atty. Gen. 373 (August 18, 1978).

28. See, text accompanying note, 76 *supra.* preceding article.

29. 22 Cal. 3d 318 (1978), 149 Cal. Rptr. 239, 583 P. 2d 1281. See, also, Solvang Municipal Improvement District v. Board of Supervisors of County of Santa Barbara, 112 Cal. App. 3d 545, 169 Cal. Rptr. 391 (1980).

30. Cal. Health & Safety Code Sections 33800 et. seq. (1978).

31. Merrill Lynch, Pierce, Fenner & Smith, Inc., California's Tax Allocation Bonds: Victims of Proposition 13, Municipal Bond Research (Oct. 1979).

32. The utility of this device is also marred by the possibility that the agency's sales tax will be construed as a "special tax" which requires a two-thirds affirmative vote under Article XIIIA, Section 4.

33. Cal. Const. Art. XVI, Section 16 (1954).

34. Lonergan v. County of San Diego, Cal. 3d. (1980), 80 Daily Journal D.A.R. 2305 (Cal. Sup. Ct., August 14, 1980).

35. See, generally, Cal. Health & Safety Code Sections 37910, et seq.

36. See, text accompanying notes, 69-71, *supra.* preceding article.

37. The attached table provides a comparison of the relative net interest cost of general obligation and revenue bonds issued by cities, schools and special districts in the 1978-79 fiscal year. As indicated in Cal-Tax Research Bulletin (August 1979), comparisons can be made by means of a Bank of America Market Index set each week on the bais of the 20-year maturity yield of a given issue in relation to similar yields of comparable issues sold in the same week. The market index permits ongoing comparisons of bond sales independent of conditions affecting the market as a whole during any particular week. On a $10 million issue with a 20-year term, a one point market index difference (64 to 65) in the example above means a $3,570 increase in the annual cost of paying off the debt and a $70,000 total increase over the full 20 years.

38. City Code of the City of San Diego, Sections 61.2200-61.2216 (1980). Telephone conversation on August 27, 1980 with Mr. Barney Allison of the law firm of Stradling, Yocca, Carlson & Rauth, special counsel to the City of San Diego. In the validating action, the City of San Diego intends to rely heavily on the provisions of Chapter 292 of the 1979 Statutes, as amended by Assembly Bill 2925 in the 1980 legislative session, authorizing a school district to issue bonds to finance the lease of school district facilities from a nonprofit corporation and to assess property owners benefitting from those facilities to repay the bonds.

39. Final Report, Commisssion on Government Reform, 68-70 (January, 1979).

40. Ch. 292, Section 24, Cal. Stats. 1978, adding California Government Code Section 26912.

41. Ch. 282, Section 59, Cal. Stats. 1979, adding California Revenue and Taxation Code Section 99.

42. See, Municipal Reorganization Act of 1977 at California Government Code Sections 35100 et. seq.

43. The negotiations process is aggravated by the fact that under California law, a city cannot terminate proceedings to annex territory to the city.

44. A California District Court of Appeal decision, City of Santa Barbara v. County of Santa Barbara, 94 Cal. App. 3d 277 (1979), 156 Cal. Rptr. 320, may provide what becomes the ultimate solution to the problem of dividing up a finite amount of property taxes by agencies providing differing service levels. The District Court of Appeal was required to resolve a troublesome provision of the California County Service Area Law (Gov. Code Section 25210.1 et seq.) which law was a legislative response to increasing inequities between residents of incorporated and unincorporated areas respecting the rendition of receipt of various municipal type services (*Id.*, at 287). Under the County Service Area Law, the City of Santa Barbara sought to establish a county service area to provide sheriff's patrol service in an unincorporated part of the county. The application was considered by the County Local Agency Formation Commission which amended the petition and approved a county service area covering the entire county. The LAFCO further recommended that the county establish zones within the county service area with differing tax rates depending on the benefit each zone received.

Under the law the county board next determines whether the services requested are extended county services. If it finds the requested services are extended county services, they cannot be financed by county general funds if the county fails to establish a county service area for the purpose of providing the services.

In the Santa Barbara situation, the county took the position that extended services meant those in excess of the level of service normally rendered by the sheriff and therefore no extended services were involved. The city took the position that extended services meant any service not being provided to the same extent on a countywide basis both within and without cities. It was conceded that sheriff's patrol services were not being provided within the city. Therefore, the city demanded that the county find the service to be "extended" and either create the county service area or stop using general funds to provide sheriff's patrol services. The trial court found the board's determination that the services were not extended to be arbitrary, capricious and without evidentiary support and ordered the board to determine the extent to which the services were extended and either provide a county service area or stop using general funds.

The court held that the county board's role was to determine whether specified services or the level thereof were being provided on a uniform basis within and without cities. If the services were being performed nonuniformly or if in certain areas of the county services over and above the normal level of services were being provided, then the county board would have the duty to find them an extended service if there was a "cognizable disparity," i.e., more than a mere difference. It would then have the duty to form the county service area or stop financing the service out of county general funds.

As a result of this case, city taxpayers will be less burdened by the costs of providing county services to unincorporated areas where the county services are not provided within cities. This case may form the basis for a future lawsuit or legislation which would provide that upon annexation of territory to a city, the county may only continue to receive property tax revenues from that territory in an amount equal to the county services provided therein. Receipt of revenues in excess of that amount would arguably have the effect of requiring the city taxpayer to fund an extended service to the unincorporated territory. See, D. Hagman, California Land Development, Public Control: Grist for the New Edition, February 5, 1980.

4

Effect on Growth, Housing and Development Mix

ROBERT H. FREILICH
STEVEN M. PERRY

Tax Expenditure and Limitation Systems

As a starting point in identifying what impact tax and expenditure limitation systems (TELS) have or will have on urban growth, housing, and development, the systems presently in effect should be classified.[1] A property tax limitation system of the California Proposition 13 type[2] possesses the following characteristics: (1) a "rollback" of the assessed valuation of the property; (2) a limitation of percentage increases in the assessed valuation of the property; (3) a limitation of the percentage increases in property tax rates; and (4) a requirement of voter approval prior to the levy of new local or "special" taxes. Alternatively, spending or "appropriation" limitation systems commonly possess these characteristics: (1) government appropriations are limited to a prior year's level,[3] (2) government spending may not exceed a specified percentage of state personal income,[4] (3) government spending is limited so that it does not

---

Dr. Freilich is Hulen Professor of Law in Urban Affairs, University of Missouri-Kansas City School of Law.
Mr. Perry is a J.D. candidate (1981), University of Missouri-Kansas City School of Law.

increase at a greater rate than the increase in gross state product,[5] (4) the spending limitation is tied to the U.S. Consumer Price Index (CPI),[6] or, (5) essentially, any combination of these methods.[7] In addition to the more clearly defined property tax and spending (expenditure) limitation systems, other systems may encompass a limitation on increases in state income tax and/or state sales tax.

The Effect of Systems on Housing and the Financing of Housing Programs—Particular Emphasis on a Property Tax Limitation System

All of the TELS described above possess characteristics which may either directly or indirectly have an effect on housing growth, housing programs, and the financing of capital facilities necessary for development. The property tax limitation system (Proposition 13 type) is focused on more closely since its effects appear to be more susceptible to analysis than other systems.

TRADITIONAL METHODS OF FINANCING—GENERAL OBLIGATION BONDS

Capital facilities such as roads, schools, bridges, water, sewerage drainage, power, and transit facilities are essential to housing and community development. Municipalities have traditionally made such facilities available by borrowing the money to build them through the issuance of general obligation bonds. These bonds are payable from and secured by an unlimited ad valorem tax which may be assessed and levied against all taxable real property within the municipality. Thus, rates and fees charged to the users of these capital facilities have been kept relatively low since the facilities are paid for by all property owners within the municipality.[8] A property tax limitation system, if engrafted, will, of necessity, abrogate general obligation borrowing if the limitation ceiling is not sufficiently high to permit the municipality to meet current operational costs and to pay debt service on the bonds.[9] The limitation will force the municipality to defer capital construction and, therefore (a) inhibit some development (particularly in newly developing areas without existing capital facilities), (b) increase borrowing costs by pledging limited tax revenues as security for the bonds, or (c) result in financing through revenue bonds.[10] This is particularly true of California's Proposition 13. In June, 1978, the California voters passed the initiative amendment to the California constitution, which drastically revamped the state's property tax system. The property tax rate to be applied by local government agencies is not limited to 1 percent of assessed value. The meaning of "assessed value" has undergone a substantial change in that the valuation of property is frozen, subject only to specified inflationary increases, as of its 1975/76 "full cash value," or thereafter the appraised value of the property when purchased, newly constructed, or upon the occurrence of a change in ownership. The 1 percent figure may be exceeded only if and to the extent that added revenues are required to discharge *outstanding* voter-approved indebtedness.[11] Local governments are precluded from replacing lost property tax revenues with other *general or property tax* sources by an absolute prohibition against imposing new ad valorem taxes on real property. Section 4 of Article XIIIA allows two-thirds of the "qualified electors" to impose *special* taxes but no definition for "special taxes" appears in the amendment.[12]

A property tax limitation system that increases the cost of borrowing will mean new or increased fees and charges for municipal services to be paid by the consumers of such services.[13]

REDEVELOPMENT FOR HOUSING IN THE CENTRAL CITY–TAX-INCREMENT FINANCING AND TAX ABATEMENT

Tax-increment financing, in states which provide for it, is a popular method of financing urban redevelopment in blighted areas of a city.[14] The assessed valuation of the property located in the blighted area is "frozen" at its existing level. Tax-increment (redevelopment) bonds are then issued to finance redevelopment. Ideally, the proceeds of the bond issue will be sufficient to redevelop the property and entice private investment in the once blighted area. Once the property is redeveloped, the difference (increment) between property taxes collected based on the assessed valuation of the improved property and those collected at the "frozen" assessed valuation are committed to retiring the bonds. Thus, a successful tax-increment financing program requires property values after redevelopment to be sufficiently higher than "frozen" levels so that the tax increments are sufficient to cover the redeveloper's net cost and interest over the period of debt service on the bonds.[15]

A property tax limitation system makes tax-increment financing much less attractive to a redeveloper and maybe even impracticable if the property under redevelopment is rendered incapable of generating the cash flow necessary to retire the tax increment bonds.[16]

Tax abatement laws provide another incentive for urban redevelopment in the central city by exempting or deferring property taxes levied on rehabilitated property. Rehabilitation programs undertaken pursuant to a tax abatement law are normally implemented through urban redevelopment companies.[17] The theory behind a tax abatement law is that property taxes discourage rehabilitation since an increase in assessed valuation after rehabilitation results in increased taxation.[18] Thus, taking a short-term view, a property tax limitation system seems to be an answer to the "distinctive" problem which tax abatement is designed to cure. However, the anticipated long-term effect of redevelopment made possible by tax abatement is increased revenue for the municipality by way of increased assessed property valuation.[19] From an ecomonic standpoint, that revenue is essential to further municipal development. Property valuation rollbacks and a limitation assessment and rates are likely to nullify the long-term effect that a tax abatement law is designed to achieve.

SITE SELECTION FOR LOW- AND MODERATE-INCOME HOUSING

Tax and expenditure limitation systems are likely to prevent housing growth in the urban fringe areas by limiting local government revenue. As a result, private developers may be forced to consider the central city area as a site for new building. Federally subsidized housing programs, however, are subject to restrictions on site selection that may be a deterrent to new construction. The Civil Rights Act of 1968,[21] Housing and Community Development Act,[22] United States Housing Act[23] and National Environmental Policy Act[24] either directly or indirectly impose an affirmative duty on developers to integrate housing and prohibit development on sites that would cause an "impaction" of minority or low-income families. In two recent cases in this area, *Karlen v. Harris* and *King v. Harris,*[26] the courts, relying on these statutes, enjoined construction of new housing in central city areas because such development would result in a concentration of minority or low-income families in the same community. The indirect effect of tax and expenditure limitation systems, therefore, may be to eliminate investment opportunities for private developers in the urban fringe areas because of the lack of local government revenue to finance capital facilities and in the central city because of site selection restrictions.

Alternatives to Raising Revenue by Property Taxation

SUBDIVISION EXACTIONS AND IMPACT FEES

Where a property tax limitation system has been implemented, housing development may be possible only if the costs of such development can be supplied by alternative sources.

A municipality may require a developer or subdivider to dedicate land or money in lieu of land in order to meet a subdivision's capital needs. The justification for these "exactions" is that the developer or subdivider should bear the cost of the burden which he had created on municipal facilities.[27] As would be expected, developers and subdividers have challenged "exactions" on constitutional grounds.[28] Where "exactions" have been upheld, the courts have required the municipality to show that the need for the exaction is either "uniquely attributable to"[29] or "reasonably related to"[30] the development creating the need.[31] Where a property tax limitation system such as Proposition 13 is in effect, subdivision exactions might be attacked as "special taxes" requiring voter approval;[32] however, in California at least, exactions were found to be valid charges imposed on subdividers and developers and not "special taxes."[33] As an alternative to raising revenue by property taxation, subdivision exactions imposed on subdividers and developers may be a less than satisfactory answer since they will probably be passed on to homebuyers in the form of higher prices.

Impact "fees" are levied against a developer by a municipality in order to recoup expenses incurred by the municipality in providing a pro-rata share of capital facilities necessary for new development, where contributions of land are not involved. Impact fees that exact an amount of money greater than the actual cost of providing facilities for new residents[34] may be held to be "special taxes."[35] There is a likelihood that impact fees used to replace general ad valorem property taxes lost under a Proposition 13 type system will be construed as "special taxes" requiring voter approval.[36] The determining factor appears to be whether such fees are used to fund projects traditionally funded by general tax revenues and which benefit the general public, as opposed to assessments for special benefit.

PUBLIC UTILITIES

Public utility law may also provide an alternative to raising revenue through property taxes so that housing development may continue. Housing development in the urban fringe areas depends on the extension of capital facilities to service that new development. Traditionally, capital facilities have been funded by general revenues, a major portion of which is composed of ad valorem taxes; however, a property tax limitation system will severely reduce the amount of funds normally attributable to these taxes. A municipality-owned utility might therefore impose user charges[38] or tap-in fees[39] to recoup this lost revenue, but such charges or fees will normally be limited to the actual cost of providing the service.[40]

The timing and location of new development may also be controlled by a municipal utility's refusal to extend capital facilities.[41] From a strictly legal standpoint, a utility's duty to serve potential customers is usually controlled by a determination that the entity was acting in a "proprietary" or a "municipal" capacity. A utility has a stringent duty to service the development if acting "proprietarily," whereas, if functioning in a "municipal" capacity, the utility may exercise governmental discretion in deciding whether to provide service. The courts, however, as a practical matter, have held municipal utilities to the same duty to serve regardless of the label applied to its function, where the utility is providing service extraterritorially.[42] The decisions in extraterritorial areas are essentially grounded in the economic and practical feasibilities of extension versus nonextension.[43] The net result is that, in the absence of a statute to the contrary, current law allows municipal utilities to refuse extension of service only for a "utility-related" reason; e.g., an insufficient expected rate of return in view of a large capital investment coupled with supply shortages is a "utility-related" reason.[44]

Thus, the concept of public utility law as an alternative to raising revenue via property taxation so that development might continue has several pitfalls, but nonetheless may serve as an alternative in two ways; first, the revenues lost because of a property tax limitation system may be recouped to a limited extent by the imposition of user charges and tap-in fees as a prerequisite to extension of capital facilities. Second, with appropriate statutory authority, public utility law may be used to control the timing and location of development and furnish a technique for directing development into areas where capital facilities are already in existence, depending on whether the utility is private or municipal and whether the extension is within or outside municipal boundaries.

GROWTH MANAGEMENT SYSTEMS

Growth management, as an alternative to raising revenue through property taxation, can achieve results similar to public utility law and, accordingly, a system's effectiveness can be greatly enhanced by coupling it with a municipal utility's authority to refuse extension of service.[46] Basically, growth management systems are comprehensive attempts to apply time and sequence methods to the development of land and to manage the character of growth within urban communities and on the urban fringe through various techniques such as zoning and subdivision regulations, exactions, fee systems, official mapping annexation, and capital programming.[47]

Where a property tax limitation system has been adopted, growth management may be able to ease the municipality's fiscal strain and avoid passing on the entire cost of capital improvement to the homebuyer by directing development into areas where capital facilities have already been constructed.[48]

Ideally then, growth management systems have the potential to allow development, yet hold down housing costs by structuring the full assimilation of population to areas already serviced or in which a plan will apply time and sequence methods to capital formation. Modern growth management systems such as those in San Diego, Minneapolis-St. Paul, and Lexington employ regional plans to effectively accommodate this result,[49] while the courts themselves are requiring that communities that regulate land do so in accord with regional general welfare. In *Southern Burlington County NAACP v. Township of Mt. Laurel,*[50] the court held that a "developing" municipality that enacts local land use regulations affecting housing construction must consider the general welfare of the region and, therefore, has a responsibility to the region in providing a regional "fair share" of low- and moderate-income housing.[51] Following the Mt. Laurel decision, the court established a standard by which municipalities were to provide their "fair share" of low- and moderate-income housing and at the same time keep the price of housing down. In *Oakwood at Madison v. Township of Madison,*[52] the court held that a good faith effort must be made toward eliminating or minimizing undue cost-generating aspects of municipal zoning ordinances so that "least-cost housing" would be possible.[53]

INCLUSIONARY ZONING ORDINANCES

In light of the property tax limitation systems that decrease local government revenue and increase the cost of housing, inclusionary zoning ordinances may serve as a limited alternative to raising revenue. Such ordinances mandate that new residential developments of a certain minimum size contain a specified portion of low- and moderate-income units and, therefore, may provide a segment of the population with housing that would otherwise be unavailable.[54] An additional feature of inclusionary regulations is a provision for "density bonuses," which are made available to developers who comply with the regulations, thereby allowing the developer to mitigate the lost profits sustained by him as a result of compliance.[55] Further, an award of a "density bonus" eliminates, to some degree, the developer's need to recoup his losses by raising the cost of units not subject to the ordinance. Generally, inclusionary zoning ordinances are upheld as valid exercises of the police power; however, a few recent decisions have held otherwise.[56]

SPECIAL ASSESSMENT

Although the scope of this article does not permit a detailed analysis of special assessment, a brief reference to it as an obvious alternative to raising revenue through property taxation should be made. Special assessment is essentially a method of imposing the cost of capital facilities or improvements directly against the adjacent property to be benefited, thereby allocating costs according to benefit.[57] Thus, the method by which revenue is raised through special assessment completely counters financing with general tax revenue, which spreads costs across all taxable property. From a constitutional standpoint, a special assessment will be upheld when it does not exceed the special benefit to the property. The owners of the property benefited by the capital improvements are required to pay only for its cost.[58]

Conclusions

The effect of tax and expenditure limitation systems, particularly a property tax limitation system, on housing development is directly related to the availability of capital facilities to service the housing development. As a result of implementing a system, the use of general obligation bonds to finance capital facilities and tax increment bonds to finance redevelopment become less promising, riskier, and, therefore, more expensive.

In addition to the diminished desirability of traditional financing methods, there is no guarantee that the alternatives to raising revenue that have been presented will provide an effective means for continued development. All of these alternatives are subject to constitutional challenge and, if invoked indiscriminately, such challenges are likely. Aside from the constitutional issues, the economic consequences of implementing these alternatives may be to directly or indirectly impose the increased cost of new housing development on the consumer. If, on the other hand, effective growth management techniques are employed, the added costs can be diminished by encouraging the development of housing in bypassed areas where capital facilities exist or to apply time and sequence methods to growth in fringe areas so that the most economical and efficient utilization of facilities is made to hold down costs.

Notes

1. *Public Administration Review,* July-August 1979, Table 1, p. 378.

2. Cal. Const. art. 13A, §§ 1-6.

3. Cal. Const. art. 13B, effective July 1, 1980 (the GANN initiative curbing governmental spending by limiting governmental appropriations to 1979/80 levels). These provisions can be even more limiting than the JARVIS-GANN, art. 13A initiative amendment. Whereas 13A limits the growth of the property tax valuation base and places restrictions on substitute "special taxes," at least special assessments have been determined to be exempt from such provision since they are not "taxes." City of Fresno v. Malmstrom, 94 Cal. App. 3d 974, 156 Cal. Rep. 777 (1979). However, art. 13B defines "appropriations subject to limitation" to include the *proceeds* of taxes and Section 8(c) of art. 13B defines proceeds of taxes to include user charges, user fees, regulatory licenses and the investment of tax proceeds. An appellate validating action will have to be brought to determine if the amendment is legally more restrictive than its 13A predecessor.

4. See, *e.g.,* Ariz. Const. art. 9, § 17, which provides: "The legislature shall not, by appropriation for any fiscal year, cause the expenditure of state tax revenues for that fiscal year to exceed 7 percent of the total personal income of the state for such fiscal year . . . except upon affirmative vote of each such appropriation of two-thirds of the membership of each house of the legislature."

5. See, *e.g.,* Hawaii Const. art. 7, § 9, which provides:

> [The] legislature shall establish a general fund expenditure ceiling which shall limit the rate of growth of the state's economy as provided by law. No appropriations in excess of such ceiling shall be authorized during any legislative session unless the legislature shall, by a two-thirds vote of the members to which each house of the legislature is entitled, set forth the dollar amount and the rate by which the ceiling will be exceeded and the reasons therefore.

See *also* Tex. Const. art. 8, § 22 (limiting the rate of growth of appropriations such that they shall not exceed the estimated rate of growth of the state's economy).

6. A constitutional amendment which would have indexed state income tax revenues to the CPI was proposed in Colorado and defeated. Pub. Adm. Rev., July/August 1979, Table 1 at 378.

7. See, *e.g.,* Mich. Const. art. 9, §§ 25-31 (Supp. 1980).

8. See Rankin, Osburn, & Rogers, "Municipal Bonds and Property Tax Limitations," 9 Envt'l L. Rev. 452, 461-70 (1979); the resultant "subsidy" to new development has been paid for by the existing neighborhoods and downtown commercial properties. This process has been analogized to "redlining" by banking and financial institutions—receiving deposits in older neighborhoods and loaning the funds in nearby developing areas—a "public redlining" process. This commentator believes that this is a major cause in the decline of older community areas. *See* note 49, *infra.*

9. *Id.*, Rankin at 470 & n. 75.

10. *Id.*, Rankin at 470-71.

11. Freilich, "1978-79 Annual Review of Local Government Law; Undermining Municipal and State Initiative in an Era of Crisis and Uncertainty," 11 Urb. Law. 547, 578 (1979).

12. Cal. Const. art. 13A, § 4.

13. Rankin, Osburn, & Rogers, *supra* note 8, at 471.

14. In California, tax increment financing is authorized by the state constitution and implemented by duplicate provisions in the state Community Redevelopment Law. Davidson, "Tax Increment Financing as a Tool for Community Redevelopment," 56 J. of Urb. L. 405, 423 nn. 133, 134 (citing Cal. Const. art. 16, § 16 and Cal. Health & Safety Code § 33670 (West 1973).

15. ABA Advisory Commission on Housing and Urban Growth, *Housing for All Under Law: New Directions in Housing, Land Use, and Planning Law,* 525-28 (1978).

16. In Amador Valley School District v. State Bd. of Equalization, 538 P. 2d 1281 (1978), the California Supreme Court was asked to determine whether Proposition 13 impaired the contractual rights of tax increment bondholders in violation of the Contracts Clause of the U.S. Constitution. The Court upheld the constitutionality of Proposition 13 and found the impairment of contractual obligation claim to be premature since a "Local Agency Indebtedness Fund" had been created from state budget surplus in order to avert such defaults on public obligations. *Id.* at 1295-98.

17. See Murphy, "State and Local Tax Incentives for Urban Growth: A Concept Whose Time Never Was?" 6 Fordham Urb. L.J. 457, 468-79 (1978). The New York tax abatement law has been in effect since 1955. The Limited-Profit Housing Companies Law, commonly known as the Mitchell-Lama Law, was enacted to facilitate the contruction of low-rent housing and rehabilitation through government financing at below market interest rates and the use of private incentives such as real property tax exemptions. N.Y. Priv. Hous. Fin. Law §§ 10-37 (McKinney 1976 & Supp. 1979). For a more complete discussion of New York's Mitchell-Lama Law, including a performance evaluation, see Sternlieb, Roistacher & Hughes, *Tax Subsidies and Housing Investment: A Fiscal Cost-Benefit Analysis,* 15-17 (1976).

18. Gupta & Rea, "The Investment Decision in the Central City: A Consideration of a Property Tax Abatement Law," 7 Fordham Urb. L.J. 253, 259 (1979).

19. *Id.* at 263 & n. 26.

20. See, Freilich, "1978-79 Annual Review of Local Government Law: Undermining Municipal and State Initiative in an Era of Crisis and Uncertainty," 11 Urb Law. 547, 570-76 (1979).

21. Civil Rights Acts of 1968, Title VIII, § 801, 42 U.S.C. § 5301 (1976).

22. Housing and Community Development Act of 1974, § 101, 42 U.S.C. § 5301 (1976).

23. United States Housing Act of 1937 § 8, 42 U.S.C. § 1437 (1976).

24. National Environmental Policy Act of 1969, § 2 42 U.S.C. § 4321 (1976).

25. 590 F. 2d 39 (2d Cir. 1978). In *Karlen,* the court found that an urban renewal program filed with HUD which proposed construction of a seventeen-

story apartment building exclusively for low-income tenants in an area already containing a high percentage of low-income housing would lead to concentration in that area in violation of the National Environmental Policy Act of 1969 and thus enjoined construction of the project. *Id.* at 45.

26. 464 F. Supp. 827 (E.D.N.Y. 1979). Here, the court held that HUD violated its affirmative duty to avoid concentration of minority or low-income families in the same community by approving federal funds for a low-income community where it was established that such construction would result in a concentration of low-income housing and would, therefore, have a "tipping" effect on the community. The Court struck HUD approval of the project and issued a permanent injunction enjoining HUD from providing or reserving federal funds for the construction of a low-income housing project at the proposed site. *Id.* at 841-845.

27. See, R. Freilich & P. Levi, *Model Subdivision Regulations Text and Commentary,* 118-29 (American Society of Planning Officials 1975).

28. For a classic article concerning the constitutional aspects of subdivision exactions, *see* Heyman & Gilhool, "The Constitutionality of Imposing Increased Community Costs on New Suburban Residents Through Subdivision Exactions," 73 Yale L.J. 1119 (1964).

29. See Krughoff v. City of Naperville, 369 N.E. 2d 892, 895 (Ill. 1977).

30. See Jenad, Inc. v. Village of Scarsdale, 18 N.Y. 2d 78, 218 N.E. 2d 673, 271 N.Y.S. 2d 955 (1966); Assoc. Homebuilders, Inc. v. City of Walnut Creek, 4 Cal. 3d 633, 94 Cal. Rptr. 630, 484 P. 2d 606 (1971).

31. Under either test, the amount of dedicated land or money in lieu of land must be kept within reasonable limits. Where the exaction is totally unrelated to the subdivision's needs, or the money collected is unlimited in amount so as to constitute a general tax rather than an exaction, the regulation or its application in the specific case will be stricken. R. Freilich & P. Levi, *supra* note 27 at 128.

32. See Cal. Const. art. 13A, § 4.

33. 62 Op. Ca. Att'y Gen. 712 (November 1, 1979). The Attorney General concluded that an exaction imposed upon a subdivider by a local agency to build improvements which will benefit the subdivided land in in the nature of a special assessment and not a special tax. Thus, it would appear that a subdivision exaction which is not more than a charge against the property for the share of costs attributable to the benefit is outside the scope of the special tax prohibition in section 4. *See also,* Trent-Meredith v. City of Oxnard, 170 Cal. Rptr. 685 (1981) extending the analogy of special assessment to subdivision exactions and finding the latter neither an *ad valorem* nor a special tax.

This "special assessment-special tax" dichotomy was examined by the California Court of Appeals in County of Fresno v. Malmstrom, 94 Cal. App. 3d 974, 156 Cal. Rptr. 777 (1979). The *Malmstrom* court upheld the county's authority to improve certain areas within its jurisdiction by imposing special assessments on the property owners specially benefited. Such assessments are not "special taxes" which are collected and earmarked for a special purpose and, therefore, are outside the scope of the section 4 requirement of two-thirds voter approval.

34. See National Science Foundation, *Local Capital Improvements and Devel-*

opment Management, 58-59 (ASPO, July 1977). *See,* Christian and Missionary Alliance Foundation v. Florida Cities Water Company, 386 So. 2d 543 (Fla. (1980).

35. See note 33 *supra* and accompanying text.

36. See 62 Op. Cal. Att'y Gen. 724 (1979), wherein the Attorney General concluded that payment of an in-lieu fee imposed by a county as a condition precedent to issuance of a building permit for construction of low- and moderate-income housing is a "special tax" within the meaning of Cal. Const. art 13A, § 4 and, therefore, requires two-third voter approval.

37. See 62 Op. Ca. Att'y Gen. 625 (1979). Here, the Attorney General concluded that school development fees charged developers to finance construction of interim school facilities could not be imposed without the voter approval required by § 4. The rationale for this conclusion is that such a fee is, in effect, being substituted for the ad valorem taxes which have traditionally been the source for financing such facilities and, therefore, should be considered a special tax requiring voter approval.

38. A municipality which owns its own water, electric, or other utility plant has the right to charge consumers who make use of its services. E. McQuillan, *Municipal Corporations* § 35.37 (rev. ed. 1970).

39. Municipalities may provide for tap-in charges for water subject only to the qualification that the fees established must be fair and reasonable and bear a substantial relationship to the cost involved in providing the service to the property owner. *Id.*

40. Fees which exceed the actual cost of providing the service are analagous to impact fees and, therefore, may be classified as "special taxes" subject to voter approval. See notes 36 & 37 *supra* and accompanying text.

41. See Notes, "Public Utility Land Use Control on the Urban Fringe," 63 Iowa L. Rev. 889, 890-91 (1978).

42. Robinson v. City of Boulder, 547 P. 2d 228 (Colo. 1976).

43. *Id.* at 900 & n. 68. A landmark decision in the "extension vs. non-extension" area is Lukrawka v. Spring Valley Water Co., 169 Cal. 318, 146 P. 640 (1915). There, the Supreme Court of California held that a private water company organized and engaged in a public enterprise, pursuant to state law, to supply the inhabitants of a community with water must extend its service to a number of inhabitants who were not receiving service where the extension was practically and economically feasible and the demand therefore was reasonable. 146 P. at 645-46. *Accord* Cedar Island Improvement Ass'n v. Clinton Elec. Light & Power C., 142 Conn. 359, 114 A. 2d 535 (1955) (compelling extension of electric service); *Contra,* Jordan v. Clarke-Washington Elec. Membership Corp., 262 Ala. 581, 80 So. 2d 527 (1955) (refusal to compel extension of electric supply where demand to do so was economically unreasonable); McMullin v. Pub. Serv. Comm'n, 7 Utah 2d 157, 320 P. 2d 1107 (1958) (refusal to compel extension of water supply).

44. Notes, "Public Utility Land Use Control on the Urban Fringe," 63 Iowa L. Rev. 889, 899 (1978). "The category of valid utility-related reasons traditionally recognized by the courts is very restricted." Also included in this category, however, is the refusal of a customer to pay his water bill as a justification for refusing to extend service.

In Robinson v. City of Boulder, 547 P. 2d 228, 229 (Colo. 1976), the Supreme Court of Colorado concluded that the City of Boulder could only refuse to extend water and sewer services to landowners for utility-related reasons and growth control and land use planning considerations are not utility-related reasons which require extension.

45. For a comprehensive listing of state statutes which give municipalities authority to control the location and timing of public utility extensions in order to implement land use control and development objectives, see Notes, "Public Utility Land Use Control," *supra* note 41 at 905 n. 97. But c.f. Crownhill Homes, Inc. v. City of San Antonio, 433 S. W. 2d 448 (Tex. 1968).

46. See notes 43-44, *supra* and accompanying text.

47. ASPO, Report Nos. 309, 310, *Urban Growth Management Systems* 35-48 (1976).

48. Notes, "Public Utility Land Use Control," *supra* note 41 at 889.

49. See, generally R. Freilich, "Land Use Controls and Growth Management: The Need for a Comprehensive View," 9 Urb. Law. V, viii-ix (1977) (response to Ellickson, "Suburban Growth Controls: An Economic and Legal Analysis," 86 Yale L.J. 385 [1977]).

50. 67 N.J. 151, 336 A. 2d 713 (1975).

51. *Id.* at 731-34.

52. 72 N.J. 481, 371 A. 2d 1192 (1977).

53. *Id.* at 1207-08. ("Nothing less than zoning for least cost housing will . . satisfy the mandate of Mt. Laurel.")

54. See, ABA Advisory Commission on Housing and Urban Growth, *Housing for All Under Law: New Directions in Housing, Land Use, and Planning Law* 584-592 (1978).

55. *Id.* at 238-39, 384. See also Oakwood at Madison v. Township of Madison, 371 A. 2d 1192, 1209-10 (1977).

56. See Bd. of Supervisors of Fairfax County v. DeGroff Enterprises, Inc., 214 Va. 235, 198 S.E. 2d 600 (1973). The *DeGroff* court invalidated the zoning ordinance in question on two grounds: First, the mandatory ordinance was outside the municipality's authority under the state zoning enabling act because the ordinance was not promulgated in consideration of the physical characteristics of the land, and second, such "socioeconomic" zoning is an unconstitutional taking without just compensation since it reduces developer profits by requiring him to sell a specified percentage of units in the development to persons of low or moderate income at rental or sale prices not fixed by a free market. *Id.* at 602. *Accord* Middlesex & Boston St. Ry. Co. v. Bd. of Alderman, 359 N.E. 2d 1279 (Mass. 1977) where the court invalidated a condition in an ordinance under which a special permit would be issued to the plaintiff only if the plaintiff would lease several apartments to the city's housing authority at reduced rents. *Id.* at 1285-86; Oakwood at Madison v. Township of Madison, 72 N.J. 481, 371 A. 2d 1192 (1977), where the court held that "least cost" housing should be implemented in lieu of an ordinance which sets up a specific formula for determining a community's fair share of lower-income housing. *Id.* at 1207-08.

57. ASPO, *Urban Growth Management Systems* 44 (Report Nos. 309, 310, 1976).

58. E. McQuillan, *Municipal Corporations* § 38.02 (rev. ed. 1970).

5

Development Agreements: Are They an Enforceable Response to TELS?

BRUCE M. KRAMER

Under an innovative law recently enacted in California, which could be the precursor of similar legislation elsewhere, local governments may enter into development agreements with developers which prohibit the local legislative body from changing the land use restrictions on a parcel prior to the vesting of development rights. However, what if subsequent legislation is passed which impairs the development agreement? Is the developer protected under the impairment-of-contracts clause of the Constitution or can the local legislative body invoke the reserved powers doctrine which protects any valid exercise of the state's police power? To answer this question, the author analyzes the leading cases on the contracts clause and the reserved powers doctrine. He also considers the applicability of judicial decisions involving the validity of contract zoning–situations where there is an agreement that purports to bind both the landowner and the local governmental agency–and conditional zoning–where the person seeking the development permission agreed unilaterally to do something but the governmental agency made no binding agreement.

The Problem

One of the ramifications of the passage in California of Proposition 13 has been the shifting of the burden to the land developer and

Mr. Kramer is professor of law, Texas Tech University School of Law.

subdivider of more of the costs of the infrastructure needed to service the development. This has obviously led to higher front-end costs for developers. Faced with these higher front-end costs, financed at even higher interest rates, the developer is going to be even more hesitant to develop and/or subdivide raw land.

An additional problem for developers is the late "vested right" rule in California and other states. Thus, the developer must add into his decision-making process the possibility that the local governmental body he is working with may change the rules on him prior to the vesting of his rights; this would leave him at the mercy of a local legislative body once the initial work and financing has been arranged.[1] In many cases where multiple permits are required, it may not be until the last permit has been approved that the right to develop will become vested.[2] Once vested, the permit and laws become unchangeable except through an eminent domain proceeding. Prior to vesting, however, the developer may already have incurred large financial liabilities.

Since the local government can change the rules of the game, the developer is in a poor bargaining position to contest those changes that are suggested by the local government. This may lead to even higher housing and building costs in the event that developers become more reluctant to act. In response to the perceived need to lessen the burden of land developers and subdividers, given the large increase in infrastructure costs being imposed on them, the California Legislature in 1979 enacted a statute which proposes to allow local governments to enter into "development agreements" which will freeze the local governmental land use regulations on the property in question.[3]

The statute requires that the developer must in "good faith" prosecute the development of the parcel. If not, the "development agreement" may be unilaterally terminated or modified. The agreement must be of limited duration, specify the permitted uses, density and intensity of such uses, maximum height and size of proposed buildings, along with the reservation or dedication of land. The agreement is to be periodically reviewed to determine the good-faith compliance by the developer. It can only be entered into after a public hearing is held and cannot be amended or canceled unless by mutual agreement of the parties. The agreement is considered to be a legislative act subjecting it to the referendum provisions of the California Constitution.[4] The agreement is modifiable to take into consideration subsequently changed state or federal laws affecting the development. No development agreement can be binding on property within the jurisdiction of the California Coastal Commission Act[5] unless the local coastal program has been approved by the California Coastal

Commission or the agreement itself receives approval of the entire Commission.

The stated purpose of the statute is to maximize the efficient utilization of land resources with the least economic cost to the public. If the purpose is to be achieved, then the enforceability of the development agreement and the remedies available after a breach must be identified. The statute merely states that the development agreement will be enforceable. That could include actions for damages, specific performance, or other contractual remedies.

The statutory scheme raises some interesting issues. The first issue deals with the contracts clause of the Constitution and its application to governmental contracts. The second issue involves the reserved powers doctrine as a limit on a government's ability to contract or bind itself. Last is the issue of to what extent the classic contract zoning cases are applicable or relevant to the development agreement.

Applicability of the Contracts Clause to Development Agreements

THE "ABSOLUTE" TEST

The Constitution simply provides that "No State shall . . . pass any . . . Law Impairing the Obligation of Contracts."[6] Although originally designed to prevent state governments from enacting debtor relief laws,[7] the contracts clause under the aegis of Chief Justice Marshall became an avenue to review public contracts and legislation as well. In *Fletcher v. Peck,*[8] Marshall held the contracts clause applicable to an attempt by a subsequent Georgia legislature to repeal earlier state land grants issued after widespread fraud and bribery were discovered.[9] Although the decision waffled on the issue of the strict applicability of the contracts clause to a contract or agreement between a public entity and a private individual, that issue was soon resolved in *Dartmouth College v. Woodward.*[10] In *Dartmouth College,* Chief Justice Marshall clearly held that the contracts clause was applicable to a state-granted charter to a private institution, namely Dartmouth College. The New Hampshire legislature was attempting to pack the trustees and change the institution into a public college in violation of some of the covenants contained in the original charter.[11] The attempt to change several of the covenants was found to be an unconstitutional impairment of a contract and thus void.

As it emerged from the Marshall Court, the contracts clause was a potent weapon to prevent state and local legislatures from changing previously granted charters, land grants, or contracts. All one had to show under *Fletcher* and *Dartmouth College* was the existence of a contract, some type of beneficial interest, and an impairment.

Seemingly any impairment would be sufficient, but in both cases you have attempts at an outright repeal of the previously granted contractual rights so the Court did not have to develop a limiting test to determine the validity of state impairments. In *Dartmouth College,* the Court also had little difficulty overcoming the problem that petitioners in the case were not parties to the original contract, nor were they the beneficial holders under the contract.

When Chief Justice Marshall retired and was succeeded by Chief Justice Taney, some limitations were placed on the "absolute" test for a contracts clause violation. In *Charles River Bridge v. Warren Bridge,*[12] The Commonwealth of Massachusetts had granted a charter to the Charles River Bridge Company to build and operate a toll bridge. Subsequently the Commonwealth issued a second charter to the Warren Bridge Company to construct a bridge which would become a free bridge after three years of operation. Charles River Bridge contended that the second charter diminished the value of its charter and thus was an impairment of contract. The Supreme Court disagreed, initially finding that there was neither explicit nor implicit grant of an exclusive charter to Charles River Bridge.[13] Opting to construe contracts between public and private entities strictly in favor of the public entity's freedom to act, the Court found no unconstitutional impairment of contract. Thus while the contract in this case was covered by the contracts clause, it had not been impaired because of the strict canon of construction that Chief Justice Taney applied.

THE SUPREME COURT'S "SLIDING SCALE" ANALYSIS

The contracts clause did not receive much judicial attention insofar as it affected public contracts for 125 years until the Supreme Court decided *U.S. Trust Co. v. New Jersey.*[14] In *U.S. Trust,* the State of New Jersey repealed certain convenants that had limited the ability of the Port of New York Authority to take over mass transit operations that were running at a deficit. The covenants were part of a bond issuance by the Port Authority. In ascertaining whether or not the repealer violated the contracts clause, the Court embarked on a new road for judicial review. The majority opinion probably set up a dual standard of review under the contracts clause. For contracts in which the government is a party and has an interest, the courts will engage in a much stricter scrutiny.[15] In this case there was no question that the plaintiffs were a party to a contract since they were bond holders of the Port Authority. There was also no question that there was a contract between the Port Authority and its bond holders since the convenant was made part of the bond agreement. There was also no arguable question that the security for the bonds had been impaired. The key issue that was resolved in favor of the bond holders was whether the impairment was unconstitutional.

In developing the test to determine when an impairment rises to the level of an unconstitutional impairment, the *U.S. Trust* Court rejected the notion that any impairment would be a violation of the contracts clause.[16] Although allegedly deferring to legislative decisions impacting on economic and social matters, the Court said that where there is an impairment of a contract it must be "upon reasonable conditions and of a character appropriate to the public purpose justifying its adoption."[17] This appears to be a means/end test, a not-too-distant departure from the usual rational basis for equal protection and due process claims in the economic and social arena. But later on the Court subtly changes the terminology used to describe what a state must show in order to sustain an impairment where its self-interest is concerned. Instead of a true means/end, rational relationship analysis the Court requires that the state action be both "reasonable" and "necessary" in serving an important public purpose.[18] The Court then repudiated its earlier statement regarding the need for deference because of the self-interest of the state in financial matters. It also rejected the "total destruction" test whereby a state could impair its financial obligations as long as they were not totally destroyed.[19] In determining what was a "necessity," the Court utilized the "less onerous alternative" formula usually reserved for strict scrutiny analysis under the equal protection clause. If less onerous alternatives are available to the state which would achieve the same policy goals and not impair the contract, then the state is no longer free to choose among alternatives because of the existence of the impairment. Especially where the impairment is substantial in nature, the state must choose the policy alternative which least impairs any existing state/private contracts.[20] The Court adopts a "sliding scale" analysis. The greater the impairment the closer the scrutiny, in addition to a heightened level of review for public contracts.

The precedential value of *U.S. Trust* was questioned because it was a plurality opinion.[21] But one year later in *Allied Structural Steel Co. v. Spannaus,*[22] the Supreme Court in a 6-3 decision reaffirmed the revival of the contracts clause as a deterrent to state and local legislation which impairs contracts.[23] Although *Allied Structural Steel* dealt with a state law which infringed the contractual rights of private parties, the Court reaffirmed the necessity and reasonableness test set out in *U.S. Trust.*[24] In fact, *Allied Structural Steel* embraces the sliding-scale approach of *U.S. Trust* to the contracts clause by equating the strict scrutiny review of public contracts with the review to be given private contracts which are substantially impaired by state action.[25] In fact, the Court suggests an even stricter review for public contracts which are substantially impaired by subsequent state action.

Thus *U.S. Trust* and *Allied Structural Steel* would aid the developer who was trying to enforce the development agreement. In this situation, it is clear that a contract has been agreed to and that the developer has a beneficial interest. By definition, an impairment has occurred and thus the sole issue is whether the impairment violates the contracts clause. As with the covenant in *U.S. Trust,* the government is acting in its own self-interest and therefore a stricter judicial scrutiny is mandated. Subsequent legislative action seeking to amend, modify, or repeal the development agreement would undoubtedly impair the obligation of the contract and if less onerous alternatives were available to the legislature to achieve the same policy goals they would have to be taken.

WAS THE IMPAIRMENT AN OFFICIAL ACT?

The contracts clause, however, does not apply to a simple breach caused by nonperformance unless accompanied by an official act or ordinance. An excellent example of discerning when a legislative act rises to the level of a constitutional impairment as opposed to being a mere breach of contract is discussed in the recent case of *E & E Hauling, Inc. v. Forest Preserve District of Du Page County, Illinois.*[26] In that case, the plaintiff entered into a contract with the Forest District authorizing it to operate a sanitary landfill within the Mallard Lake Recreational Preserve. The plaintiff was depositing both solid and liquid waste and sludge at the landfill site when in September 1978 the District adopted an ordinance which prevented further deposition of liquids in the lake. Several months later the ordinance was amended to prevent liquid or sewer sludge wastes from being dumped at the site except for septic tank dumpings approved by the County Health Department.[27] The ordinance was enforced through the use of uniformed armed attendants at the landfill. Plaintiff then brought an action in the district court claiming that his earlier contract had been impaired in violation of the contracts clause.[28]

The court had to deal with the District's claim that what had occurred, if anything, was merely a breach of contract for which the District might be liable for damages.[29] Ever since *Hays v. Port of Seattle,*[30] it has been quite clear that if the private party has a damage remedy for breach of a governmental contract he has in essence been made whole by the damage recovery and therefore his contract has not been impaired.[31] Because in this case the District in an action for breach of contract could use the passage of the 1978 ordinances as a complete defense to the damage claim, the plaintiff had made out a prima facie case of an impairment of the obligation of a public contract. Had that defense not been available, then no cause of action would have been stated.[32] Had, for example, the District merely stationed armed attendants at the preserve and prevented the plaintiff from dumping liquid or sewage sludge wastes, no cause of action would have been stated under the contract's clause. What would have been alleged would have been a simple action for breach of contract.[33] Thus in the case of a development agreement unless the municipality enacted another ordinance which would act as a defense in a breach of contract action, no constitutional clause of action would be stated. This would occur if, for example, a city official refused to sign a permit without any legislative action requiring him to refuse to sign the proffered permit.

An important caveat must be added here. In *Dartmouth College,* the Court clearly stated that the state can reserve the right to alter, modify, or change the terms of the contract and if it does so it will not be a violation of the contracts clause.[34] Under the California statute, the local government has the authority to periodically review the provisions of the development agreement and can modify or terminate the agreement if it determines that the applicant is not complying with the terms and conditions of the agreement in good faith. Obviously if the agreement allows the city to modify or alter the terms it will be of little value to the developer. Clearly, however, the statute does allow the city to opt out of some regulatory freezes otherwise subject to the development agreement. The greater the ability to modify the lesser the value of the agreement and the lesser the incentive for the developer to enter into this arrangement.

The Reserved Powers Doctrine

Even before the U.S. Supreme Court fully developed the reserved powers doctrine, the New York Supreme Court in 1826 pronounced its application to the exercise of a municipal land use power. In *Corporation of the Brick Presbyterian Church v. Mayor, Aldermen and Commonalty of the City of New York,*[35] the plaintiffs were suing the city for all alleged breach of quiet enjoyment of a lease that had been entered into in 1766.[36] The lease, signed by the city, covenanted that the lessees were entitled to use the property as a cemetery provided it was fenced and never used for private secular means. In 1823, the city aldermen of New York enacted an ordinance which prohibited the use of the premises as a cemetery. In looking at the 1766 lease, the court determined that the city legislative body had no power to make a contract "which should control or embarrass their legislative powers and duties."[37] The court concluded that the earlier legislature had no power to limit future legislative discretion by contract or convenant. The court emphasized that the city was dealing with the public health in this case. Between 1766 and 1823, the city had grown around the church which was originally located well outside the center of population.[38] Thus the express convenant of quiet enjoyment contained in the lease could not have bound future legislatures from exercising their duty to protect their public health or morals. That conclusion when later adopted by the Supreme Court became known as the reserved powers doctrine.[39]

The broadest statement of the doctrine came in *Stone v. Mississippi.*[40] In 1867, the Mississippi legislature chartered a company to engage in the lottery business for a period of twenty-five years. One year later, the Mississippi Constitution was amended and in 1870 the Mississippi legislature passed an act which in effect repealed the 1867 charter.[41] The court simply concluded that "the legislature cannot bargain away the police power of a State."[42] In this particular case, the Court was concerned with the public health and morals aspects of the police power.[43] But the Court did distinguish this case from an earlier decision dealing with the power to tax which the Court agreed the legislative body could bargain away.[44] The Court concluded that since the people cannot grant away the power to legislate under the police power, the legislature could not and the 1867 charter could thus not bind subsequent legislatures from declaring the lottery business unlawful and thus terminating the preexisting Charter.

CURRENT VIABILITY OF THE RESERVED POWERS DOCTRINE

The reserved powers doctrine is still viable today. The *U.S. Trust Co.* case recognized its continued vitality, although in dicta indicated that it would not be as effective a weapon as it once was.[45] In *U.S. Trust,* the New Jersey trial court had found that the repeal of the 1962 convenant was an exercise of the state's police power and thus entitled to insulation from contract clause invalidation under the reserved rights doctrine.[46] The court agreed with the essential statement in *Stone* that the legislature cannot bargain away the police power. The court, however, rejected the earlier categorization approach that determined the applicability of the reserved powers doctrine solely on the basis of what power was being exercised. If it was either the police or eminent domain power, the doctrine applied; if it was the taxing and spending power, a contracts clause violation might occur. But while rejecting the "formalistic" distinctions as being dispositive, they still retain some relevance in answering what the court sees as the key issue, which is whether or not an essential attribute of sovereignty has been contracted away.[47] In this case, the court characterized the covenant not as an exercise of the police power to deal with mass transit problems but as a covenant dealing with a state financial obligation which would not automatically fall under the reserved powers doctrine.[48] The selling of bonds and promises respecting the sale are not governmental attributes that are essential. But in reality it is the police power which is being restricted since options to provide mass transit for the public's benefit are being denied. Thus, while rejecting the categorization approach in theory, the court applied it to the facts in the case, lending credence to the continued vitality of *Stone* insofar as it applies the reserved powers doctrine to attempted restrictions on future exercises of the police power.

The Seventh Circuit in the *E & E Hauling* case discussed earlier[49] attempted to lay down some guidelines for the district court in determining whether or not an impairment is unconstitutional in light of the reserved powers doctrine.[50] The court first noted that the states do reserve broad powers to regulate to protect the public interest. Nonetheless, the contracts clause does place some limits on the exercise of those reserved powers. The first is that the legislation must be reasonable and necessary to meet an important social problem. Second, the severity of the impairment heightens the scope of review given the legislative act. This "sliding scale" approach was clearly delineated in the *Allied Structural Steel* holding.[51] Thus what is left is essentially a balancing test weighing the interest of the governmental body in the enactment of its ordinance with the degree of impairment of the plaintiff's contractual expectations. The court further notes that where a party has relied heavily on an obligation impaired by legislation such as in the case where express terms of the contract are involved, the burden on the state to justify the impairment becomes very onerous.[52] In the case of a development agreement, it would appear that a subsequent legislative act which impaired the agreement would carry with it a very onerous burden of showing the reasonableness and necessity of such a direct and substantial impairment.

A good example of how the reserved powers doctrine should have operated in the context of a development agreement is presented by the California case of *Carruth v City of Madera.*[53] In *Carruth,* the city and the developer entered into an agreement whereby the developer would subdivide certain land in exchange for the city's provision of certain improvements including paving streets and providing water mains and sewers. It was not until 1960 that the developer attempted to complete the subdivision although the plat had been approved in 1947. At that time the city refused to make certain improvements and the developer sued for damages and specific performance of the agreement.[54]

The agreement by its own terms did not have a termination date. The city argued that it was an attempt by one city council to bind future city councils in the exercise of police power. The court acknowledged that the contract did bind a future legislative body with respect to a police power function regarding annexation and land use. Instead of analyzing the case in light of *Stone* and the reserved powers doctrine, the court relied on an earlier California case which held that if a contract is entered into by a city which extends beyond the term of the legislative body and is fair, just and reasonable, and advantageous to the city it can be enforced.[55] The court did not discuss the problems inherent in one city council restricting the use of the police power in the future. Instead, it awarded the plaintiff damages for the delay, equal to the cost of constructing the infrastructure if the city refused to act. Clearly there is some doubt as to the validity of the arrangement since it went beyond the mere provision of services by the city by including a promise to annex and service the newly subdivided land.

A second California case dealing with several municipal promises relating to annexation and zoning also raised some of the same problems as *Carruth*. In *M. J. Brock & Sons v. City of Davis,*[56] the plaintiffs and the city entered into an annexation agreement whereby the city would annex the property and zone it so as to comport with a previous plan for development of the tract. The plaintiff then expanded substantial sums of money to install a drainage system and also made payments for multiple sewage connections. The original agreement took place in 1966 but in April 1973 the municipal city council enacted a zoning ordinance placing the area in question in an agricultural holding zone. It then refused to grant to the plaintiff any of his requested building or land use permits.[57] Although not directly before it, the court in dicta held: "Although zoning itself is not a contractual act, a municipality should not be allowed to avoid responsibility for break of specific land use agreements entered into with private parties even though the breach occurred through the process of zoning changes."[58] Thus even without the aid of the revived contracts clause the court was able to perceive a cause of action in a situation much like the development agreement.

THE CONTRACT CLAUSE VS. THE RESERVED POWER CLAUSE

The conflict between the contracts clause and the reserved powers doctrine was evident in *Sonoma County Organization of Public Employees v. County of Sonoma.*[59] In *Sonoma County,* the plaintiffs were seeking to invalidate a California statute which penalized local governments by withholding state surplus grant and loan funds if they approved any raises to their employees at a higher level than state employee raises.[60] The plaintiffs represented unions which had entered into bargaining agreements with various California governmental entities calling for specified wage increases for the 1978-1979 fiscal year. They alleged that the statute penalizing local governments was an impairment of their employment contracts and bargaining agreements.[61] The court had no difficulty finding that an impairment has taken place. The issue then became whether the impairment was constitutional.

The court initially noted the tension between the contracts clause and the reserved powers doctrine. If the contracts clause is to have any meaning it must to a certain degree limit the exercise of the police power.[62] Unfortunately, its analysis of the reserved powers doctrine ended with that simple aphorism as it began to discuss the test it would apply to determine the constitutionality of the impairment. The court could have labeled the bargaining agreements as involving the spending power that would not fall under the reserved powers doctrine. Alternatively, it could have concluded that the agreement did not deal with an essential legislative or governmental function. Instead it applied the *U.S. Trust-Allied Structural Steel* test to invalidate the wage freeze without further mention of the reserved powers doctrine. Finding that there was a substantial impairment of a contractual right to a higher wage which could not be justified by the fiscal emergency, the court declared the wage freeze unconstitutional.[63] The court placed the burden on the state to show that a true fiscal emergency existed and that there were no less onerous alternatives to the wage freeze. Because there was a massive infusion of state aid to local governments which had lost some 22 percent of their revenue-raising capacity, the court could find no reasonable and necessary basis for the impairment which it deemed to be substantial.[64] The court did not discuss the problem raised by *Stone* that if the collective bargaining agreement could be deemed an exercise of the police power, the legislative body has no authority to bind future legislative action. Obviously that would wreck havoc with public employee collective bargaining since it would allow the local governments to unilaterally opt out of a wage agreement.

The tension between the contracts clause and the reserved powers doctrine was evident but neglected in *Sonoma County.* If the development agreement is not considered an attempt to bind future legislative bodies in the exercise of the police power, it is a public contract subject to the revitalized contracts clause analysis suggested in *U.S. Trust.* On the other hand, if the development agreement is found to be an attempt to limit the exercise of the police power then it is ultra vires and void.

The situation that developed in *Avco Community Developers, Inc. v. South Coast Regional Commission*[65] may provide some insights to resolving this problem. Although *Avco* is more famous for its tough rule on vested rights,[66] there was also an issue raised regarding the enforceability of a so-called breach agreement between the Orange County Harbor District and Avco.[67] *Avco* claimed that part of the consideration to induce it to sell the county eleven acres of sandy beach at a price well below market value and to dedicate certain access to some parking areas was the promise by the county to issue *Avco* required building and development permits. *Avco* alleged that the quid pro quo for the agreement was a commitment by the county and the state to allow it to develop under the planned community zoning district. The Coastal Commission disagreed claiming the sale was merely to resolve a dispute as to prescriptive rights the public may have gained on the property.[68] The California Supreme Court found that even if Avco's allegations were true it would still not constitute a valid cause of action for estoppel or breach of contract because the government may not contract away its rights to exercise the police power in the future, in the area of land use regulation.[69] Again the analysis was absent, replaced by a simplisitic application of an aphorism. The difference between *Sonoma County* and *Avco* is the choice of aphorisms not the choice of analytical approaches. Nonetheless, there is strong precedent within California that the development agreement insofar as it prohibits the local legislative body from changing the land use regulations on a parcel prior to the vesting development rights would fall under the reserved powers doctrine, making such agreements void and unenforceable.

Contract or Conditional Zoning–
A Fruitless Search for a Common Thread

The traditional distinction between contract and conditional zoning has focused on the agreement of the public body to act or refrain from acting in the area of land use regulation.[70] Contract zoning has been described as an agreement that purports to bind both the landowners and the local government agency to an agreed set of covenants. Conditional zoning occurs where the persons seeking the development permission agrees unilaterally to do something, usually dedicating land or restricting the use of the parcel, while the governmental agency makes no binding agreement.

In either case, two issues should be prominent in deciding the validity of the agreements. The first is the reserved powers doctrine which has received surprisingly little attention in many of the court decisions. The second relates to the problem of uniformity of zoning regulations and districts which is required under the Standard Zoning Enabling Act. Given the nature of most of the covenants which place the landowner in a different position from others similarly situated, courts have had little difficulty finding the uniformity requirement violated.

In examining the approximately sixty-five contract or conditional zoning cases decided in the past fifty years,[71] there is a surprisingly even split between those case which have invalidated such arrangements and those which have either upheld the arrangement or distinguished it from the contract zoning case. In a surprising number of cases in which the court invalidated contract zoning, there is a market absence of any reference to the reserved powers doctrine.

New Jersey perhaps comes closest to the reserved powers doctrine in invalidating contract zoning decisions. In *V. F. Zahodiakin Corp. v. Zoning Board of Adjustment,*[72] the landowner was seeking to enforce a contract between himself and the city to grant it a variance so a laboratory could be built. The agreement was entered into in 1942 and would automatically terminate if the landowner sold the property or used it for other than laboratory purposes.[73] In striking down this arrangement, the New Jersey court said that basic legislative functions could not be surrendered or curtailed by bargain or contract.[74] The police power may not be subverted to private welfare but only to the public welfare. Although not identical to the reserved powers doctrine of *Stone,* the basic point remains the same, a local legislative body cannot bargain away its power to govern through the police power through a private contract.[75] The attempt to so delegate is void and unenforceable.

In *Hartnett v. Austin,*[76] a neighbor was seeking to invalidate a rezoning which had taken place pursuant to the zoning applicant agreeing to six specific conditions restricting the use of his land for a shopping center. Here the court came out quite clearly that the city could not contract away the exercise of police power and that the rezoning would have to be justified on other grounds to be proper.[77] However, in many of the cases striking down contract or conditional zoning it is very hard to determine what the precise rationale of the court is. In some cases the court may be relying on the lack of enabling authority to contract zone; in others the court may find that contract zoning is for private not public benefit and therefore not valid under the police power; in others it may be invalid as spot zoning or finally in others it may be invalid as violative of the uniformity requirements of the enabling act.[78] No clear rationale has yet been developed.

On the other side of the ledger, the courts which have upheld contract or conditional zoning have usually ignored the issue of the aplication of the reserved powers doctrine. In one of the leading case affirming the validity of contract zoning, *Church v Town of Islip,*[79] the court was faced with a contract zoning argument made by the city. In *Church,* some neighboring landowners were objecting to the rezoning of a parcel upon the condition and agreement of the landowner to restrict his building size and place fences and shrubbery around the proposed establishment before he could establish his commercial business. In responding to the contract zoning argument, the court quite frankly conceded that contract zoning was invalid since a legislative body can never bargain away or sell its powers.[80] But the court went on to say "we deal here with actualities, not phrases." Finding that there was nothing wrong or unconstitutional with the conditions or covenants, the court could not say that this was a contract in violation of the reserved powers doctrine. It would have been interesting to see how the court would have reacted if this legislative body had changed its mind and rezoned the property. The court of course did not address that issue.[81] Thus the contract zoning cases do not provide us with much guidance on the applicability of the reserved powers doctrine to the development agreement. Clearly it is a hurdle that must be cleared. The context in which the litigation arises may have something to do with the outcome. The courts seem less disposed to invalidate contract or conditional zoning cases at the request of third parties or neighbors. But the courts are also not receptive to local governments seeking to avoid contractual responsibilities. Absent a vested right to develop, the developer may have difficulty enforcing development agreements which are changed or repealed by subsequent governmental action.

Some Final Thoughts on Recent Cases

As one can readily see, the conflict between the contracts clause and the reserved powers doctrine has not alway been the subject of particularly keen judicial thought. Recently, several cases dealing with local governmental contracts have muddled their way through, raising some interesting points that may be valuable as development agreements become more prevalent.

In *Morrison Homes Corp. v. City of Pleasanton,*[82] the plaintiff was seeking damages and specific performance of several annexation agreements which the city had allegedly reneged on. Through a series of annexation agreements, the developer agreed to subdivide and improve some land in return for the city's promise to annex, zone, and provide sufficient sewage capacity in the city-operated sewage treatment plant. Unfortunately, a Regional Water Quality Board determined that the municipal plant was violating water-quality standards and at various times limited new sewage hookups to the plant until such time as the effluent was cleaned up. The city then began denying sewer connections to parts of the plaintiff's property which was subject to the annexation agreement. The corporation then instituted this action.

At first blush there are several issues which call for the imposition of the reserved powers doctrine. The agreements call for the placement of the newly annexed area in a holding or interim zone classification. Classically that part of the agreement should be held void under the reserved powers doctrine as the city cannot contract away its ability to change zoning classifications.[83] The court did not discuss the validity of the zoning part of the contract because that was not in dispute. What was in dispute was the sewer commitment and the annexation agreement. Although the court identified annexation as a legislative, police power function it refused to apply the reserved powers doctrine. While it conceded that a city could not "contract away" its governmental functions, that only applied to a total municipal surrender or abrogation of control.[84] Because in this case the annexation agreement by its own terms was consistent with the municipality's master plan and zoning ordinance, the court found no surrender of control but merely the carrying out of its governmental functions. The court failed to consider the fact that the city may for public health reasons have to limit new sewer hookups and that the hookup covenant in the annexation agreement would prevent some future legislature from exercising an essential attribute of the police power. The attempt to distinguish between the surrender of control of a police power and a limit on the exercise of it in the future appeals to be ill-founded.[85] Undoubtedly, the annexation agreement did surrender the city's ability to control new sewer hookups in the future, as they affected plaintiff's lands, which could pose a real threat to the public health of the community.

As to the annexation contracts in toto, the court found that since the annexations were carried out pursuant to the applicable state laws on annexation, they were not void and unenforceable.[86] But again the court missed the point in not raising the issue of whether the city would be liable if it by ordinance refused to annex the area. Would the city not be protected under the reserved powers doctrine? What would happen if, for example, the annexation ordinance failed to carry a majority of the city council. The court implied that the city would be liable even though annexation is a police power function which cannot be delegated away. But isn't annexation an essential sovereign, governmental power which would come under the umbrella of the reserved powers doctrine. Clearly, under the annexation agreement the city is agreeing to annex some lands at a future date binding a future legislature to that course of action regardless of the consequences.

Blithely unaware of these problems, the court affirmed the damages awarded at trial on the basis of the failure to provide the necessary hookups on demand. It did not order the city to hook up the plaintiff's lots in violation of the Regional Board's order but did require the city to "repair, rebuild, improve, maintain and operate" the sewer system in a manner consistent with the Regional Board's requirement so that new hookups could be allowed.[87] That order could cost the city thousands of dollars depending upon the required repairs or modifications needed to meet the Regional Board's demands. This plus the added expense of the daily damage recovery for failure to provide hookups will undoubtedly make a serious dent in the municipal treasury.

An interesting fillip was added to the reserved powers doctrine in the Michigan case of *Kethman v. Oceola Township.*[88] In *Kethman* the plaintiff received a variance from the local board in 1972 allowing him to have a thirty-three-foot-wide access road instead of the usually required sixty-six-foot-wide road. Less than one year later, the plaintiff was notified that the board was rescinding the "land permit" and invited the plaintiff to reapply for another variance. The plaintiff hurriedly attempted to finish the road until a stop-work order was issued. At that time, the plaintiff refiled his variance application which was turned down and instituted this litigation, claiming both a taking and a breach of contract. The trial court awarded the plaintiff $110,172.25 in damages apparently on a breach of contract theory.[89]

While finding that the township had no authority to rehear the variance approval sua sponte, the court was puzzled over the awarding of damages for a breach of contract, the court explored the existence of any contract between the township and the city by virtue of the variance and other development permits issued. Citing *Stone,* the court concluded that a licensee or permittee does not enter into a binding contract with the local government merely upon the receipt of a permit after the payment of the permit fees. To do so would violate the reserved powers doctrine and be a delegation of police power authority that would affect the public health. While the court held that the township was not free to revoke the permit at will, its attempted revocation was not a breach of contract.[90] The court did say that the damages may be available for the temporary taking but that the evidence at trial was not sufficient to show the taking of a vested property right. The court did not raise the "vested rights" issue which may have applied at the time of the issuance of the permit.

Thus in Michigan the granting of a permit if revoked illegally will not lead to damages for breach of contract but possibly to damages under the taking clause. In this case, the contract involved was merely based on the issuance of a permit and the only consideration was the payment of the permit fee. The court would have had to expand its reasoning to reach a similar result where there were other considerations on behalf of the landowner. The court nonetheless uses rather sweeping language that the legislature does not have the authority to enter into an "irrepealable contract" that would affect the public health or morals or limit the exercise of the police power.[91]

In another case dealing with breach of contract remedies, the Massachusetts Supreme Judicial Court in *Middlesex and Boston Street Railway Co. v. Board of Aldermen of Newton et al.*[92] refused to allow the developer to recover damages for complying with an illegally imposed condition on a development permit. In *Middlesex,* the city, as a condition to the granting of a building permit, required the developer to rent five units to persons who qualified for rent subsidies under the rules of the Newton Housing Authority. Rents for these five units were substantially below the rents for the remaining fifty units.[93] The court struck down the condition on the basis that the city lacked the authority under the enabling act to impose minimum numbers of low-rental units as a prerequisite to the granting of a development permit. Nonetheless the court refused to grant the plaintiffs their requested monetary damages because there was no evidence that the defendants had acted "in bad faith, maliciously or corruptly."[94] Since the Newton Housing Authority was not a party to the lawsuit, the court did not decide whether or not it would be liable for the damages suffered from the leasing of the five apartments at their direction which was illegal. Thus even where a party may allege a breach of contract, damages may not be forthcoming from the municipal treasury.

Conclusion

The use of development agreements is designed to lessen the cost of development in subdividing land for resale to the public. The success or failure of the California experiment will in large part depend on the court's application of the reserved powers doctrine. If these agreements are found to contract away essential elements of governmental sovereignty, unless *Stone v. Mississippi*[95] is overruled, they may be unenforceable. The uncertainty surrounding the enforceability of development agreements will undoubtedly act as a disincentive to their widespread use.

Notes

1. In Avco Community Developers, Inc. v. South Coast Regional Comm'n, 17 Cal. 3d 785, 553 P. 2d 546, 132 Cal. Rptr. 386 (1976), the California Supreme Court held that the petitioner did not have a vested right to develop on its parcel even though it had incurred $3 million in liabilities improving the parcel because it had not received the final building permit approval. See Hagman, "Estoppel and Vesting in the Area of Multi-Land Use Permits," 11 Sw. L. Rev. 545 (1980); Hagman, "Vesting Issue: The Rights of Fetal Development Vis-à-Vis the Abortions of Public Whimsy," 7 Envir. L. Rev. 519 (1977).

2. See Avco Community Developers, Inc. v. South Coast Regional Comm'n, note 1 *supra,* at 132 Cal. Rptr. 394-395.

3. 1979 Cal. Legis. Serv., Ch. 934, §§ 3357-3359.

4. Cal. Const., Art. IV, § 1.

5. Cal. Pub. Res. Code §§ 30000 et seq. (West).

6. U.S. Const., Art. I, § 10, cl. 1.

7. See generally Wright, *The Contract Clause of the Constitution* (1938); Nowak, Rotunda & Young, *Constitutional Law* 420 (1978).

8. 10 U.S. (6 Cranch) 87 (1810).

9. *Id.* at 142-144.

10. 17 U.S. (4 Wheat.) 518 (1819).

11. See Tribe, *American Constitutional Law* 470 (1978). See also New Jersey v. Wilson, 11 U.S. (7 Cranch) 164 (1812), where the Supreme Court struck down the repeal of a tax exemption granted by the New Jersey Legislature.

12. 36 U.S. (11 Pet.) 420 (1837).

13. *Id.* at 583.

14. 431 U.S. 1 (1977).

15. *Id.* at 25-26. See Tribe, note 11 *supra,* at 473.

16. U.S. Trust Co. v. New Jersey, note 14 *supra,* at 21. See also Home Building & Loan Ass'n v. Blaisdell, 290 U.S. 398 (1934).

17. U.S. Trust Co. v. New Jersey, note 14 *supra,* at 22-23.

18. *Id.* at 25.

19. *Id.* at 26-27. See W. B. Worthen Co. v. Kavanaugh, 295 U.S. 56 (1935); Faitoute Iron & Steel Co. v. City of Ashbury Park, 316 U.S. 502 (1942).

20. U.S. Trust Co. v. New Jersey, note 14 *supra,* at 29-30.

21. *Id.* The majority opinion was signed by only Justices Blackmun, Rehnquist, and Stevens, and Chief Justice Burger. Justices Brennan, White, and Marshall dissented, and Justices Powell and Stewart did not participate in the decision.

22. 438 U.S. 234 (1978). For subsequent applications of *Allied Structural Steel* and *U.S. Trust* in a non-land use context, see Agustin v. Queen, 611 F. 2d 206 (7th Cir. 1979); Nachman Corp. v. Pension Benefit Guar. Corp., 592 F. 2d 947 (7th Cir. 1979); Baker v. Baltimore County, 487 F. Supp. 461 (D. Md. 1980); H. Phillips Co. v. Brown-Forman Distillers, 483 F. Supp. 1289 (N.D. Wis. 1980).

23. Allied Structural Steel Co. v. Spannaus, note 22 *supra,* at 244-245.

24. *Id.* at 247-250.

25. *Id.*

26. 613 F. 2d 675 (7th Cir. 1980).

27. *Id.* at 677.

28. *Id.* at 676-677.

29. *Id.* at 679.

30. 251 U.S. 233 (1920).

31. E & E Hauling, Inc. v. Forest Preserve Dist. of DuPage County, Ill., note 26 *supra,* at 679. The court notes that *U.S. Trust* does not hold that every impairment of a contract is unconstitutional but that the *U.S. Trust* test including proper consideration of the reserved rights doctrine must be analyzed and balanced. *Id.* at 681.

32. *Id.* at 679-681.

33. *Id.* at 680 n. 6. See also Jackson Sawill Co. v. United States, 580 F. 2d 302 (8th Cir. 1978), *cert. denied* 439 U.S. 1070 (1979); St. Paul Gas Light Co. v. City of St. Paul, 181 U.S. 142 (1901).

34. Dartmouth College v. Woodward, 17 U.S. (4 Wheat.) 518, 666 (1819). See Nowak, Rotunada & Young, *Constitutional Law* 420, 424 (1978).

35. 5 Cowens (N.Y.) 538 (1826).

36. *Id.* at 539.

37. *Id.* at 540.

38. *Id.* at 542.

39. See Nowak, Rotunda & Young, note 34 *supra,* at 424.

40. 101 U.S. 814 (1880). The central theme of *Stone* had been earlier stated in West River Bridge Co. v. Dix, 47 U.S. (6 How.) 507 (1848), a Taney opinion seeking to limit the broad sweep of Marshall's statement of the contracts clause. *West River Bridge* dealt with the power of eminent domain, with Taney concluding that a charter provision that limited the state's ability to exercise the power of eminent domain was not enforceable under the contracts clause because the state could not in the first place contract away the power of eminent domain.

41. *Id.* at 815-816.

42. *Id.* at 817.

43. *Id.* at 818. In Home Building & Loan Ass'n v. Blaisdell, 290 U.S. 398 (1934), the Court upheld Minnesota's debtor relief statute partly on the basis of the state's reserved power to act in an emergency to protect the general welfare.

44. New Jersey v. Wilson, 11 U.S. (7 Cranch) 164 (1812).

45. U.S. Trust Co. v. New Jersey, 431 U.S. 1, 21-24 (1977).

46. *Id.* at 21, citing 338 A. 2d at 873.

47. The court, of course, never tells you what an essential attribute of sovereignty is, leaving those "minor" issues for future resolution. A similar approach was taken in National League of Cities v. Usery, 426 U.S. 833 (1976), where in limiting federal encroachment into areas of state sovereignty the court left the definition of important areas of sovereign power to a future date.

48. The spending power has never fallen under the reserved powers doctrine because of New Jersey v. Wilson, 11 U.S. (7 Cranch) 164 (1812), where Chief Justice Marshall held that a state could permanently grant a tax exemption that could not be subsequently repealed without violating the contracts clause. U.S. Trust Co. v. New Jersey, note 45 *supra,* at 24 n. 21. See also Georgia Ry. Co. v. Redwine, 342 U.S. 299 (1952), for a modern case holding that a state cannot repeal a previously enacted permanent tax exemption.

49. See text accompanying notes 26-33 *supra.*

50. E & E Hauling, Inc. v. Forest Preserve Dist. of DuPage County, Ill., 613 F. 2d 675, 681 (7th Cir. 1980).

51. *Id.* at 681, citing Allied Structural Steel Co. v. Spannaus, 438 U.S. 234, 245 (1978).

52. *Id.*

53. 43 Cal. Rptr. 855 (1965).

54. *Id.* at 858.

55. *Id.* at 860-861.

56. M. J. Brock & Sons, Inc. v. City of Davis, 401 F. Supp. 354 (N.D. Cal. 1975).

57. *Id.* at 357.

58. *Id.* at 361.

59. 23 Cal. 3d 296, 591 P. 2d 1, 152 Cal. Rptr. 903 (1979).

60. *Id.* at 905. As a matter of fact, the governor had vetoed the bill authoring a 2.5 percent increase for state employees, making it impossible for local governments to give their employees any raise at all.

61. *Id.* at 906.

62. *Id.* at 907, citing Home Building & Loan Ass'n v. Blaisdell, note 43 *supra.*

63. *Id.* at 908-909. But cf. Subway-Surface Supervisors Ass'n v. New York City Transit Auth., 44 N.Y. 2d 101, 404 N.Y.S. 2d 323, 375 N. E. 2d 384 (1978), which upheld a statute deferring wage increases in a collective bargaining agreement during the New York City fiscal crisis.

64. Sonoma County organization of Pub. Employees v. County of Sonoma, note 59 *supra,* 152 Cal. Rptr. at 910-911.

65. 17 Cal. 3d 785, 553 P. 2d 546, 132 Cal. Rptr. 386 (1976).

66. See *Id.* at 394-395.

67. *Id.* at 394-395.

68. *Id.* at 395.

69. *Id.* at 396, citing Miller v. Board of Pub. Works, 195 Cal. 477, 486-489, 234 P. 381 (1925). See also Caminetti v. Pacific Mut. Life Ins. Co., 22 Cal. 2d 344, 139 P. 2d 908 (1943); Maguire v. Reardon, 41 Cal. App. 595, 183 P. 303

(1916); Laurel Hill Cemetery v. City & County of San Francisco, 152 Cal. 464, 93 P. 70 (1907).

70. See 2 Anderson, *American Law of Zoning* 2d, 140 (1979). Compare *Id.* at 135-137, with 1 Rohan, *Zoning and Land Use Controls* § 5.01(2) (1978).

71. See cases cited in 2 Anderson, note 70 *supra,* at 135-145, and 1 Williams, *American Land Planning Law* 585-594 (1974).

72. 86 A. 2d 127 (N.J. 1952).

73. *Id.* at 129-130.

74. *Id.* at 131-132.

75. See also Midtown Properties, Inc. v. Township of Madison, 172 A. 2d 40 (1961), *aff'd* 189 A. 2d 266 (N.J. 1963); Houston Petroleum Co. v. Automotive Prods. Credit Ass'n, 87 A. 2d 319 (N.J. 1952).

76. 93 So. 2d 86 (1956).

77. *Id.* at 89.

78. See cases cited in 70 A.L.R. 3d 125, 167-174, 177-178, 179-186 (1972).

79. 203 N.Y.S. 2d 866 (1960).

80. *Id.* at 867-868.

81. See also Funger v. Mayor & Council of Somerset, 223 A. 2d 168 (1966); State *ex rel.* Zupanic v. Schimenz, 174 N.W. 2d 533 (1970).

82. 58 Cal. App. 3d 724, 130 Cal. Rptr. 196 (1976).

83. See Avco Community Developers, Inc. v. South Coast Regional Comm'n, note 65 *supra,* and cases cited therein.

84. Morrison Homes Corp. v. City of Pleasanton, note 82 *supra,* 130 Cal. Rptr. at 202.

85. Compare McNeil v. City of South Pasadena, 166 Cal. 153, 155-156, 145 P. 2d 32 (1913), and Wills v. Los Angeles, 209 Cal. 448, 287 P. 962 (1930), with Stone v. Mississippi, 101 U.S. 814 (1870).

86. Morrison Homes Corp. v. City of Pleasanton, note 82 *supra,* 130 Cal. Rptr. at 203.

87. *Id.* at 205.

88. 276 N.W. 2d 529 (Mich. 1979).

89. *Id.* at 530-531.

90. *Id.* at 533. See also Eastwood Park Amusement Co. v. Mayor of East Detroit, 38 N.W. 2d 77 (Mich. 1949); People v. Schafran, 134 N.W. 29 (1912).

91. *Id.*

92. 359 N.E. 2d 1279 (Mass. 1977).

93. *Id.* at 1280. Rents for the five units ranged from $180 to $202 per month while similar rents for uncontrolled apartments ranged from $425 to $475 per month.

94. *Id.* at 1285-1286.

95. Note 40 *supra* and accompanying text.

III. THE NEW JERSEY SYSTEM

6

Events Leading to the New Jersey Tax Reform Program

JEROME G. ROSE

The press has given much attention to the adoption of Proposition 13 in 1978 by which the people of the State of California amended their constitution to prohibit municipal governments from imposing a property tax in excess of 1 percent of the assessed value of taxable property.[1] By contrast, there has been relatively little national attention given to the thoughtful and comprehensive program of tax reform previously adopted by the state of New Jersey.

In its Tax Reform Program, New Jersey responded to many of the same pressures that resulted in Proposition 13 in California. However, the New Jersey program provided a more deliberate and comprehensive response to these forces. New Jersey did not limit the ability of local government to impose property taxes;[2] instead it limited the ability of government to spend the revenue raised from property taxation. At the same time, the New Jersey Tax Reform Program responded to the decision of the New Jersey Supreme Court[3] requiring a more equitable distribution of funds for the support of the public

Mr. Rose is professor of urban planning, Rutgers University.
 Mr. Rose acknowledges with appreciation the assistance of Carole Walker Baker, a student in the Rutgers graduate program of urban planning.

schools.[4] Thus, the Tax Reform Program was a comprehensive program that included the following components: (1) it provided revenue to finance public education from a state gross income tax,[5] (2) it provided for property tax relief from the revenue from the income tax,[6] (3) it provided for homestead rebates by direct cash payments to home owners,[7] (4) it provided for a procedure by which tenants could share in the property tax relief.[8]

New Jersey Spending Limitations and California Proposition 13 Compared

The New Jersey program that limits governmental expenditures is similar in some ways to the California program that limits property tax and very different in other ways. A comparison of the two programs is useful.

CALIFORNIA PROPOSITION 13

The California program contained in the Proposition 13 amendment to the state constitution[9] has four main components:

- A limitation that the tax rate shall not exceed 1 percent of the 1975-1976 market value of real estate
- A limitation on the rate of increase of the assessment of real estate from its 1975-1976 tax valuation to not more than 2 percent in any one year unless the property is sold, at which time it may be reassessed at the market value
- A requirement that any increases in local government (nonproperty) taxes must be approved in a local referendum by a vote of at least two-thirds of the voters
- A requirement that any increases in state taxes (resulting from an increase in rate or method of computation) must be approved by a vote of at least two-thirds of all of the members of the state legislature

The similarities and differences between the New Jersey and California programs will become more evident from an analysis of the events that precipitated the enactment of these programs.

THE POLITICAL AND LEGAL FACTORS THAT LED TO CHANGE

The voter attitude that led to the adoption of Proposition 13 in California has been described as a taxpayers' and homeowners' revolt against government spending[10] and an expression of "anti-government feeling–part of a tide of skepticism and cynicism."[11] These attitudes were especially prevalent in California because while residents were suffering under the burden of rising residential property taxes, the state treasury enjoyed a surplus of 5.5 billion dollars. The property tax limitation in California was thus a political protest and a mandate for change that took the form of an amendment to the state constitution that was adopted by the people of the state in a state-wide referendum.

In New Jersey on the other hand, the event that precipitated the adoption of the limitation on government spending was a constitutional crisis created by the state Supreme Court's determination that the state system of financing public education in New Jersey violated the state constitution.

It may be interesting to take note that the California Supreme Court was one of the first to respond to the legal argument that the system of school financing prevalent in most states is invalid because it violates the equal protection clauses of the state and federal constitutions. The argument is based on the fact that revenue to support the public schools is derived from property taxes within the school districts. Districts with substantial tax ratables are therefore able to spend larger sums per pupil (and presumably provide a better quality education) than districts with a lower ratio of ratables per pupil. In 1971, the California Supreme Court held that the equal protection clause is violated when the levels of spending for education depends on the wealth of school districts[12] because that system makes "the quality of educational opportunity available to a student dependent upon the wealth of the district in which he lives."[13]

In New Jersey, a court was called upon to respond to a similar challenge to the validity of the New Jersey system of financing public education. In *Robinson v. Cahill,*[14] the New Jersey Supreme Court also invalidated the school financing system. However, the *Robinson v. Cahill* decision, rendered about two weeks after the decision of the United States Supreme Court in *San Antonio Independent School District v. Rodriguez,*[15] did not hold that the school finance system violated the equal protection clause. Instead, the New Jersey court held that the New Jersey system of school finance violated an obscure and previously unnoticed provision in the state constitution that the legislature shall provide for a "thorough and efficient" system of public education.[16] The court determined that this provision required "an equal educational opportunity for children"[17] and that this constitutional mandate had not been met because of the wide disparities among municipalities in expenditures per pupil. The court also stated that the state could meet its obligation by financing education either on a statewide basis, with funds provided by the state, or by continuing the system of local finance if the state would *"compel"* the local school districts to raise the money necessary to provide the equal educational opportunity.[18]

The *Robinson v. Cahill* decision clearly moved the burden of decision into the arena of the legislature. The court reserved decision on the subject of remedy and subsequently filed a further opinion in which it said that it would not disturb the existing statutory scheme unless the legislature failed to enact, by December 31, 1974, legislation compatible with its decision.[19] The December 31, 1974 deadline passed without legislative action. In May, 1975 the Supreme Court enjoined the state treasurer and commissioner of education from disbursing funds appropriated under six categories of state aid for public education for the school year 1976-1977 and directed all of the funds appropriated for those programs to be distributed under an "incentive equalization aid" formula that would provide for a distribution of state funds more compatible with the court's decision.[20]

This decision created a constitutional crisis in New Jersey and returned the burden of decision to the state legislature. The legislature responded with a statute designed to provide for a "thorough and efficient" education for public school students through a more equitable system of distribution of funding for public education.[21] The New Jersey Supreme Court indicated its willingness to approve this law on condition that the legislature provide the necessary funding.[22] Thus, the pressure was great for the legislature to develop a program to provide new revenue. This pressure was sufficient to persuade the state legislature to adopt the Tax Reform Program, which included a state gross income tax, new state aid to municipalities, and the spending "caps" to prevent the municipal government from spending the excess funds that would result from the new state aid programs. Consequently, the New Jersey limitation on municipal expenditures was a direct consequence of the judicial response to the issue of funding of public education and is part of a comprehensive program of tax and education-funding reform in the state.

The New Jersey Tax Reform Program

LIMITATIONS ON GOVERNMENT SPENDING: THE CAP LAW

The Local Budget Law,[23] the State Expenditures Limitation Act,[24] and the Public School Education Act of 1975[25] (also known collectively as the "cap law" imposed limitations, or "caps," on municipal, county, school district, and state governmental expenditures.[26] The

Local Budget Law provides that the "final appropriations" of municipal governments may not be increased by more than 5 percent over the previous year, with certain exceptions.[27] The statute defines "final appropriations" to *exclude* certain expenditures and sources of revenue.[28] Under this provision the following types of *expenditures* are not subject to the "caps" or limitations: (1) all debt service; (2) expenditures mandated[29] by federal or state law after August 18, 1976; (3) emergency appropriations of up to 3 percent of current appropriations, if approved by a two-thirds vote and the State Local Finance Board; (4) funding of preceding year's deficit; (5) capital expenditures funded from other than the local property tax; (6) amounts paid, pursuant to a contract for water, sewer, solid waste, parking for senior citizen housing; and (7) expenditures approved by referendum.[30]

In addition to the above *expenditures* that are not included in the limitations on spending, the following sources of *revenue* also are not subject to the caps: (1) assessed value of new construction or improvements multiplied by the municipal purposes tax rate of the preceding year; (2) programs funded wholly or in part by federal or state funds; (3) reserve for uncollected taxes; (4) new or increased service fees imposed by ordinance; and (5) sale of municipal assets.

The cap law imposes a different type of limitation on county government than it does on municipal government. The limitation on municipal government is placed on municipal *expenditures;* the limitation on county government is placed on the county tax *levy*. This difference in treatment results from the property tax's constituting a relatively stable and uniform percentage of total *county* revenue (i.e., between 50 and 70 percent). On the other hand, there is a wide range of variation among municipalities in the percentage of property tax revenue of total municipal revenue (i.e., between 3.8 and 40 percent of total revenue). Because of this wide variation, a limitation on municipal property tax levy would be ineffective in some municipalities and extremely harsh in others. Consequently, a limitation on *spending* is necessary for *municipalities* but a limitation on the *tax levy* is appropriate for *county governments.*[31]

The property tax levy of county governments may not be increased more than 5 percent from one year to the next. However, certain specified county expenditures and revenue are not included in the total to which the 5 percent cap is applied. Among the exclusions from the calculation of the 5 percent cap are county debt service, revenue sharing, and emergency authorizations.[32]

The cap law treats municipal governments differently from county governments in another way. *All* county governments are subject to the 5 percent tax levy limitation, whereas some municipal governments are not subject to the spending cap. If the municipal purpose tax rate is $.10 per $100 or less, the municipality is exempt from the cap law.[33] In general, exempted municipalities are rural in character and have large amounts of non-property-tax revenue such as public utility franchise and gross receipts taxes; they are municipalities which provide minimal services and, therefore, do not need very much property tax revenue.[34]

The cap law also imposes limitations on the spending of school districts and the spending of the state government. School district budget increases are limited by a formula that is dependent on the amount of taxable real estate per pupil. The increase has varied from 3.8 percent to 40 percent. The state average has been about 7 percent.[35] The expenditures of the state government may be increased only to a percentage equal to the percentage increase in personal income of state residents in the preceding year. Thus, if the per capita income of New Jersey residents increases by 10 percent from the year preceding the base year, then the appropriations of the base year may be increased by 10 percent also. However, it is important to note that certain state expenditures are not subject to the expenditures limitation; these include state aid to municipalities, federal revenue sharing, and antirecession assistance.[36] State expenditures may exceed the caps in any given year if such increase is approved in a referendum by a majority of the voters.[37]

ADDITIONAL STATE REVENUE: THE GROSS INCOME TAX ACT

The New Jersey Gross Income Tax Act[38] is the keystone of the New Jersey Tax Reform Program. The income tax furnishes the revenue that provides for a more equitable distribution of funds for school districts, for homestead rebates, for revenue sharing with municipalities, and for state assumption of the costs of senior and disabled citizen and veterans property tax deductions.

The enactment of New Jersey's income tax law was the culmination of a long and hard-fought campaign by the governors of the state during a ten-year period.[39] Governor Brendan T. Byrne was able to achieve what his predecessors, governors William T. Cahill and Richard J. Hughes, also recognized as an essential element of any program of property tax reform.

Other sources of revenue had been considered.[40] A statewide property tax for public education would have met the need for a more equitable financing of public education but would have reinforced and perpetuated the regressive impact of property taxation. A graduated personal income tax similar to the federal income tax was considered but rejected because the working person and middle-income family would pay more than their share while the high-income taxpayer would be able to avoid taxation by special treatment of capital gains, tax exempt securities, and other tax shelters. An increase in sales tax was considered and rejected because of its predicted detrimental impact on local business and lack of support in the state legislature.

The tax that was adopted by the New Jersey legislature is a tax on the gross income less a limited number of exemptions and deductions.[41] The taxable income after subtraction of these exemptions and deductions is taxed at the rate of 2 percent of the first $20,000 and 2.5 percent of all income in excess of $20,000. The revenue derived from this tax, although slightly less than anticipated, has been nevertheless substantial. In 1979 the adjusted revenue from the gross income tax (excluding funds payable to a gubernatorial general election fund) was $845,000,000, plus an existing surplus of $117, 500,000, for a total of $962,500,000.[42]

How has this revenue been spent? The state has used the major portion of this revenue to increase its financial assistance to local school districts. In 1979, $584,900,000 was appropriated from gross income tax revenue for this purpose. The additional state funding to local school districts is designed to reduce the disparities in expenditures per pupil among the school districts and is a direct response to the decision of the New Jersey Supreme Court in *Robinson v. Cahill.*[43]

The second largest portion of the revenue from the gross income tax has been allocated to homestead rebates. In 1979, $267,000,000 was appropriated for this purpose.[44] This is a unique provision in the New Jersey Tax Reform Program. Many other states provide for an *exemption* from assessments, or a reduction in the assessed value of the house and lot on which the tax levy is applied. New Jersey provides a direct *rebate* to homeowners paid out of a property tax relief fund composed of the revenues from the gross income tax. State administration of the disbursement of the rebates is designed to avoid the risk of duplicate applications and improper payments for rental properties or second homes.[45] It also serves the political purpose of providing a twice-yearly reminder (once when the homeowner receives a homestead rebate claim form and again when he receives the check with a skillfully written "explanation") of the state program to reduce the burden of property taxes on homeowners. Most New Jersey homeowners are guaranteed a rebate of $150.00.[46]

Revenue from the gross income tax is also used to pay for the entire cost of property tax deductions of $160.00 taken by senior and disabled citizens and deductions of $50.00 taken by veterans. The state government is required by the state constitution[47] to pay for one-half of the senior and disabled citizens property tax deductions. The other half of the cost of these deductions has been paid for by the other taxpayers in each municipality. Under the Tax Reform Program[48] the entire cost of these deductions and the veterans deduction is paid for out of the property tax relief fund from revenue from the gross income tax. In 1979, the cost of this program was $54,000,000.

An additional $50,000,000 is distributed by the state from the property tax relief fund to all municipalities (except those with a tax rate of less than $1.00 per $100 of assessed valuation) under the provisions of the State Revenue Sharing Act.[49] These funds are distributed to municipalities on a per capita basis. Funds received by municipalities under the Revenue Sharing Act must be used to reduce the property tax levy.[50]

Notes

1. Cal. Const. art. XIIIA, §§ 1-6. For magazine and newspaper articles, see, e.g., "All Aboard the Bandwagon! Impact of Passage of Proposition 13," *Time,* June 26, 1978, pp. 8-11; Goldman, P. and others, "Life After Proposition 13," *Newsweek,* July 3, 1978, p. 24; "In California: Heavy Layoffs, Cutbacks in Services," *U.S. News and World Report,* June 26, 1978, pp. 19-20; Quirt, J., "After Shocks from the Great California Taxquake," *Fortune,* Sept. 25, 1978, pp. 74-7; "Budget Cuts Begun after Californians Vote to Curb Taxes," *N. Y. Times,* June 8, 1978, p. 1; "California City Growing Anxious as Layoffs Loom Under Tax Cut," *N. Y. Times,* June 23, 1978, p. 1; and "Proposition 13, in 5 Months, Has Not Spurred Major Spending Cutbacks," *N. Y. Times,* Nov. 7, 1978, p. 22.

2. Municipalities, school districts, and the state government are limited in the amount they can spend. The limitation on county government is in the form of a limitation in the amount of increase in the tax levy. The laws limiting spending were enacted within a seventeen month period and passed as part of an overall legislative plan. They are The Local Budget Law, N.J. Stat. Ann. §§ 40A: 4-45 et seq. limiting the spending of municipalities and counties The State Expenditures Limitation Act, N.J. Stat. Ann. §§ 52: 9H-5 et seq. limiting the spending of the state government; and The Public School Education Act of 1975, N.J. Stat. Ann. §§ 18A: 7A-25 et seq. limiting the spending of school districts.

3. Robinson v. Cahill, 62 N.J. 473, 303 A. 2d 272 (1973).

4. N.J. Stat. Ann. §§ 18A: 7A-25 et seq.

5. New Jersey Gross Income Tax, N.J. Stat. Ann. §§ 54A: 1-9 et seq.

6. An amendment to the state constitution requires the revenue derived from the income tax to be used exclusively for reducing property taxes. N.J. Const. art. VIII, § 1, para. 7.

7. N.J. Stat. Ann. § 54: 4-3.82.

8. N.J. Stat. Ann. § 54A: 4-3.

9. Cal. Const. art. XIIIA, §§ 1-6.

10. *U.S. News and World Report.* March 20, 1978, p. 23, and June 11, 1979, p. 24.

11. Statement of California Assembly Speaker Leo McCarthy, reported in *Intergovernmental Perspective,* Summer 1978, p. 8.

12. Serrano v. Priest, 5 Cal. 3d 584, 487 P. 2d. 1241, 96 Cal. Rptr. 601 (1971), decision on remand aff'd., 18 Cal. 3d 728, 557 P. 2d 929, 135 Cal. Rptr. 345 (1976).

13. *Id.* 18 Calif. 3d at 773, 557 P. 2d at 956, 135 Cal. Rptr. at 372.

On March 21, 1973, however, the Supreme Court rejected the *Serrano* reasoning in a Texas case, *San Antonio Independent School District v. Rodriquez* 411 U.S. 1 (1973), holding that the Texas school system of finance did not violate the equal protection clause because there was no evidence it discriminated "against any definable category of 'poor people'. . . ." The court's decision was also influenced by its awareness of the implications of the *Serrano* principle on municipal finance: if local taxation violated the equal protection clause as a method for providing for education, then it might also be an impermissiable means of financing other municipal services. The court declined to uphold the *Serrano* principle because of the "convulsive implications" of such a principle on municipal home rule. See Rose, "Property Taxes, School Financing, and Equal Protection," 2 *Real Estate Law Journal* 486 (1973).

14. 62 N.J. 473, 303 A. 2d 273, *cert. denied,* 414 U.S. 976 (1973).

15. 411 U.S. 1 (1973).

16. "The Legislature shall provide for the maintenance and support of a thorough and efficient school system of free public schools for the instruction of all children in the state . . . ." N.J. Const. art. VIII, § 4, para. 1.

17. Robinson v. Cahill, 62 N.J. at 513, 303 A. 2d at 294.

18. *Id.* at 519, 303 A. 2d at 297. The word "compel" was emphasized in the opinion.

19. Robinson v. Cahill, 62 N.J. 196, 306 A. 2d 65 (1973).

20. Robinson v. Cahill, 69 N.J. 133, 351 A. 2d 713 (1975). The court rejected the arguments that the judicial power of the state does not include the power to redistribute funds appropriated by the legislature and rejected the argument that such court order would also violate the provision of the state constitution providing that "no money shall be drawn from the State Treasury but for appropriations made by law" and that "all moneys for the support of State Government and for all other State purposes as far as can be ascertained or reasonably forseen shall be provided for in one general appropriations law covering one and the same fiscal year . . . ." N.J. Const. art VIII, § 2, para. 2.

21. N.J. Stat. Ann §§ 18A: 7A-25 et seq.

22. Robinson v. Cahill, 69 N.J. 449, 355 A. 2d 129 (1976).

23. N.J. Stat. Ann. §§ 40A: 4-45.1 et seq.

24. N.J. Stat. Ann. §§ 52: 9H-5 et seq.

25. N.J. Stat. Ann. §§ 18A: 7A-25 et seq.

26. See Laezza, John F. Jr., "New Legislation Places Limitations on County and Municipal Spending," *New Jersey Municipalities* 10 (Oct. 1976): Glaser,

Sidney, "New Jersey's Limits on State and Local Spending–A Model for the Nation?" *New Jersey Municipalities* 10 (Oct. 1980); *Report of the Joint Committee on Tax Policy,* New Jersey Legislature (June, 1979).

27. N.J. Stat. Ann. § 40A: 4-45.2.

28. N.J. Stat. Ann. § 40A: 4-45.3.

29. In New Jersey State Policemen's Benevolent Assoc. Local 29 v. Town of Irvington, 80 N.J. 271, 403 A. 2d 473 (1979), the New Jersey Supreme Court held that the cost of binding arbitration decisions are not "mandated costs" as that phrase is used in the Local Government Cap Law.

30. A municipality can increase expenditures beyond the cap limit with the voters' approval in a referendum. In 1979 there were thirty-two such referenda, of which thirteen were approved. *Report of the Joint Committee, supra* note 26, at 87.

31. *Id.* at 85.

32. N.J. Stat. Ann. § 40A: 4-45.4.

33. N.J. Stat. Ann. § 40A: 4-45.2.

34. *Report of the Joint Committee on Tax Policy, supra* note 26, at 87.

35. *N. Y. Times, Nov. 19, 1978, R E at 5.*

36. N.J. Stat. Ann. § 52: 9H-6. See also Glaser, Sidney, "New Jersey's Limits on State and Local Spending–A Model for the Nation?" *supra* note 26.

37. N.J. Stat. Ann. § 52: 9H-10.

38. N.J. Stat. Ann. § 54A: 1-9.

39. For an excellent history and analysis of the law, see Van Wagner, Richard, "The New Jersey Gross Income Tax: An Analysis from Background to Enactment," 2 *Seton Hall Leg. J* 100 (1977).

40. *Id.* at 106.

41. The original tax law was amended providing an additional $1,000 personal exemption for taxpayers who had a dependent child attending nonpublic elementary or secondary school on a full-time basis. This special personal exemption for private school students was held unconstitutional by the U.S. Ct. of Appeals and affirmed by the Supreme Court. Public Funds for Public Schools of New Jersey v. Byrne, D.C. 444 F. Supp. 1228 (1978), 442 U.S. 907 (1979).

42. *Report of the Joint Committee on Tax Policy, supra* note 26, at 9.

43. 62 N.J. 473, 303 A. 2d 273 (1973). See note 14, *infra* and accompanying text.

44. *Report of the Joint Committee on Tax Policy, supra* note 26, at 9.

45. *Id.* at 10.

46. *Id.* at 11.

47. N.J. Const. art VIII, § 1, 4.

48. N.J. Stat. Ann. § 54A: 9-25.

49. N.J. Stat. Ann. § 54A: 10-4.

50. N.J. Stat. Ann. §. 54A: 10-7.

7

Speculations on the Effect on Land Use in New Jersey

JEROME G. ROSE

One of the functions of the planning profession is to evaluate concepts and analyze data in order to make predictions of future growth and development. However, extrapolations and predictions drawn from data are not based on exact scientific principles. Rather, what makes the planning profession as much art as science is the need to postulate relations between newly created or perceived forces and the growth and development they may invoke. At an early stage of analysis, those formulations proposed tentatively (frequently by academicians) are properly characterized as "speculations."

The following are some speculations about the possible impact of governmental spending limitations on future state growth and development.

Revitalization of the Cities

There are many reasons why people, businesses, and industry left the cities in past years. High taxes are one reason why industry, stores,

---

 Mr. Rose acknowledges with appreciation the assistance of Carole Walker Baker, a student in the Rutgers graduate program of urban planning.

and homeowners have fled to the suburbs. Inadequate police protection, interrupted garbage collection, and unsatisfactory public education have caused others to leave the cities. To the extent that state revenue is distributed to municipalities in a way that helps to reduce the disparities in municipal service between cities and suburbs, the flight of business and people from the cities may abate.

However, this optimistic analysis must be qualified. Individuals frequently chose to leave the city for psychological as well as financial reasons. Before the central cities can enjoy a rebirth, the public must feel that city streets are safe, that children can receive a good education in the public schools, and that municipal services will continue to improve. To the extent that expenditures for these municipal services are limited in the suburbs by the caps and increased in the central cities because of funds provided by the state income tax, there might be some improvement in the plight of the central city. However, as noted, fiscal factors alone should not be overemphasized as the determinant of the future of the central cities.

Exclusionary Zoning in the Suburbs

Much has been said and written about zoning laws that limit the availability of land for housing or increase the cost of land and thereby make it difficult or impossible to build housing for low- and moderate-income families in the suburbs.[1] The argument is made frequently that one of the reasons that suburban municipalities use zoning to exclude new housing for families with children is because the cost of public education exceeds the revenue that may be derived from property taxes on the new development. This practice, called "fiscal zoning," is claimed to be one of the motivating forces behind discriminatory zoning laws in the suburbs.

It would seem to follow that, to the extent that state revenue is distributed to suburban municipalities, the fiscal motivation for exclusionary zoning would be reduced. However, suburban municipalities have not been prime beneficiaries of a distribution of new state revenue. In fact, the judicial decision that led to the adoption of the New Jersey Tax Reform plan requires a very different form of distribution of revenue. Under the mandated plan, the central cities, rather than the "exclusionary" suburbs are intended to be the prime beneficiaries of state revenue. The suburban municipalities receive less financial assistance and are limited in their expenditures for public education by a formula that ties increases in spending to a percentage of the annual increase in the value of real property.[2] Thus, the quest for ratables in the suburbs, and the need to consider fiscal consequences of future land use, i.e. fiscal zoning, will be increased rather than diminished by the cap limitations and Tax Reform Program.

State Leadership in Land Use Development

The limitation on expenditures by state and local governments will encourage increased leadership by the executive branch of state government in the process by which the land in the states is developed. Necessity is the mother of both invention and frugality. When funds are limited, every spending entity, be it individual, family, or government, is forced to consider how to maximize the benefits that can be derived from limited resources and how to reduce waste and inefficiency.

Financial necessity is also one of the primary reasons for long range planning. The adoption in several states of limitations on government spending appears to be a fundamental political statement that the era of automatic assent to ever-increasing governmental budgets may be coming to an end. If this is true, then state government will have no choice but to consider the impact of land use development in the state on the demand for future capital and recurrent expenditures of state revenue and to plan for the long range development of the state. In New Jersey, Governor Brendan Byrne has already begun to do so. He has on several occasions expressed his concern for the relationship between state land use development and the fiscal limitations on state government. The governor has encouraged the preparation of a state development guide plan[3] that allocates all land in the state into categories of growth, limited growth, agriculture, and open space areas. He has advocated a policy of directing federal and state aid to cities and built-up suburban areas as a means of revitalizing the cities and limiting development in the unspoiled areas.[4] He created a cabinet-level committee to take the initiative and state funds to "direct growth patterns" rather than having land use patterns simply reflect the interests of developers.[5] In his sixth annual report to the state legislature he expressed his intention to "shift growth to already developed areas and away from fragile remaining natural resources.[6]

In California as well, the state has responded to the problem of limited financial resources and urban development with a new urban strategy. The state planning office has recommended that the first priority in California urban land use be the renewal and maintenance of existing urban areas. Second, underutilized land within areas already served by utilities should be more intensely developed. Only then if development is still necessary, should open land be used, and that land should be immediately adjacent to existing urban and suburban areas. By focusing its strategy on a more compact urban environment, California's planning office hopes that money and energy can be saved, existing cities protected, and the state's diminishing open space preserved.[7]

Thus, with limited funds to spend there will be a tendency to limit the development of areas to which governmental services would have to be expanded. New highways, water supply, and sewerage treatment facilities will not be authorized as readily as in the past. Capital expenditures will be directed to older built-up areas. Local governments are going to become more dependent on state programs of financial assistance. As this financial dependence increases, there will be a greater tendency for local governments to respond to the planning leadership of the state.

Population Shifts

Limitations on expenditures by local government, together with a state policy of discouraging the extension of highway, water, and sewer facilities into new areas, will tend to limit the movement of population from the central cities to the outlying suburbs. If the quality of life in the central cities continues to deteriorate, the movement of population from the cities will tend to concentrate in the suburban communities in close proximity to older built-up areas where highways, water, and sewer facilities already exist and can be used to serve increased populations. This shift in population will be consistent with the limitations imposed by a possible shortage of gasoline and likely continued increase in the costs of fuel.

Real Estate Values

The most readily accepted principle of real estate appraisal is that the location of a property is the most significant determinant of its market value. It is also understood among real estate appraisers that the market value of real estate is an expression in money of the relative optimism or pessimism about the future prospects for growth and development of the area in which the property is located. Where there is optimism about the future of the area, property values go up; where there is a prevailing attitude of pessimism, property values go down.

The effect of the New Jersey Tax Reform Program, including the limitations of government spending, on real estate values depends on a number of factors. For example:

1. To the extent that the distribution of state revenue from the gross income tax improves the quality of life in the central cities sufficiently to create a sense of optimism about an improved future for the cities, the value of real estate in the central cities will increase. Consequently, the effect of the Tax Reform Program on central real estate will depend on whether improved governmental services in any specified area, together with the advantage of reduced property taxes, will be significant in improving the prospects for future development or redevelopment. On the other hand, there are many areas in many cities where reduced taxes and some improvement in municipal services will have very little beneficial effect upon real estate values. Thus, the effect of the Tax Reform Program on real estate values is only one of many factors to be included in the process that constitutes the art of real estate appraisal
2. To the extent that the limitation on municipal spending impairs the quality of life in suburban areas, the attractiveness of these areas will tend to be reduced to new purchasers. However, this factor may be offset by two countervailing forces. First, the reduction of property taxes will tend to enhance the value of real property in the suburbs and, second, even if the services of suburban municipalities are reduced because of spending limitations, when compared to the disadvantages of living in some central cities, the comparative advantages of suburban living may remain sufficiently significant to maintain the relatively better market value of suburban real estate.
3. To the extent that the limitation on state government spending results in the implementation of a state policy that discourages the extension of services and facilities into the underlying areas of the state, the value of real estate in these areas will be diminished. It is very likely that the prospect of reduced governmental expenditures for highways, sewer, and other services and the prospect for continued shortages and the high cost of gasoline will tend to reduce the market for and value of real estate in the outlying suburban areas.

When these factors are considered, it appears likely that the greatest opportunities for the appreciation of real estate values in the state will be in the developing municipalities outside of but in close proximity to the cities and older built-up suburbs. These are the areas where highways, roadways, sewer and water service, school buildings and other capital improvements are in place and where the capacity exists to accommodate additional population. The value of real estate in these areas will be further enhanced by the expectation of development at densities higher than existing zoning ordinances presently allow. This expectation will result from challenges to restrictive zoning of "developing municipalities" under the principle of the *Mount Laurel* decision.[8]

Notes

1. For an analysis of this issue whether exclusionary zoning laws do in fact exclude low-income persons from the suburbs, see Rose, "Myths and Misconceptions of Exclusionary Zoning Litigation," 8 *Real Estate Law Journal* 2 (1979).

2. N.J. Stat. Ann. §§ 18A: 7A-25.

3. *State Development Guide Plan,* New Jersey Department of Community Affairs, Division of State and Regional Planning, Sept. 1977.

4. "Byrne to Take Active Hand in Agency Readings," *Star Ledger,* Jan. 5, 1979, p. 5.

5. "New Growth Policy: Cabinet Level Panel to Guide State Development," *Sunday Star Ledger,* Feb. 18, 1979, p. 1.

6. "Governor Stressing Urban Rebirth in Address on Objectives for State," *Star Ledger,* Jan. 8, 1980, p. 1.

7. *An Urban Strategy for California,* Office of Planning and Research, California, 1978, pp. 9-10.

8. Southern Burlington County NAACP v. Township of Mount Laurel, 67 N.J. 151, 336 A. 2d 713 (1975).

8

Effects of the School Budget Caps

ERNEST C. REOCK, JR.

In the Public School Education Act of 1975, the New Jersey legislature responded to a decision of the State Supreme Court in the case of *Robinson v. Cahill.* Guidelines for the governance of the state's system of free public schools were provided and a revised system for financing public elementary and secondary education was established. The law called for substantially increased state support for the roughly 600 local school districts, and companion legislation instituted New Jersey's first personal income tax.

Included as a part of the law were statutory limitations placed for the first time on the annual increase in local school budgets. An unprecedented move for New Jersey, the statutory budget "caps," as they are called, extend state control over local decision making. Subsequent legislation provides similar, though far from identical, limits for municipal, county, and state budgets.

The caps are calculated by statutory formula in an attempt to limit expenditures in an objective manner. There are, in addition, two clauses providing guidelines under which the state commissioner of

---

Ernest C. Reock, Jr. is Director, Bureau of Government Research, Rutgers University. This article is based on a report prepared for the Joint Committee on the Public Schools of the New Jersey Legislature, and published in May, 1980 by the Rutgers University Bureau of Government Research.

education may exercise discretion to waive the budget cap for an individual school district and allow budgeted expenditures to exceed the cap.

The Budget Cap Formulas

The law contains two statutory formulas, one applying to school districts that have been spending at a level *below* the state average per pupil, and the other apply to districts that have been spending *at or above* the state average per pupil. Each formula may be divided into three parts: (1) the basic growth rate; (2) the equalization factor; and (3) the base budget. The formulas are shown in table 1 with the three parts labeled. In each case, the formula gives the amount by which the net current expense budget (NCEB) can be increased in dollars.[1] This can be translated into a percentage increase by dividing it by the district's NCEB for the prior year.

THE BASIC GROWTH RATE

Common to both formulas is the use of the growth in total statewide "equalized valuation" (a measure of the true value of taxable property) to calculate the basic growth rate allowed in school district budgets. Three-fourths of either the annual percentage change in equalized valuation or the average of the last three years' annual percentage changes, whichever is larger, is to be used. Since equalized valuation is used in the law as a means of estimating community fiscal resources for state aid purposes, it was adopted also as the basis for calculating permissible budget increases. The three-fourths multiplier applied to the growth of statewide equalized valuation in each formula reflects legislative concern caused by the high growth rate of equalized valuation at the time when the law was written.

THE EQUALIZATION FACTOR

Also the same in both formulas is the equalization factor, a fraction in which the state average NCEB per pupil is divided by the school district's NCEB per pupil. The use of the fraction as a multiplier is intended to help equalize school expenditures per pupil over a period of years by permitting a faster rate of budget growth for low-spending districts.

THE BASE BUDGET

Where the two formulas differ is in the base budget. For districts spending *below* the average level, the base budget is the *state average*

TABLE 1

NEW JERSEY SCHOOL BUDGET CAP FORMULAS, ACCORDING TO SECTION 25, CHAPTER 212, LAWS OF 1975, AS AMENDED

	Basic Growth Rate		Equalization Factor		Base Budget
A. For districts spending in the prior year *below* the state average NCEB* per pupil:	The larger of: 3/4 × The latest annual percentage change in statewide equalized valuation (or) 3/4 × The average of the last three year's annual percentage changes	×	The prior year's state average NCEB* per pupil / The prior year's district NCEB* per resident pupil	×	The prior year's *state* average NCEB* per pupil, times the prior year's resident enrollment of the district
B. For districts spending in the prior year *at or above* the state average NCEB* per pupil:	The larger of: 3/4 × The latest annual percentage change in statewide equalized valuation (or) 3/4 × The average of the last three years' annual percentage changes	×	The prior year's state average NCEB* per pupil / The prior year's district NCEB* per pupil	×	The prior year's *district* NCEB* per pupil, times the prior year's resident enrollment of the district

* NCEB = Net Current Expense Budget.

NCEB per pupil, multiplied by the district's prior-year enrollment. For districts spending *at or above* the average, the base budget is the *district's own* NCEB per pupil, multiplied by the district's prior-year enrollment. For these higher-spending districts, the use of the district's own budget figure does two things: (1) it provides more room for spending increases than otherwise would be the case if the formula used the state average as the base budget, and (2) it results in the permissible increase in budgeted *dollars per pupil* being the same for all districts spending above the state average level.

Waiver Provisions

Budget caps are calculated for individual districts on the basis of the formulas, which are weighted in favor of those at the lower end of spending scale. To ensure flexibility in budget limitations, two clauses were added setting guidelines under which the caps might be waived for individual districts upon request. One guideline, or reason, for waiving the cap for a district is increased enrollment. The cap formulas make no allowance for year-to-year enrollment increases when determining the allowable margin for expenditure growth. The commissioner of education, therefore, may grant an exception to the budget caps for increased enrollment that "may be reasonably anticipated in the district."

The other guideline under which the caps may be waived lacks clear statutory definition. It allows the commissioner to grant exception to the caps "having judged that a reallocation of resources or any other action taken within the permissible level of spending would be insufficient to meet the goals, objectives and standards established pursuant to this act."

In 1979, the state board of education asserted its right to hear appeals from decisions by the commissioner of education on requests for budget cap waivers, thus making the granting of cap waivers a two-tiered process.

Implementation of the Budget Caps

THE BASIC GROWTH RATE

The basic growth rate used in the budget cap formulas is the *higher* of:

3/4 of the latest annual change in statewide equalized valuation

or

3/4 of the average of the last three years' annual percentage changes in statewide equalized valuation.

Equalized valuation is calculated every year for state school aid purposes by the New Jersey Division of Taxation, and is reported on October 1.

When the budget caps were first implemented, statewide equalized valuation was near the end of a period of very rapid annual growth. The growth rate dropped sharply during the mid-1970s and then began to revive toward the end of the decade. The basic growth rate calculated for the budget cap formula, thus, was relatively liberal at first, became steadily more restrictive, and then reversed direction:

School Year	Basic Growth Rate
1976-77	8.7858%
1977-78	7.1766
1978-79	5.3585
1979-80	5.7962
1980-81	9.2290
1981-82	10.6348

Part of the growth in equalized valuation during the most recent past results from a substantial increase in property values in Atlantic County as a result of casino development there. The statewide impact of the casinos can be overestimated, however. Although the percentage growth of property valuations in Atlantic County has been spectacular, the county still constitutes only about 3 percent of total statewide equalized valuations, making its impact on the statewide total growth relatively minor.

THE BUDGET CAP WAIVER PROCESS

The combination of budget increases permitted by the statutory formula and the administration of the budget cap waiver process has been different in every year. Statewide figures showing the financial impact of these combinations are shown in table 2.

The first implementation of the budget caps took place during the winter of 1975-76, as school budgets for 1976-77 were being prepared. Because of uncertainty on the funding of the new law, most local boards of education took a cautious approach, and only a small portion of the potential budget increase capacity was used. Since then, however, they have come much closer to using the full amount permissible.

The granting of waivers has varied from year to year, generally inversely to the level of the basic growth rate. The result has been that the maximum permissible amount of annual budget increase statewide remained fairly stable through 1979-80 at about $175 million, and

TABLE 2

STATE TOTAL NET CURRENT EXPENSE BUDGETS AND INCREASES UNDER BUDGET CAPS, 1975-76 TO 1980-81

School Year	State Total of Net Current Expense Budgets	Basic Growth Rate in Formulas	Permissible Increase under Budget Caps Formulas	Budget Cap Waivers Granted by Commissioner	Budget Cap Waivers Granted by State Board	Maximum Permissible Increase, including Budget Cap Waivers	Actual Increase in Net Current Expense Budgets	Actual Increase as a Percentage: of Formula Amount	Actual Increase as a Percentage: of Maximum Permissible
1975-76	$2,089,805,917								
		8.7858%	$200,086,935 (9.5744%)	$14,115,301 (0.6754%)	––	$214,202,236 (10.2499%)	$ 67,175,417 (3.2144%)	33.6	31.4
1976-77	2,156,981,334								
		7.1766%	168,644,716 (7.8186%)	10,047,466 (0.4658%)	––	178,692,182 (8.2844%)	138,575,000 (6.4245%)	82.2	77.5
1977-78	2,295,556,334								
		5.3585%	134,940,274 (5.8783%)	42,005,379 (1.8299%)	––	176,945,653 (7.7082%)	164,371,041 (7.1604%)	121.8	92.9
1978-79	2,459,927,375								
		5.7962%	156,263,487 (6.3524%)	15,488,041 (0.6296%)	$2,023,619 (0.0823%)	173,775,147 (7.0642%)	136,220,155 (5.5376%)	87.2	78.4
1979-80	2,596,147,530								
		9.2290%	263,408,682 (10.1461%)	23,206,929 (0.8939%)	769,432 (0.0296%)	287,385,043 (11.0697%)	240,169,014 (9.2510%)	91.2	83.6
1980-81	2,836,316,544								

the utilization of that capacity ranged only from about 78 percent to 93 percent. Substantially increased growth of property values in the last two years has led to a liberalization of the budget caps for 1980-81, and an increase in the permissible and actual growth of school budgets.

Performance of the Budget Caps

The four major purposes generally acknowledged for the New Jersey school budget caps are:

1. To prevent annual budget increases that are so large as to encourage inefficiency, particularly in school districts where the flow of state aid was suddenly increased
2. To limit state liability for future financial aid
3. To assure that a substantial portion of new state aid funds is passed along to taxpayers as property tax relief
4. To encourage and permit the low-budget school districts of the state to move toward more nearly equal expenditures per pupil

PREVENTION OF LARGE AND INEFFICIENT BUDGET INCREASES

One of the most obvious original purposes of budget caps was to prevent large and potentially inefficient budget increases. In general, analyses of actual budget increases have found relatively few substantial annual increases. Even in the highest year (1976-77), fewer than 30 places had budget increases of more than 20 percent and the number has dropped to less than half that in recent years. These are mostly small school districts, where a few dollars makes a large percentage change. The number of places with million dollar increases has remained steadily at about 30, with most being large school districts where the growth represents only a small percentage change. Where a large percentage or absolute change has taken place, this has been done most often on the basis of a cap waiver authorized after budget review by the state commissioner of education. The conclusion that has been reached is that the budget caps—together with all other factors—have been quite successful in preventing excessive individual budget increases as state aid has been expanded.

LIMITATION OF STATE FISCAL LIABILITY

A second major purpose of the school budget caps was to control the growth of the state's liability for future state aid funding. The Public School Education Act provides for a guaranteed tax base system of state support in which costs are shared between the state and the local communities, with budgetary decisions being made by the local boards of education. The share of the current expense budget provided by the state government varies in inverse proportion to the wealth of the community, as measured by the equalized valuation of property per pupil. The budget caps, thus, are a means of keeping local school districts from increasing their budgets unreasonably in the knowledge that the state will pay a portion which, in some cases, may run to more than 70 percent. It is primarily for this reason that the budget caps have been applied to the same element of the total budget—the net current expense budget—that is used as the basis for calculating the state's dollar input to the school district's current expense budget.

Growth of the NCEB has a secondary impact on state fiscal liability, because categorical aid for children with specified handicaps is calculated by multiplying an "additional cost factor" for the specific handicap by the number of children in that category, and by the prior year's state average NCEB per pupil. Unlimited growth of the state average NCEB per pupil, without adjustment of cost factors, could lead to unlimited growth of the state liability for categorical aid. Thus, the budget caps serve to limit the growth of state categorical aid also.

In the fall of 1975, following enactment of the law but prior to passage of the funding legislation, a Senate Commission on Financing State School Aid was established to explore the various alternatives available for meeting the costs of the new law. The cost projections made by the commission in its final report provide the best guide to the expectations of the legislature at the time with regard to the probable future fiscal liability of the state for aid to public education. The effectiveness of the budget caps in limiting that liability can be measured by comparing actual subsequent appropriations and expenditures against the projections made by the commission.

In the area primarily affected by the budget caps—current expense equalization aid—state appropriations and expenditures have gradually fallen further and further behind the 1975 projections. The effectiveness of the budget caps in limiting growth in this area seems apparent. In categorical aid, which is affected indirectly by the budget caps, the picture is different. Here, appropriations and actual expenditures have exceeded the projections made in 1975. This is largely the result of aid for compensatory education, the calculation of which was not defined clearly by the Act. The gap here has begun to narrow, however, with the growth of firmer administrative determination of compensatory education funding procedures. Taking the two cap-related state aid categories together—current expense equalization aid and categorical aid–the state's fiscal liability has remained well below the level projected in 1975.

Other aid categories show mixed patterns. Debt service and capital outlay equalization aid, transportation aid, special costs for research and emergencies, and miscellaneous other grants-in-aid all are costing the state less than was anticipated. On the other hand, the state's contribution to the Teacher's Pension and Annuity Fund (TPAF) is ahead of the projection.

Even with rapid growth of the TPAF and unexpected costs for categorical aid, the overall cost of aid for public education to the state treasury remains below the projections of four years ago. Clearly, the budget caps–in conjunction with all other influences–have played the role intended for them in limiting state fiscal liability.

PROPERTY TAX RELIEF

A third purpose for the school budget caps was to ensure that some of the additional state aid funds made available under the Public School Education Act were passed on by the school districts to local property taxpayers in order to reduce their tax burden. This was a particularly appropriate purpose in the first year under a new and expanded state aid law, but also has applicability in subsequent years.

Table 3 shows the average state equalized school property tax rate over the 1967-80 period. The tax rate rose steadily during the late 1960s, peaked in 1971, and began a decline that has continued steadily now for nine years, the first four as the predecessor of the current Act–known as the Bateman Act–was phased in, and the last five coming under the provisions of the present law.

Not only has the state average equalized school property tax rate continued its decline, but tax rates in most communities have mirrored this decrease. The number of communities having equalized school tax rates of $2.00 or more has declined from:

210 in 1975, to
127 in 1976, to
72 in 1977, to
47 in 1978, to
23 in 1979, to
9 in 1980.

The budget caps, together with other factors, have been highly effective in providing relief from school property taxes.

TABLE 3

STATEWIDE AVERAGE EQUALIZED SCHOOL PROPERTY TAX RATE AND ANNUAL CHANGE, 1967 TO 1980

Tax Year	State Average Equalized School Tax Rate	Change	
1967	$1.64		
1968	1.80	+ .16	
1969	1.93	+ .13	
1970	2.01	+ .08	
1971	2.10	+ .09	
1972	2.04	– .06	Phase-in of Bateman Act
1973	1.96	– .08	
1974	1.81	– .15	
1975	1.76	– .05	
1976	1.66	– .10	Public School Education Act of 1975
1977	1.58	– .08	
1978	1.55	– .03	
1979	1.46	– .09	
1980	1.39	– .07	

EQUALIZATION OF EXPENDITURES PER PUPIL

A fourth purpose of the budget caps may be stated as an attempt to encourage and permit the low-budget school districts of the state to move in the direction of more nearly equal expenditures for each pupil, statewide, in order to achieve more equal educational opportunity. The New Jersey Supreme Court found the prior system of funding the public schools to be deficient on the grounds that expenditures and resources varied greatly.

The court did not clearly direct equalization of expenditures but its statements appeared to require a system that encourages low-spending school districts to use the fiscal resources made available to them under the law by increasing their budgets. High-spending school districts would have to be limited, so that the others could catch up, but there is no indication by the court that they would have to reduce their spending levels.

Several reports have found that there is a slow movement of low-budget districts toward the state average spending level when *total* school budgets are analyzed in relative terms on a community-by-community basis. However, the performance of the *budget caps* in bringing about equalization of expenditures probably should not be judged by *total budgets,* but by the equalization that has taken place in the *net current expense budget* per pupil, since this is the budget item which is limited by the budget caps. Here the results are not encouraging. As shown in table 4, the proportion of school districts having *net current expense budgets* per pupil less than 85 percent of the state average declined in 1976-77, but there has been no improvement since then. The proportion of districts budgeting at high NCEB-per pupil levels (over 115 percent of the state average) has increased over the past five years, despite the limits presumably imposed on them by the budget caps.

TABLE 4

DISTRIBUTION OF SCHOOL DISTRICTS BY LEVEL OF NET CURRENT EXPENSE BUDGET PER RESIDENT PUPIL, 1975-76 TO 1979-80

Net Current Expense Budget Per Resident Pupil	1975-76	Percentage of School Districts 1976-77	1977-78	1978-79	1979-80
More than 115 percent of state average	21.0	22.7	22.0	22.5	24.2
85-115 percent of state average	54.0	56.5	56.9	57.0	53.7
Less than 85 percent of state average	25.0	20.8	21.1	20.6	22.1
Total number of school districts	572	573	573	574	574

Note: Omitted are 20 county vocational districts; four districts that receive large amounts of federal impacted area aid under P.L. 874; the "special education" districts of Corbin City and Longport; and three districts each year that have no resident pupils. Increase in total is caused by activation of Cumberland Regional and Pinelands Regional.

Moreover, if public school pupils are tabulated, rather than school districts, there is even less progress. As shown in table 5, following a slight initial increase in 1976-77, the percentage of public school pupils receiving the benefits of dollar inputs within 15 percent of the state average has declined steadily, while the proportion of pupils at the high and low ends of the scale has increased substantially.

When the divergent trends of equalization for *total school budget* and *net current expense budget* are compared, they lead to the following conclusions:

1. The budget caps have *not* been effective in raising the relative spending level of school districts having low net current expense budgets.
2. The modest relative equalization of per-pupil *total* budgeted expenditures among districts, which has been observed, probably results from programs *outside* of the budget caps, such as state aid for special education, compensatory education, and bilingual education, which have resulted in increased total school budgets per pupil in the lowest-spending districts.

TABLE 5

DISTRIBUTION OF PUBLIC SCHOOL PUPILS BY LEVEL OF NET CURRENT EXPENSE BUDGET PER RESIDENT PUPIL, 1975-76 TO 1979-80

Net Current Expense Budget Per Resident Pupil	Percentage of Resident Pupils 1975-76	1976-77	1977-78	1978-79	1979-80
More than 115 percent of state average	16.7	19.6	18.3	18.3	21.2
85-115 percent of state average	64.7	65.2	63.6	61.9	58.6
Less than 85 percent of state average	18.5	15.2	18.1	19.8	20.2
Total number of pupils	1,420,856	1,390,360	1,347,060.5	1,307,762.5	1,262,771

Note: See table 4 for school districts omitted.

REASONS FOR FAILURE OF THE BUDGET CAPS TO RAISE THE RELATIVE SPENDING LEVEL OF LOW-BUDGET DISTRICTS

Two major factors potentially could offset the equalizing effect of the budget cap formulas: (1) budget cap waivers; and (2) the impact of enrollment decline.[2]

There always has been concern that the granting of a disproportionate number of budget cap waivers to high-spending school districts could destroy the equalizing impact of the budget cap formulas. However, this does not appear to have been the case. Both in percentage terms and in absolute dollar-per-pupil terms, budget cap waivers, as administered by the commissioner of education, have gone mostly to low-spending districts, and have strengthened the equalizing aspects of the budget cap formulas.

The same cannot be said of enrollment decline, however. Any enrollment decline results in an expanded budget cap, since the limted amount of dollar increase permitted in the budget may be spread over a smaller number of pupils. It now has become apparent that the patterns of enrollment change are closely linked to (though not necessarily caused by) budget levels. The average change in resident enrollment from September 1978 to September 1979 is shown in table 6 for groups of school districts stratified by budget levels. Almost without exception, the greater the NCEB level, the greater the average enrollment decline. The highest-NCEB places in group A had a 4.32 percent *decline* in enrollment; the lowest-NCEB places had a 0.24% *increase* in enrollment. With the enrollment decline being far greater among the high-spending school districts, it may be expected that the expansion of their budget caps will be greater. The actual impact, in terms of permissible per-pupil increases, is shown in table 7. The change is striking (see chart 1). The lowest-budget school districts—those in Group G spending at less than 75% of the state average per pupil—could increase their budgets by $153 per pupil according to the formula, and this was expanded by $23 more by cap waivers. Because they added enrollment, the total permissible increase per 1979-80 pupil, however, amounted to only $173. In contrast, the highest budget places—those in group A—had only a $106 formula cap, expanded by $5 through waivers. But their enrollment dropped so rapidly that, in terms of 1979-80 pupils, they could increase their budgets by $229 per pupil.

TABLE 6

AVERAGE ENROLLMENT CHANGE IN NEW JERSEY SCHOOL DISTRICTS, 1978 to 1979; SCHOOL DISTRICTS GROUPED BY 1978-79 NET CURRENT EXPENSE BUDGETS PER PUPIL

Expenditure Group and Relation to State Average Net Current Expense Budget per Pupil in 1978-79	Number of Districts	Average Enrollment Change, September 1978 to September 1979
A – Over 125% of Average	70	– 4.32%
B – 115% to 125% of Average	59	– 4.88
C – 105% to 115% of Average	98	– 4.35
D – 95% to 105% of Average	118	– 3.71
E – 85% to 95% of Average	111	– 3.61
F – 75% to 85% of Average	82	– 1.33
G – Below 75% of Average	36	+ 0.24
Total	574	– 3.44%

Note: See table 4 for school districts omitted.

TABLE 7

DOLLAR INCREASES PER PUPIL IN 1979-80 NET CURRENT EXPENSE BUDGETS PERMITTED BY STATUTORY FORMULAS, BUDGET CAP WAIVERS, AND ENROLLMENT CHANGE–SCHOOL DISTRICTS GROUPED BY BUDGET LEVEL

Expenditure Group and Relation to State Average NCEB Per Pupil	Number of Districts	1978-79 Average NCEB/Pupil	Increase Permitted by Budget Cap Formulas	Addition Because of Waivers	Addition Because of Enrollment Change	Total Permissible Increase Per 1979-80 Pupil
A – Over 125% of average	70	$2,504	$ + 106	$ + 5	$ + 118	$ + 229
B – 115% to 125% of average	59	2,190	+ 106	+ 4	+ 118	+ 228
C – 105% to 115% of average	98	2,005	+ 106	+ 8	+ 96	+ 210
D – 95% to 105% of average	118	1,829	+ 106	+ 16	+ 75	+ 197
E – 85% to 95% of average	111	1,647	+ 118	+ 7	+ 66	+ 191
F – 75% to 85%	82	1,466	+ 132	+ 20	+ 22	+ 174
G – Below 75% of average	36	1,266	+ 153	+ 23	– 3	+ 173

Note: See table 4 for school districts omitted.

In effect, the varying levels of enrollment decline have turned the budget cap provisions of the law upside down. The New Jersey school budget cap law, thus, has become a major obstacle to equalization of per-pupil expenditures.

Unintended Consequences

Although school budget caps appear to have achieved some of the purposes for which they were developed and to have failed in other areas, there is the possibility that they may have had unintended consequences in their impact on the educational programs of the public schools. School board members and school administrators have complained bitterly that they have had to cut back on educational programs because of the budget caps. The difficulty has been in finding some way to measure this sort of impact objectively. Attempts to evaluate programs in over 600 school districts seldom have proceeded very far. For purposes of this analysis, the dollar input to the instructional portion of the budget has been used as a substitute for evaluating programs. When placed on a dollar-per-pupil basis, using constant-value dollars, a reduction from the prior year has been taken to indicate some reduction in school program quality.

STATEWIDE IMPACT OF BUDGET CAPS ON FISCAL RESOURCES FOR SCHOOL PROGRAMS

During the early 1970s, state average instructional expenditures per pupil in constant dollars rose at about 3 to 4 percent per year (see table 8). A state aid "freeze" in 1975-76 caused this growth almost

CHART 1

Dollar Increase in 1979-80 Net Current Expense Budgets Permitted by Statuatory Formulas, Budget Cap Waivers, and Enrollment Changes

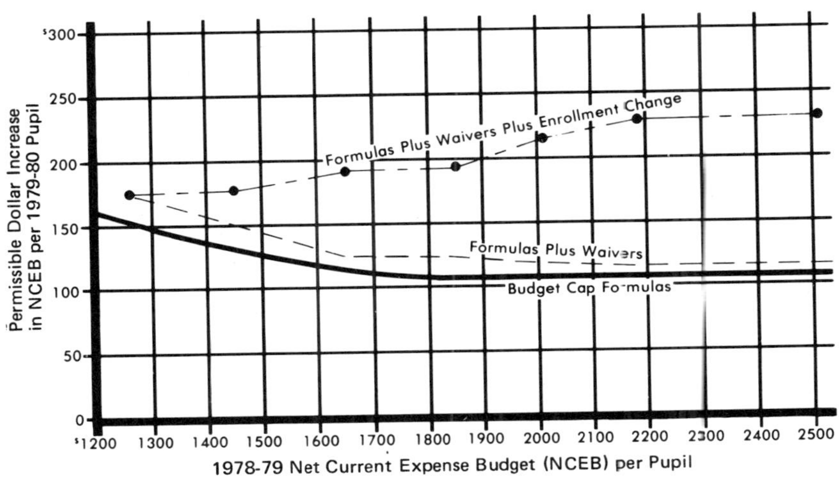

TABLE 8

STATE AVERAGE PER-PUPIL EXPENDITURES FOR INSTRUCTION IN CONSTANT 1975-76 DOLLARS; 1970-71 TO 1979-80

Year	Instruction Expenditures Per Pupil in 1975-76 Dollars	Percentage Change from Prior Year	
1970-71	$ 905.42		
1971-72	938.31	+ 3.6%	
1972-73	971.55	+ 3.5	
1973-74	1,010.19	+ 4.0	
1974-75	1,048.06	+ 3.7	
1975-76	1,050.41	+ 0.2	
1976-77	1,056.83	+ 0.6	Period of Budget Caps
1977-78 Preliminary	1,081.11	+ 2.3	
1978-79 Tentative	1,129.24	+ 4.5	
1979-80 Tentative	1,157.65	+ 2.5	

to stop, with instructional expenditures increasing only 0.2 percent that year in constant dollars. The first year under the public School Education Act—1976-77—saw only a modest resumption of growth, as many districts failed to utilize their budget cap capacity. Thereafter, instructional expenditures per pupil have increased each year, though at a somewhat lesser overall rate than before the budget caps were imposed. On a statewide basis, the budget caps appear to have reduced the rate by which the fiscal resources for school programs are growing, but they have not resulted in an overall reduction in those resources.

IMPACT OF THE BUDGET CAPS ON INDIVIDUAL SCHOOL DISTRICTS

The conclusion that there has *not* been a general statewide decline in fiscal resources available for school programs under the budget caps does not preclude the possibility that this may have happened in individual districts. To test this possibility, the constant-dollar instruction expenditure per pupil in each district was compared with the prior-year data for each of the first four years under the budget caps. In the first year of budget caps—1976-77—almost 40 percent of the school districts in the state reduced their fiscal input to instructional programs when this is measured in constant dollars on a per-pupil basis. In subsequent years, the proportion dropped to about one-fourth.

The year-to-year changes do not tell the story fully, however. Although a school district may be forced to a lower instructional expenditure per pupil in one year, it may recover in the next. In fact, this is what seems to have happened in many cases. Although roughly one-quarter of the districts have reduced their per-pupil instructional expenditures in each year, this result over the entire four-year span is less widespread. Of all school districts, about 10 percent have a long-term (1975-76 to 1979-80) decline in constant-dollar expenditures per pupil for instruction.

Although a substantial minority of the school districts had a lower expenditure level for instruction in each year, this does not necessarily indicate that the change resulted from the budget caps, since the same result could be caused by a board of education that failed to use its budget cap fully, or by an electorate that refused to approve a budget fully utilizing the caps. In order to test this possibility, each declining-expenditure district's net current expense budget (NCEB) was compared with the permissible NCEB under the budget cap to establish whether the budget cap was fully utilized. If it was *not* used fully, the amount by which the actual NCEB could have been increased under the cap was added to the instructional budget and divided by the enrollment to obtain a new, hypothetical per-pupil instruction budget which could be compared with the prior year's figure.

In the first year under the budget caps—1976-77—school budgets were adopted initially before there was assurance that the new state aid programs under Chapter 212 would be funded for the year. Many school districts, therefore, adopted very conservative budgets that fell short of the limits imposed by the budget caps. Even though legislation eventually permitted a reopening of the budget process, many districts made no change or only marginal changes in their budgets. Moreover, more than half of the school budgets submitted to referendum were defeated in 1976. One of the unique aspects of the New Jersey school budget cap is that the proposed budget must fit within the statutory budget caps *before* it is submitted to the voters. Any reduction caused by negative voter action then results in underutilization of budget cap capacity. Of the 232 school districts suffering a reduced per-pupil instruction budget in constant dollars in 1976-77, 179 were placed in this position by underutilization of the budget caps. The impact of the budget caps on fiscal resources for school programs in this year was relatively small—apparently hitting only about 9 percent of those in the state.

Preliminary data for 1977-78 and tentative data for 1978-79 and 1979-80 show a much different picture. While underutilization of the caps has been dropped, the role of the budget caps has become more important, remaining remarkably consistent at about 15-17 percent each year. In the last three years of the study period, the budget caps, in particular, appear to have had a negative effect on the fiscal resources for instructional programs in about one-sixth of the school districts of the state each year.

Again, the long-term impact is considerably less extensive, since school districts whose program is impacted in one year may recover subsequently. In about 9 percent of the school districts, the budget caps appear to have had the long-term effect (1975-76 to 1979-80) of reducing the fiscal resources for school programs.

Conclusions

School budget caps in New Jersey have achieved some of their original purposes—to prevent large and inefficient annual expenditure increases, to limit state liability for future financial aid, and to ensure that there would be some property tax relief. They have failed notably in their fourth purpose—to help move the low-budget school districts of the state in the direction of the more equal per-pupil expenditure levels.

But more than this. Not only have the budget caps failed to achieve this fourth goal but, because of varying rates of enrollment decline, the budget cap formulas have now become a positive obstacle to those low-budget school districts that might wish to bring their expenditures more nearly in line with expenditures in other places. With this development, the constitutional viability of the budget caps comes immediately into question.

Furthermore, there is evidence that the budget caps have led to a reduction in the financial resources available for school instructional programs in a significant minority of districts.

Although the budget caps are in trouble, they probably can be salvaged, and various programs of revision are under consideration. But the conclusion seems clear—unless changes of some kind are made, the school budget caps appear highly vulnerable to challenge at any time.

Notes

1. The Net Current Expense Budget of the district is the district's total current expense budget, *minus* funds received for state categorical aid programs

for pupils with special handicaps; most costs of transportation; and all other special sources of revenue, such as federal aid, tuition revenues anticipated, free balance reappropriated, and other miscellaneous revenues. It is essentially the portion of the budget that is financed by state equalization aid and local property taxes.

2. Failure to utilize the budget cap capacity is a third potential factor analyzed in the report on which this article is based. It was found to have a limited influence, except in the first year.

IV. THE TEXAS SYSTEM

9

The Texas Tax Relief Amendment: Much Ado About Nothing

BRUCE M. KRAMER

Pre-1978 Constitutional Expenditure and Debt Limits

EXPENDITURE AND DEBT LIMITS–STATE LEVEL

Even before the voters approved HJR I in 1978,[1] the Texas constitution contained a prohibition against the creation of debt at the state level, with three basic exceptions: wartime emergencies, payment of existing state debt, and the supply of casual deficiencies in revenues if the total amount of debt did not exceed $200,000.[2] Article 3, section 49, which limits state indebtedness, has been part of the Texas constitution since 1876 and has been virtually unchanged since then.[3] In addition to this strict limitation on the issuance of state bonded indebtedness bonds, the Texas constitution also prohibits the state legislature from appropriating any funds in excess of anticipated revenues.[4] This pay-as-you-go provision was added in 1942 and requires the comptroller of public accounts to estimate anticipated revenue for the upcoming biennium prior to the convening of each regular session of the state legislature. The provision also allows for a legislative override of the pay-as-you-go requirement if there is a four-fifths vote of the total members of the House and

Mr. Kramer is Professor of Law, Texas Tech University School of Law.

Senate in case of "emergency and imperative public necessity."[5] The third in the trilogy of state expenditure and debt limitations is article 3, section 50, of the Texas constitution, which prohibits the state legislature from lending or pledging the credit of the state to any person, association, corporation, or municipality.[6]

By various constitutional amendments the state has created exceptions to these strict limitations on state debt. For example, the Veterans Land Fund can issue $700 million in state bonded indebtedness for the purpose of purchasing land for eventual resale to veterans.[7] The fund was created by a constitutional amendment in 1946 that initially set a $25 million limit on indebtedness.

The constitution further provides for the issuance of state general obligation bonds to support the Texas Water Development Fund with an overall indebtedness limit of $200 million. The funds are made available to special districts and municipalities for the purpose of water conservation, reclamation, storage, and transportation projects.[8] A further amendment was added in 1962 allowing the sale of an additional $200 million for water storage transportation, treatment, and reservoir expansion projects.[9] Projects authorized under the 1962 amendment can be developed and acquired by the state and then leased or sold to others pursuant to legislative directives. In 1971 an amendment providing for an additional $200 million in state bonded indebtedness for any purpose authorized in article 3, sections 49c or 49d, was passed by the electorate.[10] In all cases state bonds for water project purposes must be authorized by a 2/3 vote of both houses of the state legislature.

Article 3, Section 49e authorizes the state park and wildlife department to issue up to $75 million of state general obligation bonds for the purpose of the acquisition of park land by the state.[11] Article 3, section 50b authorizes bonding authority of $85 million to the Coordinating Board, Texas College and University System, for the making of loans to higher education in both public and private institutions.[12] In 1969 the bond limit for student loans was increased to $200 million.[13] Finally, the commissioner of agriculture is authorized to issue $10 million in state general obligation bonds for the purpose of guaranteeing loans used for the purchase of farm or ranch real estate.[14]

Thus Texas has a history of enacting constitutional amendments to allow state indebtedness for specific purposes when they are deemed sufficiently important to state interests. However, Texas has avoided the issuance of general obligation debt to fund most of its capital development needs and has assiduously avoided the use of debt to fund current operating expenses.

In addition to the constitutional amendments authorizing the sale of state general obligation bonds, there have been several court decisions carving out other exceptions to the debt limits. In *Texas Turnpike Authority v. Shepperd,*[15] the Texas supreme court recognized the long-standing exception for revenue bonds from the prohibition against the issuance of state general obligation bonds. Since the bonds were to be payable solely from the revenues generated from the Dallas-Fort Worth turnpike and were not to be considered a debt of the state, they did not fall within the rubric of the constitutional prohibition against the incurring of state debt. In the *Shepperd* case the court drew upon its earlier decision in *Texas National Guard Armory Board v. McCraw.*[16] In *McCraw* the legislature had authorized the Board to issue $4.5 million in bonds to build several armories throughout the state. The bonds were to be paid by the leasing of the armories from the board to the state for the use of the Texas National Guard. Although the state treasury was paying the rent, and thus the bonds, the court held that the bonds were not a general obligation of the state and upon default would not constitute a debt of the state. Therefore the bonds were not covered by the constitutional prohibition against the incurring of bonded indebtedness. *McCraw* also held that long-term lease-purchase agreements, whereby the state agrees to make long-term periodic payments and receive the property at the end of the leasehold, are not a debt for constitutional purposes.[17]

EXPENDITURE AND DEBT LIMITS–SUBSTATE UNITS (counties, cities, school districts, special districts, etc.)[18]

Because of the confluence of two factors, scarcity of water and overextension of substate unit credit for the benefit of railroads, the Texas constitution was amended in 1904 to severely limit the lending of credit by substate units. Under article 3, section 52a, no substate unit may lend its credit or issue bonds unless the legislature enacts enabling authority giving that unit the ability to issue bonded indebtedness and a two-thirds majority of the resident property taxpayers in the affected substate unit approve the bond issuance. In *Hill v. Stone*[19] the requirement that a person has to render real property for taxation before voting in a bond election was declared unconstitutional. Hence, all registered voters are entitled to vote in these bond elections.

These bonds have other restrictions. Constitutionally imposed requirements limit their face value to no more than one-fourth of the assessed valuation of the real property in the substate unit. The bond monies may only be used to (1) improve rivers, canals, and streams for navigation or irrigation purposes, (2) construct or maintain irigation, drainage, or navigation structures or facilities, and (3) construct, maintain, or operate roads or turnpikes.[20] Simultaneous with the enactment of the bond sale ordinance, the substate unit must create a sinking fund for the redemption of the principal and interest of the bonded indebtedness.

In addition, counties are authorized to issue bonds for road construction and maintenance purposes after receiving a majority vote of the resident property taxpayers at a countywide election. The face value of those bonds, however, may not exceed one-fourth of the assessed valuation of the real property in the county.[21] Counties also are authorized to levy and collect taxes to apply to the interest of the bonds as they become due and to provide a sinking fund for the redemption of the bonds.[22]

An interesting problem arose when the state legislature enacted a statute that authorized counties to sell bonds for the purpose of road construction and maintenance after an election in which a simple majority of county residents favored its issuance.[23] The statute was enacted under the general authority of article 11, section 2 of the Texas constitution, which gives to the legislature the ability to provide by general law for the construction of jails, courthouses, bridges, and roads by counties.[24] This conflicted with article 3, section 52 by only requiring a simple, rather than two-thirds, majority vote of residents. The court resolved the conflict between article 11, section 2 and article 3, section 52 by refusing to allow article 3 to repeal by implication the provisions of article 11.[25] Instead the court harmonized the provisions by allowing the more lenient ones of article 11, section 2 to prevail. This interpretation validated the bond issuance for road construction purposes which was passed by a simple majority vote.[26]

In other provisions, the constitution allows the legislature to grant to counties general obligation bonding authority for such purposes as courthouse construction, park development, voting machines, and jails.[27] Counties bordering on the Gulf of Mexico are authorized to issue general obligation bonds for flood protection purposes if approved by a two-thirds affirmative vote of the residents. However, at the same time, the county must create a levy to pay the interest and create a sinking fund of at least two percent of unpaid principal.[28] Thus, counties have been authorized to issue general obligation bonds subject only to a sinking fund requirement and other applicable taxing limits.[29]

In contrast to counties, municipalities can issue general obligation bonds for any municipal purpose if they receive voter approval and create a sinking fund to pay off the principal.[30] Although article 3, section 52 also refers to cities' issuance of general obligation bonds, the courts have held that the provisions of article 11, section 5 take precedence over the more restrictive bonded indebtedness provisions of article 3, section 52.[31]

The constitution specifically authorizes cities along the Gulf of Mexico to issue general obligation bonds for purposes of flood control upon a two-thirds majority vote of the residents and the creation of a sinking fund to pay off the principal.[32] Although the authority to issue bonds is contained in the home rule provision of the constitution, the language when referring to bonding authorities refers to *any* city, not just cities that have adopted home rule charters. Municipal revenue bonds need not meet the requirements of article 11, section 5 regarding sinking funds and elections unless the city charters impose those requirements on their issuance.[33]

Article 3, section 52, which limits bonded indebtedness, specifically refers to political corporations or subdivisions as coming under its aegis. Nonetheless, independent school districts and special districts have been able to circumvent its limitations in the same manner as counties and cities. For example, independent school districts are authorized to issue bonds for the construction and equipment of school buildings and sites if an election is held prior to the issuance of the bonds and the sinking fund and interest payments for all outstanding bonds plus the new issuance can be serviced by an ad valorem tax rate that does not exceed \$1.00/\$100 assessed valuation.[34] Similarly, special districts created specially either under the constitution or by legislative enabling act can be cloaked with the authority to incur debt with individualized limitations.[35] Thus, while article 3, section 52a contains a general restriction against substate units incurring bonded indebtedness, the legislature and courts have been willing to circumvent those restrictions to allow these units to more easily incur general obligation indebtedness.

STATE TAX LIMITATIONS

Because of the patchwork nature of the Texas constitution, there exist several inconsistent limitations on the state ad valorem property tax. The original limitation was in article 8, section 9[36] which, as amended, limits the state ad valorem tax rate to \$.35/\$100 assessed valuation for general purposes. But another provision, enacted in 1951, prohibits the state from levying any ad valorem tax for general revenue purposes.[37] In addition, the state constitution prior to 1968 authorized a maximum state ad valorem rate of \$.35/\$100 assessed valuation for use in the available school fund. This was amended in 1968; the state property tax was gradually phased out so that by 1974 the available school fund revenue came out of general appropriations rather than the state property tax.[38] A further levy of up to $0.2/$100 assessed valuation was authorized to create a special fund for confederate pensions.[39] This levy was repealed by a 1968 constitutional amendment that added another provision to the already byzantine Texas constitution.[40] By virtue of that 1977 constitutional amendment the state ad valorem property tax rate was limited to $.01/$100 assessed valuation to be levied for the purpose of paying for capital improvements at specified institutions of higher learning.[41] Thus, prior to the tax relief amendment (TRA), the state's role in property tax levies was minimal.

Texas has other sources of tax revenues. It is authorized to impose an income tax, although one is not presently being used.[42] A state sales tax of 4 percent is levied, with food and drug purchases exempt from the tax.[43] The state can also impose occupation taxes as long as they are equal and uniform.[44] The state also derives substantial income from its oil and gas holdings.

SUBSTATE UNIT TAX LIMITATIONS

No county can levy an ad valorem tax rate in excess of $.80/$100 assessed valuation for its general fund, permanent improvement fund, road and bridge fund, or jury fund[45] and the tax rate must be set so as not to impair the obligation of any outstanding bonds. A county may levy an additional tax at a rate not to exceed $.15/$100 for road maintenance purposes provided that a majority of the property tax-paying voters agree.[46] After *Hill v. Stone,* the election is now open to all registered voters in the county.[47] A further levy of $.30/ $100 is authorized for the purposes of constructing and maintaining farm-to-market roads and for flood control.[48] In implementing this provision the legislature has provided for a county election to approve the levying of the tax for the above two specified purposes.[49] Thus, counties are fairly well restricted both as to the amount of money they can raise through the ad valorem property tax and the purposes for which the money can be used.

Article 8, section 9 of the Texas constitution says: "no county, city or town shall levy a tax rate in excess of Eighty cents (80¢) on the One Hundred Dollars ($100) valuation in any one (1) year for general fund, permanent improvement fund, road and bridge fund and jury fund purposes."[50] This provision has not been applied to cities because of other conflicting limitations contained in different provisions of the constitution. For example, home rule cities, which must have a population in excess of 5,000 and adopt a home rule charter, cannot assess ad valorem taxes in excess of 2½ percent of the taxable property in the city.[51] Enabling legislation repealing this 2½ percent limitation for home rule cities was found to be constitutional in the early case of *Bodenheim v. Lightfoot,*[52] even though it is in apparent conflict with article 8, section 9 of the Texas constitution. The city charter in any home rule city may contain more restrictive levy limitations if voted on by the residents of the city.

General law cities are limited by the constitution to a tax rate not to exceed 1½ percent of the taxable property of the city.[53] General law cities that choose to incorporate under the provisions of articles 1133-1153a are further restricted to a property tax levy of no greater than $.25/$100 assessed valuation.[54] This type of incorporation is authorized for cities with a population of between 200 and 10,000 who desire to use an alderman form of city government.[55] General law cities having a population between 600 and 5,000 have the option of incorporating under the provisions of articles 966 *et seq.* and can levy a property tax rate not in excess of $1.50/$100 assessed valuation.[56] If, however, the general law city has a population in excesss of 5,000 it can levy a property tax of up to $2.50/$100 assessed valuation.[57]

Independent school districts may levy a tax for the maintenance and operation of the school system if the tax does not exceed $1.50/$100 assessed valuation.[58] Property tax limits on special districts occur either in the constitution or in the legislation creating the special district. For example, countywide hospital districts that can be created by an act of the legislature pursuant to constitutional enabling authority are restricted to a property tax levy not in excess of $.75/$100 assessed valuation.[59] Navigation districts created by the legislature are restricted to a tax levy not to exceed $.20/$100 assessed valuation by virtue of the legislature's actions, although the constitution would allow for a greater tax levy.[60]

Thus, all substate units were subject to a property tax limit even before the passage of the tax relief amendment. In several cases, the limits had not been approached—home rule cities—while in others many of the substate units had been levying at the constitutional or statutory limit for a long time.

The two other major sources of revenue for substate units are the sales and occupation taxes. Cities have the option of adding a 1 percent sales tax to the state 4 percent sales tax; the tax is collected by the state and refunded to the city.[61] Counties are not entitled to recover that 1 percent for sales made in unincorporated areas. However, both counties and cities can levy occupation taxes at one-half of the state rate.[62]

STATE AND LOCAL EXPENDITURE AND REVENUES– A PERSPECTIVE ON THE CLIMATE SURROUNDING THE PASSAGE OF THE TAX RELIEF AMENDMENT (TRA)[63]

In 1977, the year before the passage of the TRA, the state of Texas had revenues in excess of $8.847 billion. The sales tax provided close to $3.5 billion of the total revenue. State property tax revenue was only $37 million, which went to capital expenditures at specified institutions of higher education. In 1976, local governments (including special districts) raised $6.2 billion in revenue, of which $2.945 billion came from the property tax and $417 million came from the sales tax. Texas local governments rely on the property tax for between 45 and 64 percent of local revenues, with smaller governments having the greatest percentage of reliance.

Texas has approximately 254 counties, 1,066 municipalities, 1,425 special districts and 1,138 school districts. The state has about $2.125 billion in outstanding debt while substate units have over $12.080 billion in outstanding debt. Of that substate total, school district debt accounts for $3.125 billion and utility-based debt accounts for $3.196 billion. By far, the lion's share of the local school district financing was raised by the property tax ($1.642 billion out of $1.912 billion raised locally in 1976).

Because neither the state nor substate units were excessively dependent on the property tax and Texas had not experienced the rapid rise in residential property values, the forces that coalesced in California to forge the adoption of Proposition 13 were just not present in Texas. Nonetheless, enough public sentiment was voiced about tax and expenditure limits so that the state legislature decided to respond through the adoption of TRA.

FINAL NOTE

To conclude that the pre-1978 Texas scheme for tax and expenditure limitations is "arcane" is to be generous. During a 1974 attempt to simplify the entire 1876 Texas constitution, it was constantly argued that the existing constitution had suffered through 212 miscellaneous, and sometimes contradictory, amendments. Under the proposed new constitution, tax, debt, and expenditure limits were clearly defined for state and substate units of government. The limits were not as severe or drastic as those contained in Proposition 13, but they were understandable. For example, the property tax rate for cities was set at a maximum levy of $2.00/$100 assessed valuation and the county rate was set at $1.25/$100 assessed valuation. In both cases the limits did not apply to payment of outstanding debt.[64] However, the proposed Texas constitution was soundly defeated by the electorate in 1974, leaving the existing 1876 constitution intact and subject to further amendment. This was the legal framework that the Texas legislature had before it when it adopted the TRA of 1978.

The Texas Tax Relief Amendment of 1978

HOUSE JOINT RESOLUTION

proposing a constitutional amendment relating to ad valorem taxation of agricultural property, exemptions of certain property from taxation, and conditions for increases in total property tax revenues.

BE IT RESOLVED BY THE LEGISLATURE OF THE STATE OF TEXAS:

SECTION 1. That Articel VIII, Section 1, of the Texas Constitution be amended to read as follows:

Sec. 1. Taxation shall be equal and uniform. All real property and tangible personal property in this State, whether owned by natural persons or corporations, other than municipal, shall be taxed in proportion to its value, which shall be ascertained as may be provided by law. The Legislature may provide for the taxation of intangible property and may also impose occupation taxes, both upon natural persons and upon corporations, other than municipal, doing any business in this State. It may also tax incomes of both natural persons and corporations other than municipal, except that persons engaged in mechanical and agricultural pursuits shall never be required to pay an occupation tax. The Legislature by general law shall exempt household goods not held or used for the production of income and personal effects not held or used for the production of income, and the Legislature by general law may exempt all or part of the personal property homestead of a family or single adult, "personal property homestead" meaning that personal property exempt by law from forced sale for debt, from ad valorem taxation. The occupation tax levied by any county, city or town for any year on persons or corporations pursuing any profession or business, shall not exceed one half of the tax levied by the State for the same period on such profession or business.

SECTION 2. That Article VIII of the Texas Constitution be amended by adding Section 1-d-1 to read as follows:

Sec. 1-d-1 (a) To promote the preservation of open-spaced land, the legislature shall provide by general law for taxation of open-space land devoted to farm or ranch purposes on the basis of its productive capacity and may provide by general law for taxation of open-space land devoted to timber production on the basis of its productive capacity. The legislature by general law may provide eiligbility limitations under this section and my impose sanctions in furtherance of the taxation policy of this section.

(b) If a property owner qualifies his land for designation for agricultural use under Section 1-d of this article, the land is subject to the provisions of Section 1-d for the year in which the designation is effective and is not subject to a law enacted under this Section 1-d in that year.

SECTION 3. That Article VIII, Section 1-b, of the Texas Constitution be amended by amending Subsection (b) and adding Subsections (c) and (d) to read as follows:

(b) From and after January 1, 1973, the governing body of any county, city, town, school district, or other political subdivision of the State may exempt by its own action not less than Three Thousand Dollars ($3,000) of the market value of residence homesteads of persons, married or unmarried, including those living alone, who are under a disability for purposes of payment of disability insurance benefits under Federal Old-Age, Survivors, and Disability insurance or its successor or of married or unmarried persons sixty-five (65) years of age or older, including those living alone, from all ad valorem taxes thereafter levied by the political subdivision. As an alternative, upon receipt of a petition signed by twenty percent (20%) of the voters who voted in the last preceding election held by the political subdivision, the governing body of the subdivision shall call an election to determine by majority vote whether an amount not less than Three Thousand Dollars ($3,000) as provided in the petition, of the market value of residence homesteads of disabled persons or of persons sixty-five (65) years of age or over shall be exempt from ad valorem taxes thereafter levied by the political subdivision. An eligible disabled person who is sixty-five (65) years of age or older may not receive both exemptions from the same political subdivision in they same year but may choose either if the subdivision has adopted both. Where any ad valorem tax has theretofore been pledged for the payment of any debt, the taxing officers of the political subdivision shall have authority to continue to levy and collect the tax against the homestead property at the same rate as the tax so pledged until the debt is discharged, if the cessation of the levy would impair the obligation of the contract by which the debt was created. An exemption adopted under this subsection based on assessed value is increased, effective January 1, 1979, to an amount that, when converted to market value, provides the same reduction in taxes, except that the market value exemption shall be rounded to the nearest $100.

(c) Five Thousand Dollars ($5,000) of the market value of the residence homestead of a married or unmarried adult, including one living alone, is exempt from ad valorem taxation for general elementary and secondary public school purposes. In additon to this exemption, the legislature by general law may exempt an amount not to exceed Ten Thousand Dollars ($10,000) of the market value of the residence homestead of a person who is disabled as defined in Subsection (b) of this section and of a person sixty-five (65) years of age or older from ad valorem taxation for general elementary and secondary public school purposes. The legislature by general law may base the amount of and condition eligibility for the additional exemption authorized by this subsection for disabled persons and for persons sixty-five (65) years of age or older on economic need. An eligible disabled person who is sixty-five (65) years of age or older may not receive both exemptions from a school district but may choose either. An eligible person is entitled to receive both the exemption required by this subsection for all residence homesteads and any exemption adopted pursuant to Subsection (b) of this section, but the legislature shall provide by general law whether an eligible disabled or elderly person may recieve both the additional exemption for the elderly and disabled authorized by this subjection and any exemptions for the elderly or disabled adopted pursuant to Subsection (b) of this section. Where ad valorem tax has previously been pledged for the payment of debt, the taxing officers of a school district may continue to levy and collect the tax against the value of homesteads exempted under this subsection until the debt is discharged if the cessation of the levy would impair the obligation of the contract by which the debt was created. The legislature shall provide for formulas to protect school districts against all or part of the revenue loss incurred by the implementation of Article VIII, Sections 1-b(c), 1-b(d), and 1-d-1, of this constitution. The legislature by general law may define residence homestead for purposes of this section.

(d) Except as otherwise provided by this subsection, if a person receives the residence homestead exemption prescribed by Subsection (c) of this section for homesteads of persons sixty-five (65) years of age or older, the total amount of ad valorem taxes imposed on that homestead for general elementary and secondary public school purposes may not be increased while it remains the residence homestead of that person or that person's spouse who receives the exemption. However, those taxes may be increased to the extent the value of the homestead is increased by improvements other than repairs or improvements made to comply with governmental requirements.

SECTION 4. That Article VIII of the Texas Constitution by amended by adding Section 21 to read as follows:

Sec. 21. (a) Subject to any exceptions prescribed by general law, the total amount of property taxes imposed by a political subdivision in any year may not exceed the total amount of property taxes imposed by that subdivision in the preceding year unless the governing body of the subdivision gives notice of its intent to consider an increase in taxes and holds a public hearing on the proposed increase before it increases those total taxes. The legislature shall prescribe by law the form, content, timing, and methods of giving the notice and the rules for the conduct of the hearing.

(b) In calculating the total amount of taxes imposed in the current year for the purposes of Subsection (a) of this section, the taxes on property in territory added to the political subdivision since the preceding year and on new improvement that were not taxable in the preceding year are excluded. In calculating the total amount of taxes imposed in the preceding year for the purposes of Subsection (a) of this section, the taxes imposed on real property that is not taxable by the subdivision in the current year are excluded.

(c) The legislature by general law shall require that, subject to reasonable exceptions, a property owner be given notice of a revaluation and of the amount of taxes that will result from the reappraised value if neither the tax rate nor the ratio of assessment in effect in the preceding year is reduced. The notice must be given before the procedures required in Subsection (a) are instituted.

SECTION 5. That Article VIII of the Texas Constitution by amended by adding Section 22 to read as follows:

Sec. 22. (a) In no biennium shall the rate of growth of appropriations from state tax revenues not dedicated by this constitution exceed the estimate rate of growth of the state's economy. The legislature shall provide by general law procedures to implement this subsection.

(b) If the legislature by adoption of a resolution approved by a record vote of a majority of the members of each house finds that an emergency exists and identified the nature of the emergency, the legislature may provide for appropriations in excess of the amount authorized by Subsection (a) of this section. The excess authorized under this subsection may not exceed the amount specified in the resolution.

(c) In no case shall appropriations exceed revenues as provided in Article III, Section 49a, of this constitution. Nothing in this section shall be construed to alter, amend, or repeal Article III, Section 49a, of this constitution.

SECTION 6. Thar Article VIII of the Texas Constitution be amended by adding Section 23 to read as follows:

Sec. 23. (a) There shall be no statewide appraisal of real property for ad valorem tax purposes; however, this shall not preclude formula distribution of tax revenues to political subdivisions of the state.

(b) Administrative and judicial enforcement of uniform standards and procedures for appraisal of property for ad valorem tax purposes, as prescribed by general law, shall originate in the county where the tax is imposed, except that the legislature may provide by general law for political subdivisions with boundaries extending outside the county.

SECTION 7. This amendment takes effect January 1, 1979.

SECTION 8. The secretary of state shall designate this proposed constitutional amendment as "The Tax Relief Amendment" and shall place the proposition prior to any other propositions on the ballot for the election to be held on November 7, 1978.

SECTION 9. This proposed constitutional amendment shall be submitted to the voters at an election to be held on November 7, 1978. The ballot shall be printed to provide for voting for or against the proposition: "The constitutional amendment providing for tax relief for residential homesteads, elderly persons, disabled persons, and agricultural lands; for person property exemptions; for truth in taxation procedures, including citizen involvement; for a redefinition of the tax base; for limitations on state spending; and for property tax administration."

Key Provisions of the Amendment

TAXATION OF INTANGIBLES

Prior to the TRA, the Texas constitution had authorized the taxation of *all* property including intangibles.[65] Intangible property includes bank accounts, stocks and bonds, life insurance policies and retirement benefits. Because of the difficulty in assessing and levying against this type of property, there was widespread lack of assessment. The courts were generally unwilling to aid taxpayers who claimed that substantial taxable property was not being assessed.[66] The TRA authorized the state legislature to exempt or tax whatever classes of intangible personal property it felt proper.

In 1979 the state legislature responded by listing five classes of intangible personal property that would not be subject to taxation:[67] (1) stock in a banking corporation; (2) intangible property of an unincorporated bank; (3) intangible property of a transportation business, including railroads, toll roads and bridges, oil pipelines, and common carriers;[68] (4) intangible property owned by insurance companies and subject to the provisions of Tex. Ins. Code Ann. § 4.01; and (5) intangible property owned by savings and loan institutions governed by the provisions of Tex. Rev. Civ. Stat. Ann. art. 852a, § 11.09.[69]

It was reported in 1969 that 2.3 percent of all local property taxes came from the taxation of intangibles. If that figures were applied to 1977 tax figures the loss would total some $80 million per year.[70] Another report indicated that independent school districts in 1975 raised $2 million from taxes on "intangibles," $33 million for taxes on bank intangibles, and $99 million on taxes from utility intangibles. That revenue is no longer possible.

PERSONAL PROPERTY EXEMPTIONS

The TRA further amended Tex. Const. art. 8, § 1 by exempting from taxation all household goods and personal effects not held for the production of income. The previous exemption was limited to $250 of household goods. The TRA required the legislature to act to implement this provision, which it did in 1979. In defining household goods and personal effects, the legislature did not include motor vehicles, boats, trailers, or other means of transportation.[71] The TRA also authorized but did not require the legislature to exempt all or part of the "personal property homestead" from taxation. This could include home furnishings, two vehicles, tools of trade, life insurance policies, current wages, and agricultural implements.[72] In implementing this provision the legislature exempted family supplies for home or farm use[73] and farm products that are produced by the taxpayer.[74] Automobiles are automatically exempted from state ad valorem taxation. Local taxing units can levy taxes on motor vehicles (not used in the production of income) if, by affirmative act, *i.e.*, ordinance or resolution, they choose to do so. Otherwise motor vehicles are exempt from local taxation.[75] The estimated loss from this exemption to independent school districts was $50 million. The loss to municipalities was not known because of the disparate practices by cities regarding the taxation of cars and other personal property.

TAXATION OF AGRICULTURAL LAND

The TRA sought to liberalize the already extant constitutional preferential treatment for certain types of agricultural land.[76] The previous exemption was considered to be too narrow because it substantially limited the persons who were entitled to the agricultural use value assessment.[77] The applicant for the prior agricultural use exemption had to show that his primary occupation and source of income was from farming, ranching, or timber production. This excluded those who had investments such as oil and gas production or outside income providing them a substantial amount of money. The TRA would allow the legislature to include more landowners in the exempted category.

The legislature has responded by broadening the definition of "open space" land for purposes of exemption.[78] Land which has been principally used for agricultural purposes for five of the past seven years in now entitled to the exemption. The landowner need not earn his principal or primary living from the farm land. The valuation is to be made using "accepted income capitalization" methods applied to the average "net to land."[79]

If all qualified agricultural landowners applied for the new exemption the estimated loss of revenue to all levels of local government would be between $250 and $400 million. The legislature appropriated for the 1980-1981 biennium $450 million to reimburse independent school districts for their lost income resulting from this and the residential homestead exemption.[80] Cities and other taxing units were not to be reimbursed for their lost revenue.

HOMESTEAD EXEMPTION

In an area already muddied by existing conflicting and ill-defined mandates, the TRA sought to further cloud the waters by adding new wrinkles and complicated definitions. Prior to 1978, local taxing units were authorized to grant an exemption of not less than $3,000 of *assessed* value for residential homesteads for persons over 65.[81] The TRA now authorizes local taxing units to extend the exemption to those receiving federal Social Security disability payments.[82] In addition, the $3,000 exemption is now on *market* value, not assessed value. Most taxing units use appraised and assessed value, not market value, on their tax rolls, which further complicates the process.

The TRA also requires that all school districts exempt $5,000 of market value on all residential homesteads.[83] This mandatory $5,000 exemption caused the school districts to lose an estimated 3-15 percent of their property tax revenues.[84] The TRA also authorizes the legislature to require further residential homestead exemptions for elderly and disabled persons. The legislature is also authorized to define the "residential homestead" eligible for the exemption.[85] The legislature could also require school districts to "freeze" property tax payments for school purposes on the residential homesteads of the elderly.[86]

The legislature responded in 1979 by requiring school districts to freeze the total annual amout of ad valorem tax paid by persons over 65 on their residential homestead at the level at which they were first entitled to the exemption, except if improvements or additions were made to the homestead.[87] The legislature increased the exemption for those over 65 to $10,000 of the appraised value of the residential homestead.[88] That is, of course, inconsistent with the TRA, which calls for exemptions in terms of market value. The local taxing unit is also empowered to enact a residential homestead exemption for the elderly. The legislature defined a residential homestead as a structure that would include a mobile home owned by one or more individuals, designed for human residence, in fact used as a residence, and occupied as the principal residence by the owner of the exemption.[89]

TRUTH IN TAXATION

One of the alleged root causes of the Proposition 13 fever was the ever-escalating local appetite for propety tax revenues fueled by an increasingly large tax base caused by inflationary land values. Although the tax rate remained the same or even decreased, because the tax base increased substantially, the local governments were able to greatly increase their revenues. Although Texas has not suffered the same increase in property values as has California, it has not been immune to double-digit inflation. Thus the TRA attempted to deal with this problem not through the limitation on the tax base but through a disclosure system designed to inform the citizenry of these "hidden" tax increases caused by an increasingly inflationary tax base. The TRA added a new constitutional provision requring that if the total amount of property taxes imposed by a substate unit exceeds the total amount of taxes imposed the preceding year, a public hearing on the proposed increase must be held.[90] In calculalting the total amount of taxes, new construction, improvements or additional property added to the substate unit are to be excluded. Finally, the TRA authorizes the legislature to require that a property owner be given a notice of a revaluation and the amount of taxes that will result from the reappraised value if neither the tax rate nor the assessed ratio is reduced. The legislature is also authorized to make "reasonable exceptions" to the notice requirement.[91]

The state legislature, in comprehensively revising the property tax system in 1979, implemented the provisions of the truth in taxation provision. The legislature also limited the ability of substate units to change the assessment ratio by mandating that effective January 1, 1981, all property must be assessed on the basis of 100 percent of appraised value.[92] It also set up the procedures for the taxing units to prepare the property tax rolls and the rax rate with provisions for the appropriate notice and public hearings in the case of tax increases.[93]

STATE SPENDING LIMITATION

In one of the few potentially significant provisions of the TRA, the proponents for tax relief still fell far short of a meaningful expenditure limitation system. The TRA provides for a limit on state appropriations from state tax revenues. Essentially for expenditures not otherwise dedicated by the constitution, which may account for 45 percent of state spending, no appropriations for a later biennium could exceed the appropriations from the immediately preceding biennium at a rate greater than the state's economic growth.[94] The TRA does not define or provide how the level of economic growth is to be determined. That problem is left with the legislature.[95] During the last biennial session the Texas Legislature, however, did not even attempt to define that term. A further escape hatch from the expenditure cap is provided by the TRA, which allows a simple majority of the members of each house to declare an "emergency" and thus override the limits placed on appropriations.[96] This simple majority override provision contrasts with the four-fifths vote required to appropriate funds in excess of predicted revenues.[97]

While the state spending provision may have a significant effect on state spending in the future, its short-term impact appears to be limited. Of course, until the legislature determines the gauge for determining economic growth, the provision cannot be implemented. Second, as long as Texas enjoys its period of significant economic growth and development, state appropriations will continue to grow at a substantial rate because state revenues are also increasing with a steady tax rate. The problem in recent years in Texas has been what to do with the expected excess revenues that have occurred over the biennium, which in recent years have totaled around $2-3 billion every two years.

PROPERTY TAX ADMINISTRATION

The TRA attempted to deal with the growing problem of unequal and unfair assessment practices widespread throughout the thousands of taxing districts in the state. For example, a 1974 study on assessment practices of independent school districts showed 32 percent of the districts assessing between 10-20 percent of market value, 21 percent at 20-30 percent and 13 percent assessing at over 50 percent of market value. The county assessment practices in most Texas counties were even more inequitable as intradistrict variances in assessment were rampant.

But again the TRA fell short of meaningful relief by merely prohibiting the state from assessing real property for ad valorem tax purposes.[98] State assessment of certain intangibles, such as common carrier rolling stock and utility intangibles, was not prohibited. Furthermore, the TRA reaffirms the county as the basic taxing unit for determining uniform and fair assessment practices.

Partly in response to the TRA, the 1979 state legislature enacted a comprehensive property tax reform measure which had been in the legislative mill since 1975. In enacting this comprehensive reform, the Texas legislature has undoubtedly sown the seeds for a new

Proposition 13 grassroots movement to spring up in 1981 and 1982, the effective date of the new property tax system.[99] The principal element of the new tax code is uniform countywide assessment that will assess all propety at 100 percent of market value.[100] Since few if any existing taxing districts assess at 100 percent of market value there will be, in 1981, a tremendous increase in the tax base of most taxing units. Adjustments will have to be made in the tax rate so that the taxing units do not receive a windfall of revenues from the vastly increased tax base. For example, in Lubbock County the county and the county hospital district assess as something less than 25 percent of market value, while the City of Lubbock and the Lubbock Independent School District assess at 60 percent of market value. If any of those taxing units wants to increase its net revenues after the 1981 reassessment at 100 percent, they will have to go through the notice and public hearing requirement mandated by the TRA.[101]

Furthermore, if the taxing units decides to adopt a tax rate that exceeds the previous year's rate by more than 5 percent, the qualified voters of that taxing unit may petition for an election to repeal their increase.[102] The petition must be signed by 15,000 qualified voters or 15 percent of the number of qualified voters on the most recent offical list of voters, whichever is less.[103] This election provision does not apply to school districts. However, school districts which increase their effective tax rate by more than 5 percent in any one year for nonemergency purposes can be subject to a petition drive for a repeal election utilizing the same standards as other taxing units.[104] Although the nonschool district petition and election covers current year tax rates, the school district petition and election would only apply to limiting the tax rate for the following year.[105]

The Real Crunch–City Taxpayer Initiatives Limiting Property Tax Rates or City Expenditures

One of the reasons that Proposition 13 fever did not result in substantial tax limitations on the state level in Texas was that the state constitution contains no provision for citizen initiative or referendum elections. However, many home rule city charters allow citywide initiative petitions to be voted on under a varied set of procedural requirements. Since 1979 there have been at least six local initiative elections attempting to limit either city taxes or expenditures. The first such tax initiative was rejected by the voters of Corpus Christi in January 1979. The voters struck down two different tax limitations, the first limiting the maximum city tax rate to \$.26/\$100 and then placing a 2 percent limit on annual increases. The second initiative proposition was sponsored by the city council and would have reduced the annual tax rate to \$.71/\$100 and limited annual increases to 2½ percent. The Corpus Christi tax rate for 1978 had been set at \$.80/\$100. The first proposition would have caused a net decrease in the city's operating income of \$7.3 million out of a total city operating budget of only \$29.3 million. Both propositions were defeated. The city council proposition, interestingly, was defeated by a larger margin than the more restrictive first proposition.

Also in January 1979, Galveston voters approved a five section initiative proposition which limits the tax rate to \$.70/\$100, a decline from the existing \$.87/\$100 rate. The estimated loss of revenue was some \$1.5 million. Other provisions limited the annual increase in city expenditures to 7 percent and the annual increase in the tax levy on individual properties to 5 percent, although the improvements and reappraisals were to be excluded.

In the city of West University Place, a residential suburb entirely surrounded by Houston, a taxpayer initiative also passed the voters in January 1979. The two propositions limited the taxes imposed for the 1978-1979 fiscal year to no greater than 10 percent more than the 1977 levy, while allowing an additional levy of \$.10/\$100 assessed valuation for the Department of Health and Sanitation. Future tax hikes were also limited to a 10 percent annual increase. The propositions approved by the voters have not been put into effect because of a ruling by the city attorney that the charter amendments violated several provisions of the Texas constitution. Nonetheless, a recently elected slate of city council members has adopted the spirit of the charter amendments by having a policy of strictly limiting city expenditures. The bond rating for the city has not changed pending the outcome of the dispute.

In Baytown, Texas, voters approved five charter amendments dealing with tax and expenditure limitations. The tax rate of the city was limited to a maximum of \$.60/\$100. The cyclical reappraisal scheme, whereby the city would reappraise 20 percent of the parcels each year, was rejected and no changes in taxable value would be permitted unless the entire city was reappraised during that same year. Taxes on an individual's property could not rise by more than 10 percent a year unless there were a general revaluation or improvements made. Finally, the tax rate limitation was held not to be applicable to taxes imposed to pay off past and future indebtedness.

The impact on Baytown's land use policies has been minimal because the \$.80/\$100 limit has not yet been reached. Baytown is still actively annexing both commercial and residential areas. Land use fees have been increased in the past year but not to replace lost funds from the initiative limitations. The bond rating for Baytown had remained at "A" and the city manager thinks that without the initiative election the rating would have increased to "AA." The city manager feels that, because the city can still raise its tax rate for the payment of bonds without any limit, its ability to finance infrastructure for an expending residential base has not been impaired and Baytown will retain an aggressive acquisition-oriented land use policy.

Initiative elections were also held in Fort Worth and Irving. In Fort Worth the initiative proposition would have rolled back city property tax revenues to the 1976-1977 levels, a loss of some $3 million. Opponents of the proposition said that it would unduly limit city growth and result in larger user fee increases as well as restrict the delivery of services to new residents and businesses. The proposition was defeated but only after the city council had agreed to adopt a policy of limiting expenditure increases to 5 percent per year for the next two successive years.

In Irving, a large suburbs in the Dallas-Fort Worth metropolitan area, a tax and expenditure limitation was approved in August. Unfortunately for the proponents of the proposition, the initiative was worded so vaguely and inartfully that in November 1979 a state district judge declared it unenforceable. Litigation continues on this issue. The charter amendment restricts the city from increasing property tax collections by more than 6 percent from the preceding year. The amendment also limited to 8 percent the annual increases in the taxes imposed on individual properties excluding improvements. Finally, the amendment exempted from taxation the first $9,000 of assessed value plus 5 percent of the value above $9,000 of the residential homesteads of the elderly. One of the arguments made in the litigation was that the tax limitations would impair the obligations of the city from paying off its existing debt since there was no provision for tax increases to pay off existing and yet-to-be-issued debt.

Conclusion

The TRA of 1978 was a product of political compromise and special interest lobbying. Several opponents called its principal purpose the defusing of the Proposition 13 fever that was spreading throughout the country at that time. The TRA tried to pacify various groups who were complaining about rising taxes and governmental expenditures. It also focused its attention on state spending, which is not dependent on the property tax. The proposed 1974 total revision of the Texas constitution that was rejected by the electorate would have accomplished more tax relief than did the special interest group –dominated TRA of 1978. The TRA of 1978 was a "political animal" and as such did more to quell public demands for tax relief than actually provide real tax and expenditure limitations.

The state of Texas, though, plays such a insignificant role in land use and development decisions that restraints on state spending and taxes will not affect land use directly. The restraints on local governments principally impact school districts rather than municipalities, which exercise most of the local governmental land use powers. The only direct impact is on agricultural landowners who can more easily receive farm use value assessment. The impact on land use of preferential assessment is a well-debated issue. The TRA has caused several municipalities to reconsider land use policy because of the loss of certain revenue sources, *e.g.*, ad valorem taxation of automobiles or certain intangibles. But in most Texas cities this impact is minimized because cities are financially sound with increasing tax bases and population.

A survey of several municipal officials indicated that most believed that the TRA and the local city tax initiatives reinforced an already existing conservative fiscal policy regarding both taxes and expenditures. In many cities user fees are being increased but clearly not as a general substitute to lost property tax revenue. The executive director of the Texas Municipal League stated that he thought that the principal constraint on citys' land use policy was not the tax or expenditure limitations but the Voting Rights Act of 1965. Many cities, including Houston, were frustrated in their annexation attempts by their need to justify and clear their annexation ordinances with the U.S. Department of Justice.

Although California substate units have had to resort to higher regulatory fees and increased use of mandatory dedication requirements for new developments to replace lost revenue, Texas substate units have hardly reacted to the passage of TRA. An awareness of the difficulty of relying on the ad valorem property tax to provide services to largely residential communities is evidenced by a small increase in the number of communities who have adopted or expanded their existing mandatory dedication policies. Evidence of this slow growth in the use of dedication requirements is shown by the introduction of developer-sponsored bills in the last two legislative sessions seeking to take away that authority from municipalities. Both attempts have failed to date. Texas municipalities are not increasing their regulatory fees in order to make up for income lost through the TRA. If any generality can be made it is that local taxpayer resistance to any increase in ad valorem taxes has probably affected more local decisions than has the impact of the TRA tax and expenditure limitations.

Municipalities in Texas are enjoying a period of substantial growth and prosperity. Although continued growth is likely to continue, there are some doubts as to whether continued growth of municipal expenditures will be tolerated by the increasingly hostile public. Recent bond elections in cities have shown voter opposition to new bonds, although the rate of disapproval for both city and school district elections is much less than in other areas of the country. Given the 1981 requirement of 100 percent assessment, most existing tax rate limitations will have little relevance because present assessments usually run substantially below the 100 percent level. I envision 1981 to be a very interesting year for substate units in Texas as property owners see a massive increase in their assessed valuation which, if not accompanied by a significant decline in the tax rate, will lead to substantially higher property tax bills. At that time I can see further attempts to limit city and state revenue and expenditures, with perhaps a more direct and substantial impact on local land use policy.

Notes

1. In 1978 the legislature passed HJR 1, popularly known as the Tax Relief Amendment. It was then sent to the voters, who approved it in the November 1978 general election. HJR 1 was in essence a series of amendments to various sections of the Texas constitution dealing with taxation of intangibles, personal exemptions, productivity taxation of agricultural land, homestead exemption, truth-in-taxation for local governments, limits on state appropriations, and property tax administration.
2. *Tex. Const.* art. 3, § 49.
3. The language of the provisions was apparently taken from the Pennsylvania constitution, except for the use of $200,000 instead of $1,000,000 for casual deficiency debt. *See,* Interpretive Commentary to Tex. Const. art. 3, § 49.
4. *Tex. Const.* art. 3, § 49-a.
5. *Tex. Const.* art. 3, § 49-a.
6. *Tex. Const.* art. 3, § 50.
7. *Tex. Const.* art. 3, § 49-b.
8. *Tex. Const.* art. 3, § 49-c.
9. *Tex. Const.* art. 3, § 49-d.
10. *Tex. Const.* art. 3, § 49-d-1.
11. *Tex. Const.* art. 3, § 49-e.
12. *Tex. Const.* art. 3, § 50-b.
13. *Tex. Const.* art. 3, § 50-b-1.
14. *Tex. Const.* art. 3, § 50-c.

15. 279 S.W. 2d 302 (Tex. 1955).
16. 126 S.W. 2d 627 (Tex. 1939).
17. *Id.* at 635.
18. In this section I will refer to all nonstate units as substate units. Because in many instances the debt and expenditure limitations differ between the various units, where necessary I will refer to the particular unit in question.
19. 412 U.S. 289, 95 S. Ct. 1637, 44 L. Ed. 2d 172, *rehearing denied,* 422 U.S. 1029, 95 S. Ct. 1617, 45 L. Ed. 2d 686 (1975).
20. *Tex. Const.* art. 3, § 52-b.
21. See reference to *Hill v. Stone, supra,* note 15 regarding the unconstitutionality of limiting bond election franchise to resident property taxpayers. *Tex. Const.* art. 3, § 52-c.
22. *Tex. Const.* art. 3, § 52-c.
23. *Tex. Rev. Civ. Stat. Ann.* art. 7048a (Vernon).
24. *Tex. Const.* art. 11, § 2.
25. Burke v. Thomas, 285 S.W. 315 (Tex. 1955).
26. *Id.* at 318-19. *See also,* Collingsworth County v. Allred, 40 S.W. 2d 13 (Tex. 1931) and Aransas County v. Coleman-Fulton Pasture Co., 191 S.W. 533 (Tex. 1917).
27. *Tex. Const.* art. 8, § 9, art. 11, § 7. See also, *Tex. Rev. Civ. Stat.* arts. 2352, 2997a, 7048a (Vernon).
28. *Tex. Const.* art. 11, § 7.
29. See text accompanying notes 45 to 49 *infra* for a discussion of county tax limits.
30. *Tex. Const.* art. 11, § 5.
31. Lucchese v. Mauerman, 195 S.W. 2d 422, *cert. denied,* 329 U.S. 812 (1947).
32. *Tex. Const.* art. 11, § 7.
33. Atkinson v. City of Dallas, 353 S.W. 2d 275 (Tex. 1962), City of Houston v. Allred, 71, S.W. 2d 251 (Tex. 1934).
34. *Tex. Educ. Code Ann.* § 20.01 (1972).
35. See, *e.g., Tex. Const.* art. 9, § 9 dealing with the creation of hospital districts.
36. *Tex. Const.* art. 9, § 8.
37. *Tex. Const.* art 8, *R* 1-a.
38. *Tex. Const.* art. 8, § 1-e.
39. *Tex. Const.* art. 7, § 17.
40. *Tex. Const.* art 3, § 1-e.
41. *Tex. Const.* art. 8, § 1-e, *Tex. Const.* art. 7, § 17.
42. *Tex. Const.* art 8, § 1.
43. *Tex. Tax. Code Ann.* §§ 20.01, 20.02 (Vernon).
44. *Tex. Const.* art. 8, § 2.
45. *Tex. Const.* art. 8, § 9.
46. *Tex. Const.* art. 8, § 9.
47. See text accompanying note 15, *supra.*
48. *Tex. Const.* art. 8, § 1-a.
49. *Tex. Rev. Civ. Stat. Ann.* art 7048a (Vernon).

50. *Tex. Const.* art. 8, § 9.
51. *Tex. Const.* art. 11, § 5.
52. 132 S.W. 468 (Tex. 1911).
53. *Tex. Const.* art. 11, § 4.
54. *Tex. Rev. Civ. Stat. Ann.* arts 1133-1153a (Vernon).
55. *Tex. Rev. Civ. Stat. Ann.* art 1146 (Vernon).
56. *Tex. Rev. Civ. Stat. Ann.* arts 1026-1027 (Vernon).
57. *Tex. Rev. Civ. Stat. Ann.* art 1028 (Vernon).
58. *Tex. Educ. Code Ann.* § 20.04.
59. *Tex. Const.* art. 9, § 5.
60. *Tex. Water Code Ann.* § 63.282.
61. *Tex. Rev. Civ. Stat. Ann.* art. 1066c.
62. *Tex. Rev. Civ. Stat. Ann.* art. 7048.
63. The figures have been compiled from the following sources. Bureau of the Census, Statistical Abstract of the U.S. (1979); Census of Governments, Governmental Finances, Compendium of Government Finance (1977); Census of State Governments, Finances of School Districts.
64. Art. IX, § 10(a) of the proposed Texas Constitution, *reprinted in G. Braden, Citizen's Guide to the Proposed New Texas Constitution,* 101 (1975).
65. *Tex. Const.* art. 8 § 1.
66. *See* Johnson City Ind. School Dist. v. Crider, 535 S.W. 2d 725 (1976) *writ ref'd n.r.e.* and Anderson County Taxpayers' League v. City of Palestine, 576 S.W. 2d 679 (1979). *But cf.,* Luloc Oil Co. v. Caldwell County, 601 S.W. 2d 789 (1980), and City of Port Arthur v. Mosely, 586 S.W. 2d 916 (1979).
67. *Tex. Tax Code Ann.* § 11.02(b).
68. *Tex. Tax Code Ann.* § 24.01.
69. *Tex. Tax Code Ann.* § 11.02(b).
70. House Study Group, Special Legislative Report, Number 35, Analysis of HJR 1 (1978).
71. *Tex. Tax Code Ann.* §§11.14; *Tex. Rev. Civ. Stat. Ann.* art. 7150.2.
72. *Tex. Rev. Civ. Stat. Ann.* art. 3836.
73. *Tex. Tax Code Ann.* § 11.15.
74. *Tex. Tax Code Ann.* § 11.16.
75. *Tex. Tax Code Ann.* § 11.26.
76. *Tex. Const.* art. 8, § 1-d.
77. Gragg v. Cayuga Independent School District, 539 S.W. 2d 861 (1976).
78. *Tex. Rev. Civ. Stat. Ann.* art. 7174A; *Tex. Tax Code Ann.* § 23.51.
79. *Tex. Tax Code Ann.* § 23.51.
80. *Tex. Rev. Civ. Stat. Ann.* art. 4366c.
81. *Tex. Const.* art. 8, § 1-b(b).
82. *Tex. Const.* art. 8, § 1-b(b).
83. *Tex. Const.* art. 8, § 1-b(c).
84. House Study Group, Special Legislative Report Number 35, Analysis of HJR 1, 22 (1978).
85. *Tex. Const.* art. 8, § 1-b(c).
86. *Tex. Const.* art. 8, § 1-b(c).
87. *Tex. Tax Code Ann.* § 11.26.

88. *Tex. Tax Code Ann.* § 11.13(c).
89. *Tex. Tax Code Ann.* § 11.13(j).
90. *Tex. Const.* art. 8, § 21.
91. *Tex. Const.* art. 8, § 21(c).
92. *Tex. Tax Code Ann.* § 26.02.
93. *Tex. Tax Code Ann.* §§ 26.01 *et seq.*
94. *Tex. Const.* art. 8, § 22.
95. *Tex. Const.* art. 8, § 22(b).
96. *Tex. Const.* art. 8, § 22(c).
97. *Tex. Const.* art. 8, § 49a.
98. *Tex. Const.* art. 8, § 23.
99. *Tex. Tax Code Ann.* §§ 1.01-43.03.
100. *Tex. Tax Code Ann.* §§ 6.01-6.02, 26.02.
101. *Tex. Tax Code Ann.* § 26.06.
102. *Tex. Tax Code Ann.* § 26.07.
103. *Tex. Tax Code Ann.* § 26.07(b).
104. *Tex. Tax Code Ann.* § 26.08.
105. Compare *Tex. Tax Code Ann.* § 26.07(b)(1) with § 26.08(b)(1).

V. THE MASSACHUSETTS SYSTEM

10

Effects of Massachusetts's Proposition 2½ on Property Tax Administration and Reform

LAURIE ANGIOLILLO-BENT

Introduction

The enactment of chapter 580 of the 1980 Acts and Resolves of Massachusetts, popularly called "Proposition 2½," has presented Massachusetts legislators with a policy debate on property tax reform. Massachusetts voters approved the tax-limiting initiative measure by a three to two margin in November 1980. In approving the measure many voters were demanding reform of Massachusetts's tax system, which relies heavily on property taxes. The purpose of this article is not to evaluate Proposition 2½ vis-a-vis other proposals for tax reform, but to make clear what the statute requires in the context of existing Massachusetts property tax laws. Where the statute is vague, infeasible, or inconsistent with other Massachusetts laws, I have proposed changes in the law. Topics pertinent to the policy debate surrounding Proposition 2½, including questions about such state and federal constitutional issues as whether the statute impairs contracts,[1] leads to inadequate funds for education,[2] or was unfairly summarized on the ballot,[3] are not within the scope of this article.

An analysis of the effects of chapter 580 would be another relevant area of inquiry in the policy debate surrounding the new law. A

Ms. Angiolillo-Bent has a J.D. from Harvard Law School.

consideration of the effects of the law, and of the alternatives to it, will be key issues in the forthcoming policy debate. The effects of the law will reverberate beyond issues of pure property taxation: The law requires property tax cuts of $332 million in fiscal year 1982, its first year in effect. These revenue losses (an average of 10 percent across the state, and far higher in the larger cities)[4] are beginning to force municipalities to cut back services and lay off workers. Because of the reduction in municipal taxing powers, credit ratings have dropped, making it harder for cities and towns to borrow money. The tax limiting measure acts as a spur to property reassessment, since communities that complete their revaluation of real property to full value assessment in time for fiscal year 1982 (which begins July 1, 1981) will minimize the impact of the tax rate limit. The measure may also create an incentive for communities to create new local taxing districts, or to switch to fees and user charges in order to take pressure away from municipal budgets. Harder to observe but no less real are the changes the law will produce in the distribution of the property tax burden an the allocation of local government services that property taxes purchase. An extensive discussion of these issues has not been undertaken in this article.

This study focuses on specific issues within Massachusetts property tax law, in an attempt to understand how those sections of chapter 580 that affect property taxes will be implemented. The following questions are addressed below: (1) How can Proposition 2½, which requires assessment at fair cash value, be implemented when many communities have not yet achieved full value assessment? (2) What effect does Proposition 2½ have on the law that permits municipalities to classify property according to use? (3) How does Proposition 2½ affect exemptions of real and personal property? (4) What limits does the measure impose on local taxing districts other than cities and towns? (5) What is the new law's effect on home rule issues?

Tax Limits in Massachusetts

DEPENDENCY ON THE PROPERTY TAX

Massachusetts relies heavily on its property tax, which is the only direct tax available for use by local government.[5] Cities and towns depend on this source of revenue because their budgets can only be financed out of departmental revenues (mostly service charges and fees), federal and state aid, and the property tax.[6] In 1971-1972, the property tax (including proceeds of the motor vehicle excise tax) provided 42 percent of all state and local revenue[7] and 86 percent of the revenue from cities' and towns' own sources.[8] In 1977, the property tax, totaling $2.8 billion, dropped slightly to 76 percent of local governments' own-source revenue.[9] In fiscal year 1977, 56 percent of all local government revenue came from the property tax. Property taxes have provided about one-half of all local government revenue for the last twenty-five years.[10] Massachusetts's reliance on property tax revenue has consistently been well above the average for the other 49 states;[11] the 1977 per capita figure of $491 was the second highest in the nation, well above the nationwide average of $289.[12]

Local governments receive money from the state as well as from property taxes. In fiscal year 1981, state aid amounted to over $1.6 billion. A large portion of this money is earmarked for state-mandated programs such as facilities and training for handicapped children.[13] State aid is allocated based on state-determined "equalized valuation" figures, which are estimates of property value computed by the department of revenue.[14] State funds are distributed in inverse relation to the equalized valuation figures—an acknowledgment that property taxes may be an inadequate source of revenue in communities with lower property values. Although state aid to local government has increased dramatically in the recent past, it has not met the need for increased local revenue. The property tax has borne this burden instead, and between 1957 and 1973 property tax collections tripled.[15]

The property tax does not fall equally on every resident of the state. There are large variations in municipal property tax rates in Massachusetts because of differences in communities' property values, need for municipal services, and level of services offered. In 1972, tax rates ranged from 9 dollars per thousand dollars of property value to 161 dollars per thousand dollars of property value, with the median at 43 dollars.[16] In part because of this feature of the Massachusetts tax system, the authors of a study conducted in 1975 by the Boston branch of the Federal Reserve Bank concluded that the state's heavy reliance on the property tax creates negative economic and social consequences. The authors of the study found that the local property tax: (1) is "regressive and inequitable"; (2) discourages investment in buildings and industry; (3) discourages effective land use planning and leads to political and social divisions; and (4) encourages piecemeal "solutions" that ignore long-term consequences.[17]

The prediction that Massachusetts's heavy property tax burden would tend to offer piecemeal solutions to the inequities it causes has been borne out by the large number of tax reform efforts that have been initiated in the recent past. Most property tax reform measures have been attempts either to alleviate the inequities in the allocation of the property tax burden or to reduce the size of the tax burden. None of these efforts has resulted in comprehensive tax reform; the results have been piecemeal, as the authors of the Federal Reserve study foretold.

HISTORY OF PROPERTY TAX LIMITS IN MASSACHUSETTS

Property tax limits in Massachusetts have a history that stretches back to 1885, when the General Court passed statutes setting a ceiling for each city on property taxes that could be collected for expenses other than those enumerated in the statute. These ceilings had to be altered frequently for individual cities. In 1913, the legislature passed a law enabling each city's council to establish by ordinance its own property tax limit. (The law did not apply to Boston, which had to seek approval from the General Court for changes in its property tax rate limit.) Finally, in 1969 the General Court even repealed the law requiring self-imposed property tax limits.[18]

Between 1932 and 1980, a total of 126 property tax limitation proposals were introduced in Massachusetts. Three-quarters of these, like Proposition 2½, applied exclusively to local fiscal matters. Until very recently, all of these property tax limitation measures failed to pass, although several received serious consideration.[19]

In 1979, Governor Edward King submitted legislation to the General Court that would have required local governments to stay within levels equal to their fiscal year 1979 budgets, appropriations, and property tax levies. For this reason, it was referred to as a "zero cap" measure.[20] During negotiation, the zero cap was changed to a 4 percent limit, which allowed budgets, appropriations, and property tax levies to reach 104 percent of the previous year's level. Enacted in May 1979 as 1979 Massachusetts Acts, chapter 151, the law affected local governments for fiscal years beginning after June 30, 1979 and ending on or before December 31, 1981.[21] Since fiscal years in Massachusetts run from July 1 to June 30, the 4 percent limit was in effect for fiscal years 1980 and 1981. It ends before Proposition 2½ comes into effect beginning fiscal year 1982.

Several other tax limitation measures were proposed at the same time as Proposition 2½. One, the Massachusetts Teachers Association's initiative petition, was billed by its proponents as a "stop Proposition 2½" measure. This initiative, a weaker tax limit than Proposition 2½, was placed on the electoral ballot after defeat in the legislature. Massachusetts voters rejected the initiative on November 4, 1980.

Two constitutional amendments affecting property taxes have recently been under consideration. One, sponsored by a tax-relief interest group called Citizens for Limited Taxation, (hereinafter referred to as "CLT") would have placed a constitutional limit on state spending and on property tax revenues.[22] The CLT amendment was rejected in the state legislature's constitutional convention session in November of 1980. The other constitutional amendment, also supported by CLT, was cosponsored by the Associated Industries of Massachusetts and the Massachusetts High Technology Council. This amendment, which would limit state and local revenues, took a reading in 1980 and awaits further consideration.

DESCRIPTION OF PROPOSITION 2½

Property tax limitation measures can restrict taxing procedures in different ways. A *rate* limit sets a ceiling on the rate at which property can be taxed. Proposition 2½, for example, sets a rate ceiling of $25 of tax for every one thousand dollars of property value. A property tax *levy* limit constrains the total amount of revenue a government can obtain from property within its boundaries. Chapter 580 sets a levy limit of 102.5 percent of the previous year's levy. Within these two broad categories, tax limits can take different forms. A rate limit may be "categorical," "specific," or "overall" in type, depending on whether the limit is based on the use of the tax monies, the type of government body setting the tax, or the total tax burden on an area or property type. A categorical limit restricts the amount of tax that can be levied by a particular kind of governmental unit for a particular purpose. A specific limit restricts the total rate that can be levied by a specified class of local government. (Proposition 2½'s rate limit is of this latter type.) Finally, an overall limit restricts the total amount of tax that can be imposed on a particular area or type of property.[23]

Chapter 580 is an initiative measure that was presented to the legislature, with the necessary 60,000 signatures, by CLT. The General Court's joint committee on taxation reviewed the initiative bill and recommended against passage. Following that advice, the state house of representatives voted the bill down by 146 to 5. The CLT gathered the 10,000 additional signatures necessary to place the initiative bill on the 1980 state election ballot, and on November 4, 1980, Massachusetts voters passed the act by a three to two margin.

The law contains thirteen sections, amending diverse chapters of the Massachusetts statutes. Sections 1 and 12, which will be discussed below, are the two sections that most directly affect property taxes. The other eleven sections contain a medley of provisions whose only similarity is the goal of tax reduction. These sections include the following, among others: a provision prohibiting the state from imposing costs on local governments without local approval; a provision enabling cities and towns to revoke, within certain restrictions, their acceptance of optional state laws; a provision repealing the fiscal autonomy of school committees; a provision reducing the automobile excise tax from $66 to $25 per one thousand dollars of valuation; a provision repealing binding arbitration for police and firefighter unions; and a provision allowing home renters to deduct 50 percent of the rent for state income tax purposes.

The provision that gives the measure its name, Proposition 2½, amends chapter 59 of the Massachusetts General Laws, which governs the assessment of local taxes. The section provides that the total taxes in a fiscal year assessed on real and personal property by the commonwealth or any other governmental entity within the commonwealth shall not exceed 2½ percent of the full and fair cash value of that property. The section provides that cities and towns may override the rate limit provision by a two-thirds vote at a November election. If a municipality's tax rate exceeded 2½ percent on December 4, 1980, the date the law went into effect, the statute requires an annual reduction of 15 percent in the tax rate until the 2½ percent limit is reached. Any city or town whose property taxes in fiscal year 1979 were less than 2½ percent of full and fair cash value must take the 1979 rate as its tax rate ceiling. If the current tax rate of such a municipality is above the 1979 rate the city or town must reduce the rate by 15 percent each year until it reaches its 1979 level. Section 1 also contains a levy limit requiring that the total property taxes assessed by the state or any governmental entity within the state, with respect to any city or town, not exceed 102.5 percent of the previous year's levy unless two-thirds of the persons voting on the issue shall approve a higher amount for municipal taxes. Finally, Section 1 permits the 2½ percent rate limit to be decreased in a city or town by a simple majority vote.

Section 12 prevents the cities and towns from making heavy use of user fees to ease the financial squeeze caused by the rate and levy limits. The section imposes a four percent ceiling on increases over the previous fiscal year in costs, charges, or fees assessed by governmental entities on cities or towns. In addition, such governmental entities may not charge more than the cost of providing any good or service.

The rest of this article addresses issues raised by sections 1 and 12 of chapter 580, the two sections that most directly affect property taxes.

Property Assessment in Massachusetts

CONSTITUTIONAL AND STATUTORY REQUIREMENTS

The Massachusetts constitution requires that all taxes levied in the state be "proportional and reasonable."[24] It also requires each individual of the society "to contribute his share."[25] These two requirements have been interpreted to mean that the same proportional rate must be applied to all taxable property within the taxing district; however, because of local fiscal freedom, tax rates vary across the state.[26] The requirement that property be taxed at a fixed proportion of value first became a part of Massachusetts government in the Province Charter of 1691, and has been retained in substantially the same form since then. In the nineteenth century the Supreme Judicial Court stated that the rule was based on the assumption that the value of an individual's property and the benefits the individual received from government were directly related.[27] Several consequences flow from the requirement that assessments, rates, and taxes be proportional. One is that the tax rate must be a fixed proportion of the property's value (the "proportionality" requirement). Another is that all property, with narrow exceptions, must be taxed (the "universality" requirement). A third is that all classes of property must be taxed at the same rate (the "uniformity" requirement).[28]

Property taxation is governed by statutory, as well as constitutional constraints. The Massachusetts laws require that all property be assessed at fair cash value.[29] (Other phrases used synonymously with "fair cash value" in the Massachusetts statutes and case are "full and fair cash value," "full value assessment," and "100 percent property valuation.")[30] The statute and the constitution, read together, require that property be assessed at a uniform percentage of value, and that that uniform percentage must be fair cash value.

Although the requirements of full value assessment and uniform assessment are linked, they are separate concepts.[31] For example, one can assess all real property at 50 percent of fair cash value, thereby meeting the uniformity condition but not the condition of assessment at full value. Likewise, one can assess property at full value and subsequently apply different tax rates or different percentages of value to different classes of property for tax purposes, thereby achieving full value assessment but not uniformity. (Differentiating among types of property either by applying different tax rates or by taxing at different percentages of value is a classification approach to property taxation.) In 1978, Massachusetts voters ratified on amendment to the constitution that permitted the legislature to classify property for tax purposes: to "assess, rate and tax" property according to use.[32] A classification law implementing this amendment became effective January 1, 1980.[33]

ACTUAL ASSESSMENT PRACTICES IN MASSACHUSETTS

Property taxes in Massachusetts are levied by the board of assessors of each city or town. The cities and towns themselves are the principal taxing units, but the board of assessors also levies taxes for special tax districts. The board of assessors of each city and town reports to and takes direction from the commissioner and the department of revenue (formerly the department of corporations and taxation); that state agency takes primary responsibility for ensuring that proper assessment and collection procedures have been followed.[34]

There is no single proper assessment procedure for real estate. Appraisers rely on some combination of three basic methods: comparison of market data for other similar property; capitalization of income from the property; and replacement cost less depreciation.[35] The choice of method or methods must depend on what information is available to the assessor. For example, the market data method may not be feasible for types of real estate that are not sold very often. As the techniques available to boards of assessors become more sophisticated, asessing methods will improve the accuracy. Some communities have developed multiple regression formulas, based on numerous determinants of property value, that can make the assessing process faster and more accurate.[36] Computerization of the assessment process permits a municipality's board of assessors to assess each parcel of real estate more frequently, which increases the accuracy of the process, for one major source of inaccurate assessment is the change in property values that can occur between assessments, particularly when assessments are several years apart.[37] Regardless of what method is used, assessors are legally obligated to assess each parcel of property at its full and fair cash value. An assessor who does not follow the statutory requirements can be fined up to $1,000 and imprisoned up to six months.[38]

Until January 1, 1980, the effective date of the classification law, Massachusetts law required both uniformity and full value assessment in its property taxes. In practice, however, neither requirement was met. There is ample evidence of systematic biases in the assessment of real property in Massachusetts. Henry Aaron and Oliver Oldman, in a 1963 study comparing assessed value to sale value for Boston property, concluded that single-family homes were assessed at substantially lower percentages of value than commercial property. The authors found that the relation of assessment value to sales value was 44.2 percent for single-family residences, and 77.8 percent for commercial real estate. The Aaron and Oldman study uncovered lower assessment percentages for high-priced property than for low-priced property, and found lower assessment ratios for high-income neighborhoods than for low-income neighborhoods.[39] Similarly, David Black found that neighborhoods containing deteriorating structures, a high density of nonwhite racial groups, low family income and property values, and high population densities tended to be assessed at higher ratios than other neighborhoods.[40] The biases detected in these and other studies have indicated a trend of assessing low-priced residences at a higher percentage of value than high-priced residences, apartment buildings at a higher percentage of value than single-family homes, and commercial and industrial properties at a higher percentage of value than residential properties.[41]

One likely cause of these biases is the infrequency of assessment. The frequency of property assessment is not evenly distributed across types of property. The results of a study by Michael Woodbury showed that of 200 random properties located in Boston, 70 percent of the assessed valuations were not changed between 1955 and 1968, and another 15 percent had their assessed valuation changed only once in that period. Woodbury found that homes were revalued much less frequently than commercial properties.[42] Different assessment frequencies among types of property can create assessment bias. In addition, assessment lag may affect different properties differently: properties that are increasing in value will be underassessed relative to other properties, and properties that are decreasing in value will tend to be relatively overassessed. One would expect these two effects to contribute to assessment bias, and in fact one analyst computed that as much as 53 percent of the differentials in assessment ratios between classes of property may result from assessment lag.[43] Desire on the part of assessors to reduce the burden on homeowners and to place the property tax burden on income-producing properties is another source of assessment bias.[44] Still another cause of assessment variation may be the use of tax incentives that benefit certain types of property. For example, the tax incentives given to encourage new commercial construction in the city of Boston created an assessment gap between old and new commercial property that was even larger than the gap between residential and commercial property.[45] Finally, the fiscal autonomy of cities and towns which allows each community to determine its own assessment patterns leads to assessment variation as well as tax rate variation.[46]

The variation in assessment percentages in Massachusetts violates both the statutory requirement of assessment at full and fair cash value, and the constitutional requirement that property is assessed at a uniform percentage of value. Full value assessment and uniformity are separate concepts, as noted above, but studies of assessment variation indicate that nonuniform assessment frequently accompanies assessment below fair cash value.

The conditions of underassessment and nonuniform assessment, besides violating the laws, create a number of inequities for Massachusetts taxpayers. One is that those properties assessed at relatively higher percentages of fair cash value will pay more than their proportional share of the tax. Since these taxpayers are not assessed at the statutory rate of 100 percent valuation, they may believe that they are paying less than their proportionate share, and hesitate to appeal their assessment, when in fact they are bearing more than their share of the tax burden. Another inequity caused by the combination of underassessment and nonuniformity occurs when the average assessment percentage of the real estate in one community is a higher fraction of value than in another community. Since state aid is distributed according to a formula that is inversely related to community property values, the higher a community's assessed property value, the less state aid it will receive. (For purposes of this aid allocation, the state used equalized valuation figures, as noted above, and these figures are based on a community's assessed values.) Intercommunity assessment differences create another inequity: property tax exemption given to the elderly and some widows are based on fixed property value ceilings and therefore become less valuable as the assessment percentage goes up. These exemptions will be less valuable to those living in high-assessment communities than to those living in low-assessment communities.

Massachusetts's property tax system, as it is currently administered by fiscally autonomous cities and towns, creates inequities in two ways: through the structure of the tax system itself, and through uneven application of the tax laws. The property tax system, as it is currently structured in Masachusetts, produces the least amount of revenue in communities that need it most, since those communities, particularly cities, with small tax bases and low-income residents, are often the communities with the greatest need for government-provided services. Moreover, once a tax rate and tax base gap forms between communities, demographic trends will widen it.[47] Although assessment reform that increases all assessment percentages to full market value does not alleviate the inequities inherent in the tax structure, it can reduce the inequities caused by differential assessment ratios.

LEGAL REMEDIES FOR DISPROPORTIONATE ASSESSMENT

Taxpayers who feel that they have been adversely affected by disproportionate assessment practices have two judicial remedies available to them. They can seek an abatement from the board of assessors of the tax levied on them[48] or they can request an injunction against the tax plan through a suit brought by ten taxpayers.[49] While either remedy may satisfy the taxpayer who has been assessed at a higher than average ratio of fair cash value, there are important differences between them. A procedural difference is that an abatement, as the Supreme Judicial Court held in 1973, is an administrative remedy, and one seeking an abatement must exhaust administrative remedies before seeking judicial intervention.[50] Of the two remedies, an abatement is easier to obtain, for one need show only that one person—oneself—has been overassessed.

To obtain an injunction, on the other hand, one must prove the existence of an assessment plan or pattern that both violates the constitutional proportionality requirement and discriminates against the taxpayers. Although this standard creates a heavier burden for the taxpayers, it also creates a more lasting remedy, since the court requires a city or town found to be in violation to reassess its property.

The two remedies, tax plan injunction issued by a court of equity, and tax abatement issued by the board of assessors, were the primary enforcement tools for the constitutional uniformity requirement and the statutory full value assessment requirement. The history of their use in the last twenty years is briefly discussed below.

Injunctive relief for disproportate assessment practices first became a reality in 1961, when the Supreme Judicial Court decided *Bettigole v. Assessors of Springfield.*[51] The plaintiffs in *Bettigole*, who were individual, fiduciary, and corporate owners of multifamily dwellings, challenged the Springfield board of assessors' practice of classifying real estate into six categories and taxing each category at a different proportion of full value. As stipulated in an agreed statement of facts, the Springfield assessors would determine the fair cash value of each parcel of property, and then tax it at the previously determined proportion of full value based on category of use. The court found that because the plaintiff's multifamily dwellings were taxed at a higher proportion of fair cash value than were other residential premises, plaintiffs would pay more in taxes than if all parcels of real property were assessed at fair cash value. The court declared that the practice of classifying property in this way violated the "proportional and reasonable assessments" clause of the Massachusetts constitution[52] as well as article ten of the Declaration of Rights,[53] which provides that "each individual of the society has a right to be protected by it in the enjoyment of his life, liberty and property, according to standing laws. He is obliged, consequently, to contribute *his share* to the expense of this protection. . . .[54] (Emphasis in opinion.) The court also found that the classification approach violated the intent of the property tax assessment statute, which required the "assessors of each city . . . [to] make a fair cash valuation of all the estate, real and personal, subject to taxation therein."[55]

The importance of the *Bettigole* decision lay in the remedy fashioned by the court, one readily applied to the facts in this case: to "enjoin execution of the unconstitutional assessment scheme and to declare it to be a nullity."[56] The court required the Springfield board of assessors to apply a new tax rate to the fair cash value of each parcel of real estate. These fair cash values had already been ascertained, so determining the amount of tax due was a matter of introducing a new value into the computers' calculations. Because the tax rate had been calculated but not yet levied the court in *Bettigole* was able to enjoin the procedure without causing undue hardship to the city government.

Several cases decided after *Bettigole* modified the use of the injunctive remedy applied in *Bettigole.* A 1964 case held that the taxpayer could not obtain a tax plan injunction without showing that the tax assessors had committed a "deliberate and substantial violation"[57] of the proportional assessment requirements and that injunctive relief was practical.[58] The Supreme Judicial Court, in two subsequent cases, however, increased the availability of injunctive relief by disclaiming the necessity of finding an intentional plan of discrimination,[59] and finding that injunctive relief would be practical if the injunction applied to future assessments, rather than to the current year's assessments.[60]

The Supreme Judicial Court also encouraged the use of tax abatements to correct excessive taxes caused by overassessment and disproportionate assessment. In 1965, the Court eased the taxpayer's burden of proof in suits to obtain abatement,[61] and made the abatement remedy available even to taxpayers whose property was assessed below full value, if the assessment was above the average percentage of full value assessed for other taxpayers in the community.[62]

Despite the judiciary's attempt, by expanding abatement and injunction remedies, to resolve the related problems of assessment of property below fair cash value and lack of assessment uniformity, both of these problems persisted after *Bettigole.*

In *Town of Sudbury v. Commissioner of Corporations and Taxation,*[63] the Supreme Judicial Court, recognizing that many communities departed from uniform and full value assessment, devised a new remedy for the violations. The Town of Sudbury brought suit to alleviate inequities in state aid caused by assessment inequalities between communities. The distribution of that aid is based on a formula that varies the amount of aid inversely with the value of a community's assessed real estate, as measured by equalized valuation. The practice of basing state aid on community assessment figures has the anomalous effect of reducing state grants for communities that revalue their real property to full and fair value, while maintaining the level of aid to communities that continue fractional assessment practices. As the Court noted, more than half of the cities and towns in the commonwealth had recently undergone revaluation, but others continued to classify property and to assess property at fractions of its value.[64] In 1972, the ratio of assessed value to estimated sale value varied between 19 percent and 100 percent in Massachusetts.[65] The differences in assessment practices between communities meant that the fixed dollar amount exemptions granted to the elderly and others were worth less in cities and towns that revalued to assessments at one hundred percent of value.[66] The result, stated the court, "is discrimination against those cities and towns whose assessors act lawfully, in favor of those whose assessors engage in the illegal practice of fractional valuation. The findings also show that fractional valuation makes the equalization task much more difficult, if not impossible."[67]

To redress these inequities, the Town of Sudbury sought declaratory and injunctive relief against the Commissioner of Revenue.[68] The court refused to grant injunctive relief, noting that the commissioner and the department stood ready to do their duties as defined by the court. These duties, as laid out by the court, included statutory powers the commissioner apparently had never exercised, including the power to require of assessors "such action as will tend to produce uniformity throughout the commonwealth in valuation and assessments;"[69] the power to prosecute an assessor "for any violation of law relative to the assessment of taxes for which a penalty is imposed;"[70] and the power to appoint new assessors to replace those who failed to perform their duties."[71] Essentially, the *Sudbury* decision forced the commissioner and the department to abandon their chosen advisory and educational roles in favor of active enforcement of the commonwealth's statutory and constitutional requirements of uniform assessment at full and fair cash value. In so doing, the court rejected judicial remedies as ineffective and instead placed its reliance on administrative enforcement.[72]

ASSESSMENT, REVALUATION, AND PROPOSITION 2½

The *Bettigole* decision created new incentives for cities and towns to revalue their real estate to one hundred percent valuation. In the five years before Bettigole, 32 of Massachusetts's 351 cities and towns carried out revaluation programs; in the six years following *Bettigole*, 177 did so.[73] Despite the apparent flurry of revaluation activity, most communities revalued their real estate only reluctantly. Revaluation was a costly process that was often out of date only a year afterwards.[74] Revaluation usually resulted in a decrease in the community's share of state school aid funds, state lottery proceeds, and gas tax funds, three categories of state aid that account for more than half of all state aid. Revaluation also decreased the worth of property tax exemptions. Finally, revaluation, since it often raised property taxes for homeowners (who were the primary beneficiaries of assessment below full value) decreased residential property values, that, if capitalized, created a windfall loss for homeowners.[75] It is no wonder that Boston's mayor declared in 1971, "[Revaluation is] a requirement I will drag my feet on as long as I can for the benefit of the city."[76]

After the *Sudbury* decision, it became increasingly difficult for cities and towns to drag their feet on revaluation. *Sudbury* arose because some cities and towns revalued their real property faster than others, and found that state aid allocations penalized them relative to cities and towns that were not revaluing their real property. The *Sudbury* decision made very clear that assessors who failed to value property at fair cash value were violating the law and that the commissioner of revenue had a duty to prosecute them. Cities and towns began to take very seriously the requirement of one hundred percent valuation. *Sudbury* did not remove the disincentives for revaluation, but it raised the penalties for not doing so.

Notwithstanding the increasing efforts of cites and towns to meet market value assessment requirements, a large percentage of Massachusetts's 351 cities and towns will not be assessed at fair cash value in fiscal year 1982, the first year that Proposition 2½ is in effect. According to figures compiled in February 1981 by the department of revenue, 101 communities had certified local revaluations for fiscal year 1981 and 126 more will be certified as revalued for fiscal year 1982. The remaining 124 communities, as of February,

1981, did not have revaluations less than two years old.[77] Yet Proposition 2½ requires that the total taxes assessed by any taxing district within the state shall not exceed 2½ percent of the full and fair cash valuation of real estate and personal property. Proper implementation of the law depends on a condition—assessment of real property at full and fair cash value—that does not presently exist in all municipalities in Massachusetts.

The department of revenue has devised an administrative means to value real property in cities and towns that do not currently assess their real property at full and fair cash value. In those cities and towns that completed a reassessment project as of January 1, 1981, the commissioner will, if the assessments satisfy the standard of full and fair cash value, certify this valuation to the Board of assessors, and the community may then levy taxes based on Proposition 2½.[78] This group of cities and towns poses no problem in this regard for implementing Proposition 2½.

A second group of municipalities—those that were certified as revalued as of January 1, 1980—can meet certification requirements for fiscal year 1982. Some of these cities and towns have computerized their property tax assessments and can update their assessments based on recent market data. If the commissioner can certify that the updated valuations meet standards of one hundred percent assessment for fiscal year 1982, these cities and towns will be able to implement Proposition 2½ based on their assessments. Other cities and towns assessed at one hundred percent valuation for fiscal year 1981. These towns may increase assessments by a uniform percentage factor. To use this approach, they must submit by March 31, 1981 a form to the state bureau of local assessment indicating all residential property sales. The state bureau will conduct a statistical assessment-sales ratio analysis of residential and land sales to determine what percentage increase, if any, is warranted. For other classes of property (i.e., commercial, industrial, and personal) the local assessors must document their proposed assessment increases.[79] The commissioner will then certify the valuations reached in these communities as fair cash valuation.[80]

Group three consists of cities and towns currently in the process of revaluing their real property, whose revaluation program will be complete prior to fiscal year 1982 tax billing. If these communities qualify for certification by the commissioner, they will be able to apply the tax limit to their newly completed valuations.[81]

The cities and towns in each of the categories above, all of whom have recently completed or will soon complete revaluation programs, will reach a valuation of their property that is certified by the commissioner as full value assessment, and can implement Proposition 2½ based on their assessed property values. The rest of Massachusetts's cities and towns will not be certified at full value assessment for fiscal year 1982. These communities pose a problem for meeting Proposition 2½'s requirement of assessment at full and fair cash value. The department of revenue proposes to use the state 1980 equalized valuation figures for these cities and towns, increased by 13 percent and any growth in the tax base as the result of new construction or alterations, as a proxy for full and fair cash assessed values.[82] The 13 percent factor was reached because it is the statewide average inflation factor for market sales in the two years since the equalized valuation figures were compiled.

The equalized valuation figures are a poor surrogate for market value assessments. The 1980 equalized valuation figures, based on market data compiled between January 1, 1978 and June 30, 1979, may be as much as 20 percent below current market values, because of inflation.[83] For example, an assessor in Cambridge, which is completing a program of full market valuation, estimates that its real property is worth between $1.6 and $1.8 billion; the state equalized valuation figure for Cambridge in January 1980 increased by 13 percent for fiscal year 1982, is $1.45 billion.[84] Similarly, the Medford 1980 equalized valuation figure increased by 13 percent for use in 1982 would be $941 million, significantly less than the figure of $1 billion that resulted from Medord's recent revaluation program.[85] The uniform 13 percent figures buries inter-municipality differences in the rate of inflation and growth, and is added to a valuation figure that is itself only a rough estimate of value.

One state official has recognized the inadequacy of the equalized valuation figures for use instead of full value assessments in calculating tax limits under chapter 580. Noting in the fall of 1980 that equalized valuation figures lagged ten to twenty percent behind actual values he stated: "Our equalized valuations are a program for the distribution of state aid. Period. They are not an assessment of full and fair cash valuation."[86]

Proposition 2½, as written, does not violate the standard of assessment of real property at full and fair cash value. Rather, the problem lies in the fact that proposition 2½ cannot be implemented until the requirement of assessment at fair cash value has been met in all Massachusetts cities and towns, an accomplishment that has not yet been reached. The department of revenue proposes to implement Proposition 2½ using equalized valuation rather than fair cash value in a substantial number of Massachusetts cities and towns, in violation of the language of chapter 580, which requires the rate limit to be based on full and fair cash valuation.

Because the use of equalized valuation figures in calculating the tax levy limit does not meet the terms of Proposition 2½, the implementation of Proposition 2½ undertaken by the department of revenue is open to challenge.[87] The harm that could be caused by the application of the 2.5 percent tax rate limit to an inaccurate tax base might be substantial. If the equalized valuation figure employed in a city or town is lower than the tax base would be under fair cash value, the resulting levy limit would be correspondingly lower. Municipal officials forced to cut property tax revenues below the level mandated by Proposition 2½ might sue the department of revenue; so might municipal employees who lose their jobs under tighter than necessary revenue constraints. On the other hand, if the equalized valuation figure in a city or town exceeds the fair cash value of the real estate in that community, taxpayers in the community might object because their tax will be higher than the statute permits. Notwithstanding the problems inherent in the department of revenue's use of equalized valuation figures as a substitute for full and fair cash assessment, it is difficult to see what alternatives the department has for those communities that have not yet reached full value assessment. Faulty as the equalized value figures are, they come closer to approximating one hundred percent assessment than do unrevalued assessments, which in some cities were as low as one-fifth or one-fourth of full value.[88]

The levy limit, which compounds problems caused by the use of equalized valuation figures in fiscal year 1982, also creates tax base problems even in those communities whose 1982 property tax revenues are based on full and fair cash value. The levy limit makes no allowance for growth in the tax base, whether from new development, growth in industry or commerce, or inflation. The 1982 property tax collections, increased by 2½ percent each year, set the limit for future property taxes.

A third section of chapter 580 is just as problematic as the requirement of full and fair cash valuation and the levy limit. The statute requires any city or town whose taxes in 1979 were less than 2½ percent of the 1979 full and fair cash property valuation to limit itself to "that lesser percentage."[89] This section of the statute is impossible to apply in those communities that were not assessed at fair cash value in fiscal year 1979, since they do not have the full value assessment figures, and there is no adequate substitute for them. Equalized valuation figures are subject to the same objections for retoractive application to 1979 as for application in 1982. Without the full value assessment figures, it is impossible to compute what the tax rate would have been if it were based on those figures. Without such information, it is impossible to detect which communities had a total tax levy in fiscal year 1979 below the levy that would have resulted from a tax rate of 2½ percent of full and fair cash value.

RECOMMENDATIONS

Based on the problems in the application of chapter 580 that are discussed above, some recommendations can be made for amendments to the law. In its requirements of full value assessment, Proposition 2½ does not violate existing state statutes, but it cannot be implemented as its terms require because it does not recognize the underassessment of property that prevails in many Massachusetts cities and towns for fiscal year 1982. In order to be fully implemented, the statute should be amended to allow for the use of substitutes for full value assessment such as state equalized value, or to allow for alternative ways of calculating the applicable tax limit. Similar alternatives should be found for calculating the lower 1979 rate limit. As the statute is written now, the 1979 lower limit cannot be applied because it cannot be computed. Finally, modifying the levy limit could lessen the arbitrary results caused by the inflexible use of 1982 tax collections as the base for future tax collections. At the very least, chapter 580 should be amended to permit communities whose 1982 tax collections are based on equalized valuation figures to incorporate increases warranted by full and fair cash assessment into the tax base, once the community completes its revaluation program. A further alteration to permit adjustments to the tax base that reflect new development or real growth would give the law more flexibility without violating the law's tax-limiting purpose.

Property Classification

HISTORY OF THE MOVEMENT TOWARD CLASSIFICATION

The increasing insistence on full value assessment by Massachusetts courts and, after *Sudbury,* state agencies, was met in the legislature by a movement towards classification of property by use. The Supreme Judicial Court's steadfast interpretation of the "proportional and reasonable" clause of the state constitution as requiring uniform assessment meant that classification would require a constitutional amendment. A constitutional amendment that would have given the legislature power to classify real property according to use was passed by the legislature in 1968 and 1969, but was rejected by a nearly two to one margin in the polls in 1970.[90]

After the decision in *Sudbury,* however, the proponents of classification met with greater success in their movement for a classification amendment. Ratified by voters in 1978, the Classification Amendment authorized the legislature to "assess, rate and tax" property according to use.[91]

A defacto system of classification existed in Massachusetts despite the constitutional uniformity requirement. Generally, residential property was assessed at a lower fraction of full value than commercial and industrial property, with single-family residential homes assessed at lower percentages than apartment buildings, and homes in wealthy neighborhoods assessed at lower percentages than homes in less well-to-do neighborhoods. Once the *Sudbury* decision threatened to end this de facto classification, support for a legal classification system grew. The uniform and full value assessment requirements, to which the *Sudbury* decision had given new teeth, meant that the tax burden would shift from business toward residential property owners. To combat this shift, Massachusetts Fair Share and the AFL-CIO, among other groups, lobbied for passage of the classification amendment.[92]

In anticipation of its passage, the legislature passed an act to implement classification (the "shelf legislation"),[93] which required assessors to classify real property into one of four classes (residential, commercial, industrial, or open space). Each of these categories was to be taxed at a specified percentage, but only after the commisioner had certified that all real estate in the community was assessed at fair cash value. Because of technical problems, among them the failure to include personal property in the classification scheme, implementation of the shelf legislation was postponed from January 1, 1979 to January 1, 1980; before the new implementation date was reached, the law was repealed.[94]

THE CURRENT CLASSIFICATION LAW

The legislature replaced the shelf legislation with the current classification law,[95] which became effective January 1, 1980. The law leaves some discretion to the board of assessors and local government to determine biennially what percentage of the local tax levy shall be borne by the different classes of real property.[96] There are four categories of use: residential, open space, commercial, and industrial.[97] and the classification law gives some discretion to communities to vary the fraction of the tax levy borne by open space and residential property. It is important to note that the current classification law, rather than varying the fraction of assessed value to create classifications, requires full cash valuation; the variation in tax borne by different classes of real property is created by variation in the percentage of the tax rate that applies to it.

CLASSIFICATION AND PROPOSITION 2½

The Committee on Taxation reviewed Proposition 2½ when it was a bill presented to the legislature. The Committee, in its report to the House of Representatives, expressed concern about the effect the measure would have on the classification law: "the voters in 1978 overwhelmingly passed the classification amendment which is just beginning to become operational in some cities and towns. If H. 5933 [Proposition 2½] becomes law, classification will be drastically affected and residential properties will pay a greater proportionate share of the tax burden .... As written the proposal will wipe out classification."[98]

The committee's concern was unwarranted. Proposition 2½ and the recently enacted classification law do not inherently conflict. Both laws require property to be assessed at fair cash value, and both, as part of chapter 59 of the Massachusetts General Laws, apply the same definitions of property. Both can be implemented by a community without creating a statutory conflict. The two laws apply to different aspects of the tax determination process. The classification law permits, without requiring, a municipality to exercise some discretion in the allocation of the property tax burden among four different categories of real property. The classification law speaks only to the allocation of a property tax levy, not to its size or rate of growth. Proposition 2½, on the other hand, limits the size and growth of the property tax levy, but not its allocation.

Proposition 2½ provides that "the total taxes assessed under any provision of this chapter by the commonwealth or by any city, town, county, district, authority or other governmental entity upon real estate and personal property as defined in this chapter shall not, in any fiscal year, exceed two and one-half percent of the full and fair cash valuation thereof."[99] Thus, so long as the ratio of the total tax levy to the total tax base does not exceed 2.5 percent, this clause of the statute is met. The 2.5 percent limit is an aggregate limit, not a limit on each parcel of property. Proposition 2½ does not restrict the allocation of the tax burden within the limit, and in that sense does not interfere with the classification law.

While chapter 580 and the classification law have been shown to be consistent in concept and implementation, the classification law narrows the possible interpretations of the application of the rate limit to real and personal property. The wording in chapter 580 referring to the 2½ percent tax rate limit is ambiguous with regard to the allocation of the tax burden between real and personal property. The statute provides that the total taxes assessed by a governmental entity "upon real estate and personal property . . . shall not exceed two and one-half percent of the full and fair cash valuation thereof. . ."[100] This section leaves unclear whether the levy limit is to be calculated as 2½ percent of the real property plus 2½ percent of the personal property in a taxing district, or 2½ percent of the aggregate of real and personal property.

The former approach could create a conflict between Proposition 2½ and the classification law. The classification law requires a board of assessors to calculate the fraction of the total tax levy borne by each of five types of property: personal property, and four classes of real property. Under the classification law, personal property is expected to bear the fraction of the tax levy equal to its ratio to *all* property, real and personal, in the taxing district, after an adjustment is made for the fact that residential and open space real estate are taxed at less than their ratio to all property. The classification law combines real and personal property together. In order to be consistent with the classification law, Proposition 2½ must be interpreted to do the same.

To conform to this constraint, the rate limit clause of Proposition 2½ must be read to mean that the total taxes assessed shall not exceed two and one half percent of the *combined* full and fair cash valuation of real and personal property. To interpret the statute otherwise (i.e., to require a tax levy limit of 2½ percent of real property plus 2½ percent of personal property) could well lead to conflicts between the two laws.

The Effect of Proposition 2½ on Property Tax Exemptions

The same constitutional clause establishing that all property must be taxed at the same proportional rate, read to mandate uniformity of taxation, has been interpreted to require universality of taxation as well. Just as classification has emerged as an exception to the uniformity requirement, limited exceptions to the universality rule have developed over the years. In 1912 an amendment to the Massachusetts constitution was passed that permitted forest land to be taxed in a way that would "develop and conserve the forest resources of the commonwealth."[101] Gradually the number of exemptions to the property tax has increased. Exemptions from property tax include the following: property used for public or semiprivate purposes,[102] household furniture and personal effects,[103] the property of taxpayers who are in certain conditions of hardship.[104] These exemptions, which have not been judicially challenged, are based on the rationale that such property should not be used to meet public expenses.[105]

The language of chapter 580 leaves uncertain the question whether exempted property is to be included in the tax base for purposes of calculating the tax limit, a problem that was noted in the report made by the Committee on Taxation about Proposition 2½.[106] The relevant clause reads, "The total taxes assessed under any provision of this chapter . . . upon real and personal property as defined in this chapter shall not, in any fiscal year, exceed two and one- half percent of the full and fair cash valuation thereof. . . . "[107] The definitions of real and personal property in Massachusetts General Laws chapter 59, referred to in the clause quoted above, specifically exclude exempted property. The statutes provide that "real property for the purpose of taxation shall include all land within the commonwealth . . . unless otherwise exempted from taxation under other provisions of law."[108] The statute defining personal property includes as taxable personal property goods, chattels, money and effects, including ships and vessels; money at interest and debts due; and stocks and bonds. The statute excepts from taxable personal property exempt personal property.[109] It seems fair to conclude then, that the tax base, for purposes of calculating the rate and levy limits, does not include exempt property.

Proposition 2½ does not directly interfere with property tax exemptions. The law may, however, inhibit the use of residential exemptions permitted by the classification law, of up to ten percent of the average assessed value of residential real estate.[110] Since exempted real property cannot be included in the tax base, pressure on a municipality to enlarge the tax base as much as possible may prevent city or town governments from granting these optional exemptions. Other exemptions to real and personal property are not optional, and they will not be directly affected by chapter 580. Indirect effects may occur due to chapter 580. For example, if municipal services previously purchased with property tax revenues are provided on a fee or charge basis, property tax exemptions will be worth less. As property tax rates go down, property tax exemptions become less valuable.

Proposition 2½ and Taxing Districts

One of the most ambiguous aspects of Proposition 2½ is the effect it has on governmental entities other than cities and towns. The rate and levy limits mandated in chapter 580 are to be applied to the "commonwealth or . . . any city, town, county, districts, authority or other governmental entity. . . ."[111] The statute leaves unclear how the limits are to be calculated or applied. In addition to the inclusion of some taxing districts in the tax rate and levy growth limits, Proposition 2½ affects local government units in other ways. Section 12 of chapter 580 places a four percent cap on annual increases in charges imposed on cities and towns by counties, districts, public authorities, or other governmental entities. Proposition 2½ also repeals the school committee fiscal autonomy law, and so grants to municipal governments the power to set public school funding levels.

The 39 cities and 312 towns of the commonwealth are the main beneficiaries of the property tax, but the other local government entities (12 counties, 75 school districts and 328 special districts) also get most of their revenue from the property tax.[112] The mechanics of the revenue process vary among these different governmental entities. The assessment of a governmental unit may be in the form of a fee for service that is charged directly to the individuals within the district, or it may be levied against a city or town. If it is levied against a city or town, the amount may be determined using one of three bases: the state tax apportionment; a formula designed for the particular governmental entity; or a charge for expenses incurred or services performed.[113]

County and regional transit authorities obtain their revenues from cities and towns, using the state tax apportionment. Counties assess their costs on the cities and towns within each county's borders.[114] Each county prepares its own budget, which must be approved by both houses of the state legislature. The portion of the approved county budget that is not met by special state aid is then levied against the cities and towns within the county. The assessment on each city and town is made according to the legislature's latest apportionment of state and county taxes.[115] Regional transit authorities, like counties, levy automatically against member communities for their revenues.[116] Municipal governments cannot control the size of the levy of either counties or regional transit authorities.

Beach districts, regional refuse districts, and regional police districts assess member cities and towns for the expenses of the district, each using a slightly different formula. Beach districts allocate their costs based on state and county valuations; refuse districts may exercise discretion in the methods they use to allocate costs; and police districts use a formula based on state equalized valuation figures, population, and road length to distribute their costs among the cities and towns they serve.[117]

Water districts in Massachusetts can collect revenue in one of two ways. Under both approaches, the water district charges the property directly rather than through the city or town taxing mechanism. Water rates may be assessed as charges to individual parcels of property; the charge, if not paid, may be added to the city or town property tax for an individual parcel of real estate. Water districts may also meet their revenue needs by a property assessment, determined by either property size or value, that is uniformly applied to the real estate in the water district.[118]

Fire districts assess taxes to support their functions "in the same manner as town taxes."[119] Fire districts use a property tax system parallel to city and town property tax collections, but separately administered.

Chapter 580 implicitly distinguishes between those governmental entities that directly assess taxes on real property, which are subject to the 2.5 percent limit on both tax rates and levy growth, and those governmental entities that assess costs, charges, or fees on cities or towns, which are subject to the 4 percent limit on increases over the previous year's charges. Beyond this broad distinction, Proposition 2½ makes no reference to the different modes of taxation among the counties and special districts, and this omission renders the statute obscure as to how it affects relations between municipal governments and other local governmental entities, such as regional transit authorities, refuse districts, police districts, water districts, and fire districts.

Local governments may not clearly fall on one side or the other of the above distinction. The question has already arisen in the case of regional school districts, which neither assess taxes directly against residents nor request an amount certain from municipal governments. Regional school districts determine their operating budgets and apportion the costs among their member communities. Each city or town has discretion over payment of the costs: since school committees no longer have fiscal autonomy,[120] payment of those costs is subject to appropriation by municipal governments. The commissioner of revenue recently concluded that because of this distinction, regional school districts were not subject to the four percent limit imposed by section 12 of chapter 580.[121]

In addition, how the tax limit should be applied to the different governmental units that directly assess property taxes is unclear. The 2½ percent cap in the statute is applied to the "total taxes assessed . . . by the Commonwealth or by any city, town, county, district authority or other governmental entity upon real and personal property. . . ."[122] This clause appears to require that the 2½ percent limit be applied to each governmental unit separately. Yet the statute does not provide a procedure for gradually decreasing taxes to the 2½ percent level for any governmental unit except cities and towns. Moreover, the lower 1979 levy limit, applicable to cities and towns, does not apply to governmental units other than cities and towns. Finally, the limit of tax growth to a 2½ percent increase each year "with respect to any city or town"[123] is confusing because some governmental units that assess property taxes encompass several municipalities. The strongest interpretation of this tax growth limit appears to be that each governmental entity that assesses property taxes is subject to an individual levy limit of a 2½ percent increase over the previous year, and the limit for a governmental entity that encompasses several municipalities is calculated separately for the property in each member city or town.

RECOMMENDATIONS

Amending section 1 of chapter 580, as it applies to local governments, would help to clarify exactly what standards local government entities are required to meet. The different possible interpretations could make a substantial difference to taxpayers and community governments. If, for example, the levy and rate limits are interpreted to apply separately to each governmental entity, special taxing districts could be developed that would take on some of the expenses currently being paid by cities and towns, thus effectively raising the amount of property taxes paid. This maneuver would make no difference if all entities are combined for purposes of the rate and levy limits. If a new taxing district, entitled to a separate 2½ percent tax rate limit, were created, chapter 580 does not indicate how the levy limit would apply since there would be no previous tax to use as a base. Proposition 2½ does not specify the mechanics of the application of the tax rate and levy limits to various governmental entities. Questions on this aspect of the law will remain until the statute is modified.

Proposition 2½ and Home Rule

In its adverse report to the legislature on Proposition 2½, the Joint Committee on Taxation expressed concern about the effect Proposition 2½ would have on local self-determination, noting that the bill "requires greater state involvement in the decision-making process at the municipal level, thus. . . abrogating the concept of 'home rule.'"[124] In fact, the effect of Proposition 2½ cannot be classified easily as favoring or disfavoring the concept of municipal home rule, because the statute does both.

Broadly speaking, home rule refers to control over local matters by municipalities, rather than by state government. The home rule movement has been an active one: 55 constitutional amendments and 12 statutory enactments were introduced between 1956 and 1974, each designed to limit the duties and expenses the state could impose on local governments.[125] In 1966, the Massachusetts voters ratified a Municipal Home Rule Amendment to the Massachusetts constitution.[126] This amendment restricts the general court's power over cities and towns to those laws that affect at least two municipalities, with certain exceptions, thereby limiting purely local legislation by the state.

High property taxes provided some of the impetus toward home rule legislation. Proponents of these measures complained that state legislative enactments that mandate additional local spending contributed to property tax increases.[127] The 1966 Home Rule amendment only weakly restrained state-mandated local spending, and the drafters of Proposition 2½ sought to reduce state-imposed pressure on the property tax by requiring the state to fund any cost obligations it imposes on any city or town.[128] In this respect, Proposition 2½ increases local control over local issues.

Yet Proposition 2½ also reduces local discretion over local finances by imposing a state-wide tax rate and tax levy limitation on local governments. In this respect the law works against local home rule. Proposition 2½, itself a statewide measure, mandates continuing state involvement in local taxes, through the supervision of local tax levies by the state department of revenue. Proposition 2½ shifts responsibility for the level of local services away from local determination: unless cities and towns vote to override the rate and levy limits, the amount of local services will be set by the funding level, rather than the other way around. Moreover, by limiting local funding sources, the act forces local governments into increasing dependency on state and federal aid. (Ironically, the act works directly to reduce some federal aid that is contingent on the local property tax effort.)

Conclusion

Proposition 2½ is the latest addition to a recent series of judicial and legislative changes in Massachusetts property tax laws. As a result, just when many Massachusetts communities are simultaneously reaching full valuation, and classifying their property (legally) for the first time, they must also apply a 2½ percent rate and levy limit to their property taxes. The intent of this article has been to clarify how Proposition 2½ affects those and other existing property tax laws.

Textual analysis of the statute has pointed up areas where the statute's meaning is ambiguous. Because Proposition 2½ is an initiative measure, there is no legislative history to clarify the law's meaning where the law is ambiguous. In some instances, the number of possible interpretations has been narrowed by potential conflicts with another law. In these instances an interpretation consistent with both laws has been indicated. Sections where changes might clarify the meaning of the law have also been suggested. The recommendations contained in this article, and summarized briefly below, are designed to further the intent of Proposition 2½ by pointing out technical flaws, not to change it substantially.

Proposition 2½, which requires that the tax rate and levy limits be applied to property assessed at full and fair cash value, does not conflict with current assessment laws, which also require full assessment. However, the statute does not acknowledge the reality of underassessment in many cities and towns. Because many municipalities will not be fully assessed for fiscal year 1982, the statute should be amended to allow the use of some alternative to fair cash valuation (for example, state equalized valuation figures) until reassessment has been completed. This flexibility should also be extended to the levy limit, which currently requires the use of fiscal year 1982 as a base year, even in those communities that did not reach full assessment in time for fiscal year 1982. A substantive change, but one that does not violate the intent of Proposition 2½, would be to allow an adjustment for real growth in the tax base before the levy limit is applied each year. A change in the calculation of the tax rate percentage of fiscal year 1979 will be required to implement the section of the new law establishing a rate limit lower than 2.5 percent in some communities; those communities not fully assessed in 1979 cannot compute that lower percentage.

The property classification law, which permits property used for different purposes to be taxed at different rates, is consistent with Proposition 2½. The classification law gives local governments some discretion over the allocation of the tax levy, while Proposition 2½ limits the rate of tax and the rate of growth of the tax levy. To avoid conflict with the classification law, however, Proposition 2½ must be interpreted to apply to a tax base of combined real and personal property. Proposition 2½ does not interfere with existing tax exemptions: the tax base for the purpose of calculating the 2½ tax rate and levy limit does not include exempt property. However, the tax limiting measure may prevent local governments from exercising an optional residential exemption permitted by the classification law.

The language of Proposition 2½ as it affects taxing districts other than cities or towns should be clarified. As written, the law broadly differentiates between governmental units that assess taxes directly on property and those that receive revenues from cities and towns. The law does not differentiate among the various tax mechanisms within those two basic categories. It has been inferred that the tax limit applies separately to each taxing district that taxes property directly; this section of the law should be rewritten for greater specificity as to which governmental entities are subject to which limits. In addition, the law should be amended to indicate how new taxing districts may be established.

Notes

1. Cases brought by the Massachusetts Coalition of Police, AFL-CIO, Massachusetts Teachers Association, and the International Brotherhood of Police Officers raise this issue. A Superior Court judge has ruled that the measure meets state and federal constitutional requirements. The decision will probably be appealed. *Boston Globe,* April 2, 1981 p. 1.

2. *Webby v. King,* presently before the Massachusetts Supreme Judicial Court.

3. A suit brought by the Massachusetts Teachers Association raised this issue. See note 1 above.

4. *Boston Globe,* March 7, 1981 at 1.

5. Robert W. Eisenmenger et al., *Options for Fiscal Structure Reform in Massachusetts* (Boston: Federal Reserve Bank of Boston, 1975), p. 65. (Note that the motor vehicle excise tax is levied by the state.)

6. Massachusetts Department of Corporations and Taxation, *Massachusetts Property Tax Law Handbook* (Boston: Commonwealth of Massachusetts, 1978) p. 3.

7. U.S. Advisory Commission on Intergovernmental Relations, *The Property Tax in a Changing Environment* (Washington, D.C.: U.S. Government Printing Office, 1974), p. 123.

8. Eisenmenger, *Options,* p. 65.
9. U.S. Department of Commerce, *1977 Census of Governments* (Washington, D.C.: U.S. Government Printing Office, 1977), Vol. 4, no. 5, p. 104.
10. Id. In 1973, 50 percent of local government revenues came from the property tax; in 1953 that figure was 58 percent. Eisenmenger, *Options,* p. 41.
11. Id.
12. Legislative Research Council, *Report Relative to Limiting Taxation and Spending by State and Local Governments* (Boston: Commonwealth of Massachusetts, 1980), p. 340.
13. Boston Globe, January 18, 1981, at 33.
14. Mass. Gen. Laws Ann. ch. 58 § 10C.
15. Legislative Research Bureau, *Report Relative to Restricting the Application of State Laws Adding to Local Government Costs,* House Report No. 5841 (Boston: The Commonwealth of Massachusetts, 1975), p. 44.
16. Massachusetts Taxpayers Foundation, *Massachusetts Tax Primer: A Review of Massachusetts Taxes and Spending* (Boston: Massachusetts Taxpayers Foundation Research Publication, 1973), p. 18.
17. Eisenmenger, *Options,* p. 41.
18. The information in this paragraph is taken substantially from Legislative Research Council, *Limiting Taxation,* p. 332.
19. The information in this paragraph is taken substantially from *id.* pp. 333-338.
20. Id., p. 344.
21. Mass. Gen. Laws Ann. Appendix to ch. 58, §§ 1-16.
22. Massachusetts House of Representatives, No. 5015, 1980.
23. Roland B. Welch, *The Property Tax Under Pressure: A Policy Maker's Guide* (Cambridge, Mass.: Lincoln Institute of Land Policy, 1980), p. 12.
24. Mass. Const. Pt. 2, c.l., Art. 4.
25. Mass. Const. Pt. 1, Art. 10.
26. The Special Commission to Develop a Master Tax Plan, *First Report of the Special Commission to Develop a Master Tax Plan Relative to Constitutional Limits on the Tax Power,* Senate Report No. 126 (Boston: Commonwealth of Massachusetts, 1969), pp. 31-32.
27. Id., pp. 13-14.
28. Id., p. 19.
29. Mass. Gen. Laws Ann. ch. 59 § 38.
30. "Assessment" is the valuation of property for tax purposes. Fair cash value assessment means assessment at market value. It refers to the amount that a buyer willing but not compelled to buy would pay to a seller willing but not compelled to sell. *Assessors of Quincy v. Boston Consolidated Gas Co.,* 309 Mass. 60, 34 N.E. 2d 623 (1941), *Boston Gas Co. v. Assessors of Boston,* 334 Mass. 549, 137 N.E. 2d 462 (1956).
31. The economist Henry Aaron has stated that "assessment at full value is mathematically irrelevant to equitable distribution of property tax burdens within a single jurisdiction . . . ; in a purely technical sense, equal value assessments are all that matter." Henry Aaron, "Some Observations on Property Tax Valuation and the Significance of Full Value Assessment," in *The Property Tax and Its Administration,* ed. Arthur D. Lynn, Jr., p. 156.

32. Mass. Const. Amend. Art. 112.

33. Mass. Gen. Laws Ann. ch. 40 § 56.

34. Commerce Clearing House, *Guidebook to Massachusetts Taxes,* (Chicago: Commerce Clearing House, 1975), p. 168.

35. Massachusetts Department of Corporations and Taxation, *Property Tax Law Handbook,* p. 16.

36. Rudolph Russo, Cambridge Board of Assessors, interview held at the Unitarian-Universalist Church, Cambridge, Massachusetts, March 22, 1981.

37. Timothy Greene, *Revaluation of Real Property in Massachusetts Cities and Towns* (Lynn, Mass.: Massachusetts Public Finance Project, 1974), p. 5.

38. Mass. Gen. Laws Ann. ch. 41 § 30.

39. Oliver Oldman and Henry Aaron, "Assessment-Sales Ratios Under the Boston Property Tax," 18 *National Tax Journal* 41-43 (1965).

40. David Black, "The Nature and Extent of Effective Property Tax Rate Variation within the City of Boston," 25 *National Tax Journal* 203-210 (1972).

41. Greene, *Revaluation,* p. 4.

42. Diane B. Paul, *The Politics of the Property Tax* (Lexington, Mass.: D.C. Heath & Co., 1975), p. 9.

43. Greene, *Revaluation,* p. 6.

44. The Boston Board of Assessors used the owner's ability or willingness to pay taxes as one determinant of assessed property valuation, according to a study of the city's assessing practices undertaken by a consulting firm at the request of the Boston Finance Commission. The Board of Assessors used the following seven methods to assess real property: (1) income approach; (2) use of gross income multiplier or percentage of gross rent; (3) a percentage of the purchase price; (4) a percentage of the cost new; (5) a guess as to the maximum amount the owner would pay without complaining or initiating a tax appeal; (6) use of any method the assessor believes will pass the scrutiny of the Appellate Tax Board; (7) proportional return. Paul, *Politics of the Property Tax,* pp. 6-7.

45. Id., p. 32

46. The assessment variation among communities, and the bias this created in state equalized valuation figures, was challenged for the first time in *Town of Sudbury v. Commissioner of Corporations and Taxation,* 366 Mass. 558, 321 N. E. 2d (1974), discussed infra.

47. For further discussion of inequities caused by reliance on the property tax see Eisenmenger, *Options,* footnote 6. One scholar theorized that those who pay higher taxes are those with inelastic demand functions for areas where property taxes are highest–usually city locations–merchants and business, and Blacks and other non-whites. See Paul, *Politics of the Property Tax,* pp. 41 *et seq.,* footnote 56.

48. Mass. Gen. Laws Ann. ch. 59 § 59.

49. Mass. Gen. Laws Ann. ch. 40 § 53.

50. *Sears, Roebuck and Co. v. Somerville,* 363 Mass. 756, 298 N.E. 2d 693 (1973).

51. 343 Mass. 223, 178 N.E. 2d 10 (1961).

52. Mass. Const. Pt. 2, c.l, Art. 4.

53. Mass. Const. Pt. 1, Art. 10.

54. *Bettigole v. Assessors of Springfield,* 343 Mass. 223 at 230-231, 178 N.E. 2d 10, 14 (1961), citing Mass. Const. Pt. 1, Art. 10.

55. Id. at 231, 178 N.E. 2d at 15, citing Mass. Gen. Laws Ann. ch. 59 § 38.

56. Id. at 236, 178 N.E. 2d at 18.

57. *Leto v. Board of Assessors of Wilmington,* 348 Mass. 144, 143, 202 N.E. 2d 922, 925 (1964).

58. Id.

59. *Bennett v. Board of Assessors of Whitman,* 354 Mass. 239, 237 N.E. 2d 7 (1968).

60. *Bennett v. Board of Assessors of Whitman,* 354 Mass. 239, 237 N.E. 2d 7 (1968) and *Coan v. Board of Assessors of Beverly,* 349 Mass. 575, 211 N.E. 2d 50 (1965).

61. *Shoppers World v. Board of Assessors of Framingham,* 348 Mass. 366, 203 N.E. 2d 811 (1965).

62. Id.

63. 366 Mass. 558, 321 N.E. 2d 641 (1974).

64. Id., at 560, 321 N.E. 2d at 645.

65. Kathy Hellenbrand Rocklen, "Equality in Property Taxation—The Law, Practice and Prospects," *New England Law Review* 617 (1976), p. 634.

66. *Town of Sudbury v. Commissioner of Corporations and Taxation,* 366 Mass. 558, 560, 321 N.E. 2d 641, 644 (1974).

67. Id. at 566, 321 N.E. 2d at 647.

68. The commissioner and department of corporations and taxation were renamed the commissioner and department of revenue, respectively, by 1978 Mass. Acts. ch. 514.

69. Mass. Gen. Laws. Ann. ch. 58 § 1.

70. Id.

71. Mass. Gen. Laws. Ann. ch. 41 § 27.

72. After the *Sudbury* decision, abatement cases continued to be brought, but they were no longer used as tools to enforce the one hundred percent valuation requirement, since responsibility for insuring fair cash valuation had been passed to the commissioner of revenue. Several developments in the post-Sudbury abatement cases will be briefly noted here. The Supreme Court Judicial Court enlarged the abatement remedy in *Tregor v. Board of Assessors of Boston,* 1979 Mass. Adv. Sh. 770, 387 N.E. 2d 538 (1978), by holding that a disproportionately assessed taxpayer was entitled to an assessment ratio equal to the class of taxpayers assessed at the lower rate in the city. To counteract *Tregor,* a provision was included in the new property classification law, Mass. Gen. Laws Ann. ch. 58 § 14, effective immediately, that established damages in abatement cases as the amount by which the taxes paid exceeded the average tax in the municipality. Most provisions of the statute were upheld in a case in which the Supreme Judicial Court also set 1983 as a property revaluation deadline. *Keniston v. Board of Assessors of Boston,* 1980 Mass. Adv. Sh. 1485 407 N.E. 2d 1275.

73. Paul, *Politics of the Property Tax,* p. 37.

74. Rocklen, "Equality in Property Taxation," p. 633, citing Sudbury Master's Report.

75. Greene, *Revaluation,* p. 12.

76. Paul, *Politics* of the Property Tax, p. 63.

77. Massachusetts Department of Revenue, *Sudbury Compliance Report,* February 14, 1981.

78. L. Joyce Hampers, Commissioner of Revenue, *Memorandum to Boards of Assessors,* February 24, 1981, p. 2.

79. Id.

80. Mass. Gen. Laws Ann. ch. 59 § 2A, ch. 58 § 1.

81. L. Joyce Hampers, Commissioner of Revenue, *Memorandum to Boards of Assessors,* February 24, 1981, p. 3.

82. Id., p. 4.

83. John Ryan, Massachusetts Bureau of Local Assessment, telephone interview, April 3, 1981.

84. Rudolph Russo, Cambridge Board of Assessors, interview held at the Unitarian-Universalist Church, Cambridge, Massachusetts, March 22, 1981.

85. *Boston Globe,* October, 1980.

86. *Boston Globe,* October, 1980, quoting Charles Hoen, Assistant Chief of the Department of Revenue's Bureau of Local Assessment.

87. The town of Newton has already challenged the use of equalized valuation figures for this purpose in a suit filed in Suffolk County. Docket No. 80-195. Briefs are due to be filed in April, 1981.

88. Rudolph Russo, Cambridge Board of Assessors, interview held at the Unitarian-Universalist Church, Cambridge, Massachusetts, March 22, 1981.

89. Mass. Gen. Laws Ann. ch. 59 § 21C (3).

90. Paul, *Politics of the Property Tax,* p. 65.

91. Mass. Const. Amend. Art. 112.

92. Kenneth Grace, "Proposition 2½ in Massachusetts: Another Proposition 13 or a Tax Reform Measure with Constitutional Problems?, 15 *New England Law Review* 309, 311 (1980).

93. 1978 Mass. Acts ch. 580.

94. 1979 Mass. Acts. ch. 797 § 23.

95. Id., Mass. Gen. Laws Ann. ch. 59 § 2A.

96. Mass. Gen. Laws Ann. ch. 40 § 56.

97. Mass. Gen. Laws Ann. ch. 59 § 2A.

98. Legislative Research Council, *Limiting Taxation,* p. 374, quoting Massachusetts Joint Committee on Taxation's Report to the Legislature (House, No. 6368, 1980).

99. Mass. Gen. Laws Ann. ch. 59 § 21C, added by 1980 Mass. Acts. ch. 580 § 1.

100. Id.

101. Mass. Const. Amend. Art. 41.

102. Mass. Gen. Laws Ann. ch. 59 § 5.

103. Id.

104. Id.

105. Special Commission, *Master Tax Plan,* p. 28.

106. Legislative Research Council, *Limiting Taxation,* p. 374, quoting Massachusetts Joint Committee on Taxation's Report to the Legislature (House, No. 6368, 1980).

107. Mass. Gen. Laws Ann. ch. 59 § 21C, added by 1980 Mass. Acts. ch. 580 § 1.

108. Mass. Gen. Laws Ann. ch. 59 § 2A.

109. Mass. Gen. Laws Ann. ch. 59 § 4.

110. Mass. Gen. Laws Ann. ch. 59 § 5C.

111. Mass. Gen. Laws Ann. ch. 59 § 21C, added by 1980 Mass. Acts. ch. 580 § 1.

112. U.S. Department of Commerce, 1977 Census of Governments, vol. 4, no. 5, p. 166.

113. Department of Corporations and Taxation, *Property Tax Handbook,* p. 76.

114. Mass. Gen. Laws Ann. ch. 58 § 17A.

115. Mass. Gen. Laws Ann. ch. 35 §R 28, 31, 35.

116. Mass. Gen. Laws Ann. ch. 161B § 9.

117. Mass. Gen. Laws Ann. ch. 40, §R 12B, 44F; ch. 41 § 991.

118. Mass. Gen. Laws Ann. ch. 40 §R 42A-D, 42G-1.

119. Mass. Gen. Laws Ann. ch. 48 § 73.

120. 1980 Mass. Acts ch. 580 §§ 6-8.

121. L. Joyce Hampers, Commissioner of Revenue, *Memorandum to Local Government Officials,* January 19, 1981.

122. Mass. Gen. Laws Ann. ch. 59 § 21C, added by 1980 Mass. Acts ch. 580 § 1.

123. Id.

124. Legislative Research Council, *Limiting Taxation,* p. 374.

125. Legislative Research Bureau, *Restricting the Application of State Laws,* pp. 14, 17.

126. Mass. Const. Amend. Art. 89.

127. Legislative Research Bureau, *Restricting the Application of State Laws,* p. 16.

128. Mass. Gen. Laws Ann. ch. 29 § 27C, added by 1980 Mass. Acts ch. 580 § 2.

VI. THE VARIETY OF CONSEQUENCES OF TAX AND EXPENDITURE LIMITATIONS

11

Effect on Metropolitan Growth: The Washington, D.C. Area

ROYCE HANSON

Tax and expenditure limitations are based on fundamental distrust of the guts and frugality of elected government. They assume that mayors and councils, governors and legislatures, will be unable to resist other interest group appeals for beneficial programs or do not have the intelligence or fortitude to manage the public enterprise prudently. There is, of course, some basis for this. Far too many elected officials would rather rely on a charter or constitutional amendment as an excuse for saying "no" than to directly confront excessive demands on the public purse and risk alienating constituents. TELS allow representatives to have it both ways—to be for popular programs, but unable to fund them.

TELS undermine the strength of representative government through plebescitary budgeting. Modern democracy relies for its resilience on accommodation and compromise; bargaining, if you will, among claimants for public favor. The budget and the fiscal system are primary instruments of that bargaining process. Bargaining, by its nature, is a long, continuing, messy process. It is not easily subjected to arbitrary limits such as are imposed by a TELS

Mr. Hanson is chairman, the Maryland-National Capital Park and Planning Commission.

amendment. Essentially, TELS embalm one interest group's ideas of what is important into the structure of the process.

The result is a decline rather than an increase in accountability of government. The demanding groups will continue to demand. Generally, the demands will be met, but not through the politically visible process of the general budget. Instead, we shall see a trend toward more costly, less responsible quasigovernments such as authorities and special districts. Instead of taxes, we can anticipate a growth in exactions and fees, which shift the fiscal burden, at least temporarily.

From the viewpoint of substantive policy, as distinguished from governmental processes, TELS clearly threaten programs aimed at imposing the balance of social justice. And, in metropolitan areas, TELS can be expected to produce some unfortunate distributive effects on the pattern of growth and the resolution of urban problems.

In metropolitan Washington, for example, all local governments face serious fiscal problems, without TELS. The Greater Washington Research Institute estimates that by 1985 the combined cumulative revenue shortfall for all area local governments will be running at three billion dollars a year, even if the only expansion of services is to serve new development.[1]

New growth will not be able to supply the revenue. The same study estimates that to provide a 1 percent expansion of revenue for the region, new growth would have to produce 40 million dollars in added taxes.[2] Since any likely TELS would probably reduce the revenue yield of new growth (at least after the first year), what is unlikely under existing law becomes impossible with TELS.

This kind of pressure on the local fisc is quite likely to lead to demands for a classified property tax to reduce the pressure on the residential property taxpayer, or at least on the *existing* taxpayer. A classified tax is not likely in either Maryland or Virginia, and quite clearly not in the District, because of fear of its distributional effect if one jurisdiction does not enact it and the others do. If adopted, policy would be slanted toward nonresidential development and this has myriad chances for bitter opposition in local application even if heralded in principle.

In the face of such bleak fiscal forecasts, it does not appear that the pressure for expenditure increases by local government will subside in the decade ahead. Some very substantial costs are now built into the metropolitan political economy. Others will be generated by national and international events well beyond the control of local governments.

The infrastructure of the central city and suburbs is aging. Some of it is literally disintegrating. The poor condition of bridges is obvious, as is that of streets. The water distribution and sewerage systems leak or break down. In addition, new national standards for health or safety require much more sophisticated construction and management of infrastructure systems.[3] Waste water treatment, water supply and treatment, sludge disposal, solid waste disposal, storm water management, noise standards in roadway construction, and the capital and operating costs of the subway system are separately impressive. Combined, as a regional capital cost and with resulting operating costs, they are almost overwhelming. Part of that overwhelming sensation derives from the realization that all of these activities tend to be high energy users. In addition, the construction price index has moved well ahead of the CPI, and construction also involves energy costs and petroleum products, such as asphalt.

In spite of educational facilities being less needed than in past decades because of relative or even absolute declines in school-aged children, almost all of the urban and suburban school systems can expect fairly steady increases in education budgets to be built into the system. Because the school systems are static, new teachers are not being hired and the older teachers are reaching the top of their salary grades. In Montgomery County, Maryland, for example, 36 percent are in the last step of their grades.[4] This also means that regular cost-of-living increases, public contributions to benefit systems, and anything else based on a flat percentage of salaries will have a greater absolute budget impact than in past decades when a large proportion of the teaching staff was young and mobile. Teachers are not moving on; there is no place to go.

One continuing source of pressure on local treasuries will be vested retirement systems created in the 1960s and early 70s when local salaries were relatively low, and early or generous retirement was an offset.[5] Even though recent amendments reduce benefits for new employees now coming aboard—at a time of reduced hiring—the old retirement plans remain effective for almost all current employees and they must be full funded.

One natural impulse in the face of TELS is to repair to the state capital and Washington to find transfer payments to replace the restricted local revenues. Although there are some at the state level, particularly a substantial surplus in Maryland, the most likely prognosis is that transfers will decline, perhaps absolutely. One clear example of this can be found in transportation trust funds. In Maryland, the trust fund has been depleted by support of mass transit and a decline in revenue resulting from fuel conservation programs. The gasoline tax is fixed, rather than being a percentage of the price per gallon. The result is that higher costs at the pumps do not generate more revenue. The loss is the more devastating in the face of gasoline conservation and the effect of inflation on purchasing power.[6]

This absence of funding for necessary capital improvements to the transportation system is exacerbated by the almost geometric escalation of operating costs for public transportation. In many metropolitan areas, we are belatedly transferring much of the transportation budget from the people as individual consumers to the people as taxpayers. The difference is politically and fiscally significant. Even though the average person may statistically pay less for public transportation than for operation of a private automobile, the perception of the cost is far different. The almost invisible cost of paying for travel at the gas pumps, the repair shop, and the tire store is converted into a cumulative tax bill—frequently as an addition to the property tax. This not only is politically visible, it squeezes other candidates for public funding. The demand for increased transit service is unlikely to abate. The suburbs, particularly, will face relatively high costs because of lower residential densities that offer less patronage per mile of route and, therefore, higher fuel and labor costs per passenger. Rolling stock is also escalating in price because of increasing materials cost, but even more so because of federal requirements for equipping vehicles to serve the handicapped and to reduce air pollution.

In the face of these exogenous and indigenous pressures to increase local expenditures, combined with failure of commensurate growth in federal and state transfer payments, particularly as the federal government grapples with the simultaneous need to control inflation and growing military expenditures, there is little chance that the total demand on local budgets will be reduced. In a metropolitan context, separate, local TELS will further skew existing trends favoring the jurisdictions that already have stronger tax bases. Those most able to provide services and facilities will be even more attractive to fiscally beneficial development such as high-technology industry, professional offices, high-quality shopping centers, and high-income residences. Tax rates will be lower in these jurisdictions because their tax bases —even with TELS—will appreciate more rapidly than those of the less affluent jurisdictions. Thus, the poorer jurisdictions will fall further behind and become less attractive to new growth that could expand the tax base.

This point can be illustrated by looking at the effect of TELS on development. New growth requires public infrastructure—particularly transportation, assuming sewer and water can be made available. In Prince Georges County, any capital programming for more than the current budget year has, for all practical purposes, been terminated because of the limits that the TELS adopted there in 1978 have placed on increasing the bonded debt capability of the county. No new debt can be incurred because the so-called TRIM (Tax Reform In Maryland) limits property tax revenues to the level collected in 1978.[7] This, in effect, prevents the county from pledging its full faith and credit to the redemption of bonds, according to its bond counsel. At the very best, the bond rating is reduced, actually *increasing* the cost of any capital improvements. Long-term planning simply cannot go forward. The county cannot assure anyone that it can or will provide the infrastructure necessary for development that might otherwise expand the tax base. In fact, in Prince Georges County there is no point in expanding the tax base since the absolute limitation on revenues makes it unusable except as a very marginal reduction of the tax rate; it cannot be used to finance new or better services.[8]

Since the total property tax revenue cannot increase, the county will be increasingly unable to finance public transportation service. The consequence will probably be a reduction in service, rather than an increase, which will make it even less desirable for both commuters and new employment centers. The private cost of living in the county will increase as public service declines.

Water and sewerage costs are not directly affected by TRIM, as they are financed through a separate district, the Washington Suburban Sanitary Commission. Its bond ratings, however, are indirectly influenced by the financial posture of the two counties it serves. Fees and rates are likely to increase, however, to pay for new treatment requirements.[9] User rates will increase proportionately as new growth declines since the county will have a considerable amount of excess capacity, the debt for which will have to be retired by fewer users than was contemplated when it was built—before TRIM.

The effect of TELS on schools is to prefer development that is inhospitable to school-aged children. TELS, combined with the general aging of the population in established communities, could help give an advantage to new development aimed at single- and other all-adult households. Such households, however, tend to want other high-quality services unlikely to be provided, such as public transportation and intensive recreation programs or facilities. As pointed out above, school expenditures will, nonetheless, decline only slightly because of the seniority of the remaining teaching staff and other built-in costs.

A common companion of the TELS psychology is a strong prejudice for no-growth policies or actions that favor only luxury growth.[10] Of the two, no-growth is more likely. High-quality growth is particularly sensitive to the quality of services provided in a community. To avoid a deficit from new housing, Prince Georges officials calculate that they need (in 1979 terms) their new houses to be assessed at a minimum of $80,000. This requires a house that markets at $200,000.[11] Given the service environment, any substantial amount of such development is highly unrealistic. Even if successful, it would generate other costs by emphasizing large-lot sprawl. Such development is even more unlikely when one realizes that it will also bear a higher proportion of recreational costs through exactions and shifting the cost of facilities, their maintenance, and programs to private homeowners associations.

Although attracting high-quality development to a jurisdiction that has shot itself in the fiscal foot is illusory, success can probably be attained in excluding further less costly housing—up to some legal or constitutional threshold. In other words, zoning policies designed to attract the rich will probably fail, but they will succeed in reducing housing opportunities for the less affluent.

Another effect of TELS is to impair long-range planning and growth management processes. For such systems to succeed, it is essential that a strong commitment be made to sustain a staff capable of devising and maintaining a strategic approach. Intelligent growth and fiscal planning is antithetical to TELS, which tend to be a visceral response to an immediate perception. By undermining capacity to deal with long-term infrastructure and service financing, TELS destroy a principal tool of effective growth management. In fact, it makes impossible approaches that rely on the legal theory that development can be timed and balanced on the basis of a long-term plan for providing public facilities. No such plan can exist. And the staff effort to undertake careful long-range planning tends to be viewed by TELS advocates as unneeded, or worse. It is an early candidate for extinction, thereby terminating the capacity to think ahead.

Like most quick fixes, TELS carry with them a lot of slow tortures. The following generalizations about their effect on local government and the distribution of development in metropolitan Washington seem reasonable.

TELS will be most damaging to those local governments, such as Prince Georges County and Baltimore City, which most need new growth and redevelopment. This is likely because the loss in yield from the property tax will not be offset by an equal or greater increase in transfer payments and because urban costs will increase at a faster rate than revenue growth. This will occur even where the greatest possible efficiencies are achieved in governmental functions. Even the most doctrinaire apostles of TELS have not predicted more than a 10 percent reduction in costs of government. Many of the activities they most want reduced are not financed primarily by local revenues—welfare, for example. TELS seem to have, politically, a ratchet effect. Once introduced, they intimidate officials from opposing them even if they acknowledge their unfairness or unworkability. As the state tries to fill the revenue gap, it is subject to attack and the TELS notion escalates to the state. In the 1980 Maryland General Assembly, TELS measures were reported favorably by the House Finance Committee and were defeated only after a concerted effort by the leadership and governor, aided by Prince Georges County, which would have been in desperate fiscal condition without access to the state surplus. Neither the surplus, nor the ability of the leadership to forestall fiscal posturing by the legislature can be permanently guaranteed. A statewide TELS measure, especially one that limits state revenue or expenditure, or both, would be devastating to those poorer jurisdictions that rely heavily on transfer payments from the state. Another effect of TELS is to increase the burden on the less affluent and on the residential sector of the tax base. Industrial and commercial property is already relatively underassessed. So are higher valued homes. Systems that either restrict growth in assessments or collections shift the burden increasingly onto the less wealthy.

TELS will exacerbate the deterioration of infrastructure and limit new growth-sustaining infrastructure, substantially increasing future costs. In many cases, timely public investments can actually reduce maintenance costs, which are reflected in the operating budget. Similarly, good maintenance can obviate the need or reduce the cycle of replacements. Two of the earliest targets of TELS are inevitably maintenance programs and new capital expenditures. Both build higher future costs into government.

To meet this problem, local governments are forced to rely on user fees and exactions from builders. Fees and exaction rarely pay the real costs of new public improvements, and they generally fall short of meeting maintenance costs. By increasing the consumer cost of development they also have, over time, a substantial effect on the social equity of a community. Services tend to become private rather than public, and only the affluent can have good roads, parks, libraries, and schools.

Effective and socially equitable growth management and planning systems are impeded. In Maryland and Virginia, the system of countywide services and planning has prevented the kind of exclusionary development policies that operate in many areas. Any trend toward increased use of special service districts and private services will increase development costs through both delay and special assessments or fees. Planning for economic balance will not be encouraged. Such efforts as Montgomery County's moderate-price dwelling unit program could be endangered.[12]

General purpose local government will be undermined. One way to avoid TELS is to create special tax districts whose levy is separate from the governmental unit subject to the tax or expenditure limit. This was, in fact, the pattern of governance that developed between the Great Depression and the 1950s, resulting in part from millage limitations imposed on local governments. This system of invisible government has recently been in some decline as successive studies showed that it was fiscally inefficient and politically nonresponsible. Much recent federal intergovernmental legislation was aimed at strengthening general purpose government and undoing the damage done by categorical grants. TELS will help reverse this trend.

Finally, one of the most pernicious effects of TELS is to divert attention from the most fundamental problem in local government finance: the disparity between the local economic base and the tax base. The former is the system for generating and distributing wealth. The latter is only the legal authority to tax some of that wealth. In almost all instances the distribution of the tax base falls regressively on the economic base. In most urban jurisdictions, property is the major part of the tax base but is not nearly so important in the entire economic base. This very fact fuels the political demand for TELS, even though the principal beneficiaries are the wealthiest people. What is needed is a far less rigid system in most states for matching the local tax system with the local tax base. The problem for the unimaginative is that this is not conducive to uniformity among jurisdictions. Some local governments should rely on property, some on sales, some on income taxes. Some might well use value-added taxes or severance taxes far more heavily than they are now permitted to do.

Surely we have the sense and skills to do the necessary fiscal surgery to produce efficient government without using a cleaver. We should also keep in mind that fiscal conditions have substantial consequences for the management of metropolitan growth.

Notes

1. Dearborn, *Financing Washington Area Local Governments in the 1980s,* (1980), p. 19.

2. Ibid.

3. As an example, the cost of upgrading the District of Columbia's Blue Plains wastewater treatment plant is estimated to be $213,828,000 (Montgomery County, Md., *Recommended Capital Improvement Program, Fiscal Years 1981-86,* vol. 2, PDF, p. 5019). Partially as a consequence of such costs, plus the cost of other treatment facilities and processes, the Washington Suburban Sanitary Commission in 1979 imposed a System Expansion Offset Charge (SEOC) on all new development of about $1,500 per single family dwelling unit.

4. An even larger percentage of administrative personnel is at the last step in grade (Salary, Administration, Certification and Records Section, Montgomery County Public Schools. March, 1980).

5. "Public Workers' Pensions Strain Cities and Increase with Inflation" *The New York Times,* May 19, 1980, p. 1.

6. It is estimated that in the 1979-80 period as much as 25 percent of the purchasing power of the fund has been lost.

7. Testimony of the Prince Georges County government before the Special Joint Committee on Tax and Spending Limitations, Annapolis, Maryland., July 31, 1979.

8. Ibid.

9. n. 3, *supra.*

10. D.R. Mandelker "The Catch-13 in Proposition 13: Higher Development Charges Raise New Questions for Courts," *Environmental Comment,* July, 1979.

11. Residential property in Maryland is assessed at 40 percent of market value.

12. Under this local law, in any development of more than fifty units 15 percent of all units must be produced to market within moderate price ranges established by the county executive. A development using the MPDU "Option" receives a density bonus of 20 percent. (Chapter 25A, *Montgomery County Code,* 1972: sections 59-C-1.6, 59-C-2.42, 59-C-6.215 [b], 59-C-7.14 [b] and [c], *Montgomery County Code,* 1972 [Zoning Ordinance] provisions for residential zones). The theory of the law is that the density bonus offsets the costs of providing the moderately priced unit. Increases in development costs, at a minimum, put pressure on the MPDU prices to rise.

12

Effect on the Poor

HOWARD CHERNICK
ANDREW RESCHOVSKY

Introduction

During the past several years the legislatures or the voters in several states have dramatically reduced reliance on the property tax as a means of financing local government services. Efforts to limit the use of property taxation currently continue in several other states.[1] These property tax limitation measures have generally taken the form of levy or rate limits, or restrictions on the size of the property tax base. California's Proposition 13, approved by the electorate in

Mr. Chernick is with the Office of Income Security Policy, U.S. Department of Health and Human Services. Mr. Reschovsky is a member of the department of economics, Tufts University. The authors would like to extend their thanks to Martin Holmer, who first suggested the application of microsimulation to the analysis of the property tax, to participants in seminars at the RAND Corporation and the Institute for Research on Poverty, and to participants in the November, 1980 meeting of the Committee on Urban Public Economics, in New Orleans. They would also like to thank Heather Pritchard for her invaluable computer assistance and David Carroll for his excellent research assistance.

June 1978, was the largest and most prominent of these property tax limitation initiatives. By limiting the rate of property taxation to 1 percent of market value, and by placing restrictions on the growth rate of the assessed value of real property, Proposition 13 resulted in an initial $7 billion reduction in property tax revenues.

The tax limitation movement, and Proposition 13 in particular, has generated a good deal of interest and analysis. A considerable amount of research has been conducted concerning the aggregate economic and political impacts of tax and expenditure limitations.[2] However, very little attention has been paid to the *distribution* of impacts across various economic and demographic groups.[3] This paper will attempt to ascertain the impact of tax limitations on the rich and the poor, the young and the elderly, and on households in their roles as homeowners, renters, landlords, and owners of capital. We shall use California's experience with Proposition 13 as a type of case study to help us explore the distributional impacts of tax limitations.

A major impetus for the passage of Proposition 13 by California's voters was the rapidly rising property tax burdens faced by many homeowners. Although per capita local government expenditures grew at only moderate rates during the years prior to 1978 (see Shapiro, Puryear, and Ross, 1979), residential property taxes grew rapidly during this period primarily because of the increasing importance of residential property in the total property tax base of California. The rapid rise in market value of residential property in many parts of California, the enforcement beginning in the early 1970s of the state constitution's "uniformity clause," requiring that all types of property be assessed at the same fraction of market value, and the lag in some communities in reducing tax rates in response to substantially higher assessed values have all contributed to the growth of the residential share of the property tax base from 48.4 percent in 1975 to 55.6 percent in 1978.[4]

An important question in evaluating the effectiveness of Proposition 13 is thus its impact on residential tax burdens. We are interested not only in the effect of Proposition 13 on the average tax burden but also on the pattern of property tax relief generated by Proposition 13. For example, we wish to ask whether high-income homeowners received more tax relief than lower-income households, or whether landlords benefited at the expense of tenants.

Our central focus in evaluating Proposition 13 is its impact on tax burdens, rather than its impact on the provision of public services. In 1978 the California state government had a $7 billion income tax surplus that enabled the state to "bail out" local governments by replacing a substantial share of lost property tax revenues with funds drawn from the state surplus. The result of a large and continuing state surplus is that cuts in local government expenditures have been relatively small, implying that the major direct impact of Proposition 13 has been the generation of widespread tax relief. This conclusion is reinforced by a recent study by Berkeley Planning Associates (1980) that found that in the two years following Proposition 13 cuts have been made in "peripheral" services such as summer schools and recreation, while the level of basic services has remained about the same.

In order to ascertain the pattern of tax relief generated by Proposition 13 it is necessary to determine the changes in tax liabilities faced by individual households. We believe that household data are necessary to carry out this type of analysis precisely because the property tax is such a complex institution. Tax rates are set by literally hundreds of different local governments. Valuation of the tax base is also subject to considerable discretion, and local assessors do not always follow uniform criteria. Additional variations in effective tax rates have been introduced through a variety of tax relief programs targeted to specific demographic groups or tenure classes. Commonly available data on community-wide average tax liabilities are not sufficient to analyze such a complex system.

In essence, Proposition 13 involved a massive change in the structure of the property tax. In order to accurately assess the impacts of this change, it is necessary to model the property tax—with all its complexities—as it existed before the imposition of Proposition 13. In this paper we develop a microsimulation model that allows us to exploit a rich set of household data, and accurately represent the myriad of institutional details that characterize the property tax. Our microsimulation model is an elaborate device that mimics in great detail the working of the property tax system.[5] For example, starting with detailed economic and demographic data for a given household, the microsimulation model allows us to calculate its exact property tax liability by accounting for the nominal tax rate, and the assessment practice faced by that household. Appropriate adjustments in tax liabilities are made if a household is eligible for senior citizen property tax relief programs or homestead exemptions that are available under California law. Our microsimulation model also includes detailed models of both the federal income tax and the California state income tax systems. The model in effect goes through every step that a family would follow in calculating their own income taxes. Thus, it is possible for us to calculate the exact increase in federal income tax liability a family will face when property taxes are decreased. Naturally, only families who own their own houses and itemize deductions will experience a change in federal income taxes through changes in property tax deductions. By using a data sample that is representative of the entire population of California, the model allows us to simulate with a high degree of accuracy the impact of any change in the tax system on the residents of California.

Determining the impact of any tax policy on household tax liabilities is only the first step in analyzing the distributional impact of a tax change. A distinction must be made between the distribution of tax liabilities and tax *incidence*. While liability refers to the actual direct payment of the tax, incidence refers to the ultimate burden of a tax. For example, whereas a landlord is always liable for property taxes levied on his real estate, in many circumstances, it is his tenants who bear all or most of the burden of the tax in the form of higher rents. Under such circumstance the incidence of the property tax on rental property thus falls on the tenant.

Our microsimulation model allows us not only to calculate tax liabilities but to build in various assumptions about the incidence of the property tax. For example, we are able to model the shifting of the property tax from landlords to tenants, and the shifting of property tax on business property from property owners to the consumers of goods produced on the taxed property.

Most previous studies of the property tax or of property tax reform have either used aggregate data or have ignored some important institutional details of the property tax.[6] The detailed model presented in this paper will allow us to disentangle the various elements that play a role in determining the distributional impacts of Proposition 13 and to contrast the pattern of property tax burdens that would have existed in California in 1978 had Proposition 13 not been passed with the actual tax burdens imposed under the provisions of Proposition 13.

This article is divided into five sections. In section II we discuss the incidence assumptions that underlie the model. In section III we briefly describe the property tax system in California and the major elements of our model of that system. We next use the model to analyze the pattern of changes in property tax burdens. In section V we summarize our results and discuss their implications for the tax limitations enacted in other states.

Property Tax Incidence Assumptions

The choosing of appropriate incidence assumptions depends to a large degree on the time period one chooses to analyze. This can best be seen through several examples. The initial impact of a large reduction in property tax rates will be to increase the net income of landlords. However, the resulting higher rate of return on rental property should spur new construction and generate an increased supply of rental units. This increased supply will place a downward pressure on rents and, over time, shift a significant portion of the benefit of the tax reduction to tenants. Another example involves the incidence of a property tax reduction on nonresidential property. The initial impact will be to increase the rate of return to the owners of business property. However, if one allows a sufficient period of time and one assumes that capital is highly responsive to differences in return, the initially higher return to capital within California from the lowered property tax liabilities will induce capital to flow into the state and lower the higher California rate while slightly increasing the rate of return to capital in the rest of the nation.

Our choice of incidence assumptions with which to analyze Proposition 13 is influenced by our belief that the responses of individuals and business firms to a major tax change are likely to be quite slow. This is particularly true with responses involving decisions to move and involving the workings of the housing market. For these reasons, we believe it is important to explicitly study a "transition period" of perhaps ten years following the imposition of a major tax change. This is particularly true in the case of Proposition 13, as the property tax reduction was large ($7 billion in the first year) and policy decisions over the next few years, either by the voters directly or through their elected governments, are likely to be strongly influenced by the currently perceived incidence of the tax change.

The dominant view of economists concerning the incidence of the property tax has changed during the past ten years. The prevailing viewpoint, based primarily on the work of Mieszkowski (1972), is that the property tax should be considered in two parts: the *average* of all locally levied property tax rates, and deviations from the national average. In a reasonably competitive world, with a fixed stock of capital, the incidence of the national average property tax will fall on all owners of capital. This will occur because capital will flow out of the taxed sector (real estate), raising the net rate of return in the taxed sector and lowering it elsewhere. As most capital is owned by high-income people, the incidence of this portion of the property tax is strongly progressive (pro-poor). However, the property tax is not a uniform national tax and the deviations from the national average tax rate will fall on the consumers of housing. Thus, if high income households spend a smaller proportion of their income on housing consumption than the poor, the incidence of this portion of the property tax will be regressive. However, if housing consumption rises proportionately faster than income, the incidence of the deviations will be progressive.[7]

Most tax limitation initiatives, including Proposition 13, involve changes in local tax rates but a relatively minor impact on the national average tax rate. Therefore the incidence of the residential property tax changes on homeowners will fall primarily on the consumers of housing. The distribution of benefits from Proposition 13 to homeowners will thus be distributed in proportion to their tax liabilities prior to the enactment of Proposition 13. Those households paying the most property tax prior to 1978 will receive the greatest direct benefit from Proposition 13.[8]

The passage of Proposition 13 resulted in an immediate reduction in property tax liabilities of approximately $7 billion, split almost evenly between residential and nonresidential property. We will consider, in turn, the incidence of the tax reduction on owner-occupied housing, renter-occupied housing, and on nonresidential real estate.

OWNER-OCCUPIED HOUSING

The distribution of homeowners' tax reductions depends on the property tax liability faced by each household prior to the enactment of Proposition 13 and on the year in which their current house was purchased.[9] Proposition 13 requires that houses be assessed for tax purposes at 25 percent of their 1975 market value, plus 2 percent per year, unless they are sold. Whenever a house is sold its assessed value changes to 25 percent of the sales price and is incremented at 2 percent per year until its next sale. This provision can produce a substantial variation in tax liabilities depending on the frequency of sale. For example, consider two identical houses, one purchased for $50,000 in 1975 and the other purchased for $100,000 in 1978.[10] Without Proposition 13, both owners would have faced identical tax bills, but with Proposition 13 the 1978 tax liabilities, excluding the homestead exemption, would be $530.60 and $1,000 respectively. Tying the increase in assessed value to resale implies a systematic increase in effective tax rate differentials between frequent and infrequent movers. Though it has been little noticed, this reassessment rule may discriminate against the poor over time. Since the rate of price appreciation often tends to be lower for low-value properties (Peterson et al., 1973), during the period between sales this provision may raise the effective tax rates faced by the poor owner relative to the rest of the population.

Proposition 13 provides homeowners in California with tax savings from a reduced tax rate (to 1 percent) and a reduced assessed value. The second savings resides with the current owner and cannot be passed on to a new owner, who must pay property taxes on the basis of an assessed value determined by his purchase price.[11] To the extent that reductions in tax liabilities resulting from Proposition 13 are capitalized in housing prices, those people owning houses in California when Proposition 13 was passed will receive a capital gain equal to the discounted value of the tax rate savings plus the buyer's willingness to pay for the 2 percent annual limitation on future increases in assessed value.

The above discussion overstates the homeowner tax relief generated by Proposition 13. The deductibility of property taxes in calculating both federal and state taxable income implies that the reduced level of property taxation will increase many homeowners' federal and state income tax liabilities. Our simulation model will explicitly account for the interaction between the property tax and state and federal income taxes.

RENTER-OCCUPIED HOUSING

Economists generally assume that tenants bear a substantial portion of the burden of the tax rate differentials within a state and between that state and the rest of the nation, with the owners of capital bearing the remaining part.[12] However, renters bearing part of the burden of the property tax does not imply that they will reap the benefits of the tax reduction brought about by Proposition 13. The immediate impact of Proposition 13 is to reduce the tax liability of landlords. The extent to which lower taxes will be passed on to tenants depends on the response of both the demand and the supply of rental housing to rent levels and to the rate of return on rental housing. In the short run, it is unlikely that rents will be dramatically reduced. This is particularly true in light of evidence of excess demand for rental housing in many parts of California. The slower the supply response in the rental housing market, the longer the period until renters will share any benefit from Proposition 13.

The direct impact of Proposition 13 is to increase the rate of return on rental housing. This should increase the incentive for developers to build rental units. However, Proposition 13 tends indirectly to discourage the building of new rental units and increases the cost of those that are built. By mandating a maximum 1 percent tax rate, Proposition 13 places a ceiling on the property tax revenue that can be raised from a new rental housing development. The resultant increase in the cost-revenue ratio for new development should decrease the incentive for local governments to permit new rental units. Even in the absence of stringent property tax limitations, most local governments perceive, perhaps incorrectly, that new rental development increase their financial burdens by more than the new developments generate in new tax revenues. The increased fiscal burdens are generated either through the requirements of new infrastructure, e.g., new schools, or through higher municipal operating costs. These perceptions often lead local governments to prohibit new developments by using available zoning and land use controls, or alternatively, local governments require developers to increase the price of rental units by requiring them to provide more public infrastructure or by adding new development fees. Misczynski (1981) reports that a number of cities conducted cost-revenue studies on development projects after the enactment of Proposition 13. The conclusion of all these studies was that "new development was a net fiscal loser." Local government's response to this perception has been to raise hurdles in the way of development and in effect make the supply of new rental units considerably more inelastic. This suggests that a substantial portion of the Proposition 13 induced property tax reductions will remain with landlords.[13]

The rule that increases assessments by only 2 percent per year unless a property is sold may both favor and discriminate against the poor. Insofar as rental properties sell less frequently than owner-occupied properties, renters, who are more likely to be poor, will benefit. However, if high-value rental properties appreciate more rapidly than low-value properties, then the effective tax rates of poor renters will increase relative to the rates faced by higher-income renters.

NONRESIDENTIAL PROPERTY

As the focus of our analysis is on California residents, we must determine the extent to which property tax reductions on nonresidential property accrue to owners of California business property, are shifted forward to consumers in the form of lower product prices, backward to factors of production, or are exported to non-California residents.

The initial impact of reduced property tax rates will be reflected in higher business profits.[14] The extent to which these higher profits are translated into lower consumer prices depends on several factors. Lower product prices are more likely if a product market is local, i.e., within-state, rather than national. For a product produced for a competitive national market, increased production within California is unlikely to be sufficient to substantially affect product prices. For products produced for a national market, where California's production tends to dominate the market, lower taxes may reduce costs sufficiently to lower product prices. Kimbel, Shih, and Shulman (1979) suggest that such an excise tax effect may occur for some specialized agricultural products such as artichokes. Finally, the shifting of reduced property taxes to consumers depends on the market structure within each industry. The reduction in property taxes will increase profits; the greater the degree of monopoly power, the less forward shifting of these profits to consumers is to be expected.[15]

A significant portion of the benefit from the reduction of nonresidential property taxes accrues directly to non-Californians, either in their role as owners of California businesses, or consumers of California-produced products. Furthermore, the higher profits attributed to Proposition 13 result in increased federal corporate and personal income tax liabilities for Californians.[16] In other words, a significant portion of the seven billion dollar tax reduction generated by Proposition 13 will be "exported" to residents in other states. The literature on interstate tax exporting is lean. The most recent comprehensive study of exporting was carried out by Charles McLure (1967).[17] Following McLure's general strategy (although not all his exact shifting assumptions), we estimate the proportion of nonresidential property tax reductions exported from California.[18]

Within California, the reduction of taxes on nonresidential property that is passed back to consumers in the form of lower prices is allocated to California households in proportion to their estimated consumption expenditures. The increase in business profits accruing to California residents as a result of Proposition 13 is allocated to households in proportion to an estimate of their capital and rental income.

Modeling the Property Tax System

In this section we describe the property tax system in California as it existed prior to the imposition of Proposition 13 and then briefly describe the methodology we employed to model this system. Although the variation in tax rates across jurisdictions is smaller in

California than in many other states, 12½ percent of California families lived in communities with effective rates of less than 2 percent, while nearly 20 percent faced effective rates of over 3 percent.[19] By law, all real property in California is supposed to be assessed at 25 percent of market value. Despite the generally high quality of assessments in California, State Equalization Board officials admit to some systematic regressivity in assessment ratios. This results primarily from generally higher rates of appreciation in higher-value homes coupled with built-in lags in the assessment process. This feature of the property tax results in lower effective tax rates for high-valued houses within a given community.

The California legislature has enacted several provisions designed to reduce residential tax burdens. Since 1972 each homeowner is eligible for a $1,750 homestead exemption. This implies that the assessed value on which each homeowner's tax is levied is reduced by the amount of the exemption. Renters are eligible for a state income tax credit of $37. California was also one of the first states to enact "circuit breaker" legislation to aid both senior citizen homeowners and renters.[20]

We have constructed a microsimulation model of the property tax system that incorporates interjurisdictional variations in tax rates, current assessment practices, the homestead exemption and circuit breakers discussed above, and the shifting and exporting assumptions discussed in the previous section. The data base for the microsimulation model is the California subsample of the 1975 Survey of Income and Education (SIE), a national survey of 200,000 households conducted by the U.S. Census Bureau. The California sample is composed of 4,205 households containing 5,400 families. The survey includes detailed demographic, income and occupational data on each family, location information, and data on rents and housing values. The SIE identified thirteen separate SMSAs in California. Of these thirteen, households in the six largest, comprising 80 percent of the metropolitan population of the state, are identified by suburban or central city location.

The SIE contains no data on property taxes. Thus, in order to calculate tax liabilities, each household was assigned the property tax rate appropriate to its location.[21] Simulated property tax liabilities (though not the final incidence), are computed by multiplying the assigned nominal tax rate by the assessed value of each house. For renters, the appropriate assessed value is obtained by capitalizing gross rents paid, using a gross rent multiplier assumed to vary positively with the level of rent.[22] Average assessed values are derived from a special survey conducted in 1976 by the State Board of Equalization. Assessment-sales price ratios are allowed to vary by county of residence and (inversely) to the value of the property, with the most expensive houses being assigned ratios a maximum of 20 percent below the county average assessment-sales ratio. Property tax liabilities are computed net of the relevant renters' credit, homeowner exemptions, and senior citizen assistance program. The residential property tax module was validated by comparing the simulated totals to the actual property tax collections for owner- and renter-occupied property.

The actual incidence of the property tax obviously depends on a number of shifting assumptions. The property tax module is constructed so as to allow us to test alternative assumptions concerning the shifting of the property tax burden between landlords and tenants, and between consumers and the owners of capital. The ultimate incidence of the property tax depends also on its interaction with state and federal income taxes. In order to take account of the deductibility of property tax payments from state and federal income taxes, we link our microsimulation model of the property tax system to detailed models of the state and federal income tax systems.[23]

Finally, in order to simulate the impact of Proposition 13, the 1975 SIE data base is aged to 1978 values, using standard demographic and economic aging techniques and actual 1978 property tax rates. The pre-Proposition 13 case is simulated by calculating the tax liabilities that would have existed in 1978 had Proposition 13 *not* been passed. To calculate 1978 post-Proposition liabilities, new tax rates and new assessed values had to be assigned to each household. To allow for the financing of existing debt service, effective tax rates in 1978 were slightly in excess of the 1 percent statutory limit. In order to assign assessed values it was necessary to determine the frequency of sales of residential real estate. Accurate data on sales frequency is not available. However, based on 1970 U.S. Census data for California SMSAs, Wallace Smith suggests an 8 percent annual turnover rate, implying on average a move every 12½ years.[24] Based on data from the Census Bureau's 1977 Annual Housing Survey (1979), and from several sources within California, we assumed that the probability of sale increased each year until a house was sold, and that frequency of sale is substantially lower for elderly than for younger homeowners and for rental units as compared to owner-occupied units. Those housing units that did not change ownership between 1975 and 1978 were assigned their 1975 assessed values inflated at a rate of 2 percent a year.

In order to analyze the distributional impact of Proposition 13, we employ two analytical approaches. First, we compare conditions in California in 1978 following the imposition of Proposition 13 with conditions that would have existed in California had no tax limitations been enacted. This approach emphasizes the impact of the changes that occurred because of Proposition 13. It is, however, highly unlikely that in the absence of Proposition 13 California would not have limited taxation in some alternative way. Our second approach is thus to compare the $7 billion property tax reduction resulting from Proposition 13 with an equal dollar tax reduction generated by a cut in a mix of alternative tax instruments. By comparing two equal sized tax cuts we were able to carry out what economists refer to as a differential tax incidence study. As our alternative tax cut, we have chosen the specific cuts that we believe the legislature would have been most likely to enact had Proposition 13 not been approved by the voters of California. Our alternative tax cut included a 20 percent reduction in *residential* property taxes, a 1½ percentage point cut in sales taxes, cuts in miscellaneous excise taxes, and nearly 50 percent cuts in both corporate and personal income taxes.

The Impact of Proposition 13: Results

In this section we present our simulations of the incidence of Proposition 13. The emphasis will be on results reflecting what we believe to be the most plausible set of assumptions about shifting of tax reductions among California residents and exporting to non-California residents.

The set of assumptions used in our basic simulation reflect the view of the property tax outlined in the previous sections. That view has two central tenets: first, that inter- and intrajurisdictional differences in tax rates are largely shifted forward to the consumers of housing; second, that the local economy reacts with considerable sluggishness in attaining a new long-run equilibrium after an abrupt tax change such as Proposition 13. The forward shifting assumption implies that the incidence of the change in taxes in owner-occupied residential property is equal to the change in tax liabilities. To characterize the slow economic response, the following assumptions are made: in the residential sector, 80 percent of the reduction in tax liabilities on recent property is allocated to landlords, while only 20 percent is rebated to tenants. The asymmetry of response between the equilibrium situation and the transitional period is reflected in the assumption that, prior to Proposition 13, 75 percent of the tax on rental property is shifted forward to tenants. In allocating the reduction in taxes on business, 63 percent is assumed to be retained by firms in the form of higher profits, while 37 percent is shifted forward to consumers through price reductions. To distribute the business tax reduction to California owners and consumers, 38 percent of the nonshifted portion is assumed to accrue to the owners of capital in California, while 76 percent of the price reduction is realized by California residents in their capacity as consumers; 41 percent of the aggregate tax reduction accruing to landlords is exported from California.

Table 1 summarizes the aggregate tax reductions resulting from Proposition 13. The reductions generated by our model correspond closely with estimates made by the California State Equalization Board and Franchise Tax Board. Gross property tax liabilities on owner-occupied housing units were reduced by nearly two and one-half billion dollars, or by 49 percent of their pre-Proposition 13 level. Proposition 13 resulted in proportionately greater reductions in homestead exemptions and senior citizen assistance, slightly reducing the *net* amount of homeowner property tax relief. This reduction in homeowner property tax relief was partially offset by an increase of $401 million in federal income tax liabilities, and $93 million in state income tax liabilities. These increases result from lowered itemized deductions for homeowners who choose to itemize. Adjusting for those federal and state income tax offsets, Proposition 13 resulted in a 35 percent reduction in homeowner property taxes.

Tax liabilities on renter-occupied housing units were reduced by 65 percent. Following our standard assumptions, nearly 50 percent of this aggregate reduction accrued to Californians who are owners of rental property. Only 20 percent of the total, or $300 million, was returned to renters, while the remaining portion was exported to non-California owners of rental property. Of the total $3.44 billion reduction in nonresidential property taxes because of Proposition 13, 48 percent is exported to non-California residents, 24 percent accrues to Californians in their role as owners of businesses, and 29 percent benefits California consumers.

In order to analyze the distributional impacts of these tax reductions we have divided our sample into thirteen income classes.[25] California is a relatively high-income state. In 1979 median income was $22,249, compared to a nationwide median of $20,022. Although in 1978 slightly more than a quarter of California households had incomes below $10,000, and approximately the same number had incomes between $10,000 and $20,000, nearly 40 percent of the households had incomes between $20,000 and $50,000 per year.

As our simulation results will demonstrate, the final distributional impact of Proposition 13 is a result of the interaction of several

TABLE 1
PROPERTY TAX REDUCTIONS DUE TO PROPOSITION 13

	1978 Pre-Proposition 13	Changes Due to Proposition 13	% Changes Due to Proposition 13
Gross Residential Property Tax	$7,408,286,000	−$3,983,002,000	− 53.8
Gross Property Tax: Owner-Occupied Units	5,114,776,000	− 2,496,422,000	− 48.8
Homestead Exemption	868,875,000	− 501,974,000	− 57.8
Homeowner Senior Citizen Assistance	61,242,000	− 39,061,000	− 63.8
Net Property Tax: Owner-Occupied Units	4,184,659,000	− 1,955,386,000	− 46.7
Federal Income Tax and offset against Lower Homeowner Taxes	25,980,932,000	+ 401,495,000	+ 1.5
State Income Tax and Offset against Lower Homeowner Taxes	5,120,602,000	+ 92,946,000	+ 1.8
Gross Property Tax: Renter-Occupied Units	2,296,208,000	− 1,489,229,000	− 64.8
Renter Senior Citizen Assistance	4,621,000	0	− 0.0
Net Property Tax: Renter-Occupied Units	2,291,587,000	− 1,489,229,000	− 65.0
Property Tax Allocated to Tenants	1,717,535,000	− 297,845,000	− 17.3
Property Tax Allocated to Landlords	338,690,000	− 702,916,000	− 207.5
Reduction in Business Property Tax		3,440,000,000	
Retained by Business Firms (63%)		2,167,000,000	
Allocated to California Residents (38%)		814,276,000	
Shifted to Consumers in Form of Lower Prices (37%)		1,273,000,000	
Allocated to California Residents (76%)		983,736,000	
State and Federal Income Tax Offset against Higher Business Taxes		369,848,000	

Source: Model-simulated totals

factors. In order to fully understand the reasons for the results, and to help disentangle a number of these factors, it is important first to look separately at the impact of Proposition 13 on homeowners, on tenants, on landlords, and on owners of nonresidential property. This is accomplished in tables 2, 3, and 4. Each of the tables presents average tax changes for all households in each income class–table 2 for the residential property tax, table 3 for the nonresidential property tax, and table 4 for property tax changes.

As would be expected, the dollar amounts of the Proposition 13 generated tax reductions for both owners and renters increases with income. Because housing consumption increases with income, total property tax payments prior to Proposition 13 were higher for higher-income households. Tax rate reductions thus tend to generate tax cuts in rough proportion to prior levels of taxation. Because tenants are assumed to receive only 20 percent of the tax reductions on their housing units, tenant tax cuts are quite small relative to the average homeowner tax cut. The average tenant tax cut is $83, while the average homeowner tax reduction is $434. Although these dollar amounts are important, the distribution of absolute tax cuts tells us little about how fairly these cuts affect households with different levels of income. Data on the *percentage* reductions in property taxes provide a much clearer picture of relative tax cuts received across income classes. For homeowners, the largest percentage tax cuts accrued to the poorest households–those with incomes below $6,000. Although the differences across income classes are not very large, the average tax cut was 47 percent, and the percentage cuts decline slightly as income rises to about $20,000. The percentage tax reduction for homeowners is fairly constant for all incomes above $20,000. The majority of all California homeowners (63 percent) have incomes within this higher income range.

For renters, the pattern of percentage property tax reductions is extraordinarily stable across income classes. Except for the poorest renters with incomes below $4,000, most tenants, regardless of income, benefited from an approximately 19 percent cut in property taxes.

The impact of Proposition 13 on the portion of the residential property tax borne by consumers of housing can be summarized by adding together the impacts on homeowners and renters. The effect of Proposition 13 on landlords will be considered separately. In order to understand the pattern of residential tax changes it is necessary to pay close attention to the tenure status across income classes. As is expected, the lower incomes are dominated by renters, while the higher incomes are the almost exclusive domain of owners. Nearly 65 percent of renters in California have incomes below $15,000,

TABLE 2

CHANGES IN THE RESIDENTIAL PROPERTY TAX RESULTING FROM PROPOSITION 13

Household Income	Average Change in Homeowner Property Taxes		Average Change in Renter Property Taxes		Average Change in Residential Property Taxes		Income Tax Offset against Property Tax	Average Percentage Change in Property Tax Net of Income Tax Offset: Homeowner	Average Percentage Change in Property Tax Net of Income Tax Offset: Residential
$2,000-3,999	$– 220	– 53%	$– 50	– 24%	$– 93	– 31%	$ 0	– 53%	– 31%
4,000-5,999	– 268	– 56	– 62	– 20	127	– 31	0	– 56	– 31
6,000-7,999	– 293	– 51	– 70	– 19	–159	– 32	0	– 51	– 32
8,000-9,999	– 315	– 54	– 67	– 19	–167	– 33	1	– 54	– 33
10,000-11,999	– 416	– 55	– 72	– 19	–184	– 30	4	– 53	– 30
12,000-14,999	– 403	– 52	– 81	– 19	–204	– 31	6	– 50	– 30
15,000-19,999	– 417	– 48	– 88	– 18	–273	– 35	23	– 45	– 33
20,000-24,999	– 414	– 44	– 96	– 17	–296	– 34	46	– 37	– 29
25,000-34,999	– 443	– 44	–118	– 18	–363	– 38	88	– 33	– 29
35,000-49,999	– 527	– 42	–161	– 18	–471	– 38	174	– 26	– 25
50,000-99,999	– 595	– 40	–178	– 18	–545	– 37	269	20	– 20
More than 100,000	–1062	– 45	–365	– 17	–975	– 41	675	– 12	– 13
Average	– 434	– 47	– 83	– 19	–278	– 34	58	– 38	– 29

TABLE 3

CHANGES IN THE NONRESIDENTIAL PROPERTY TAX RESULTING FROM PROPOSITION 13

Household Income	Average Tax Change Allocated to Business Owners	Average Tax Change Allocated to Consumers	Average Residential Tax Changes Allocated to Landlords	Income Tax Offset against Changes in Column 1 and 3
$2,000-3,999	$– 2	$– 30	$– 1	$ 0
4,000-5,999	– 10	– 38	– 6	0
6,000-7,999	– 18	– 48	– 13	1
8,000-9,999	– 27	– 58	– 23	3
10,000-11,999	– 17	– 68	– 14	3
12,000-14,999	– 24	– 81	– 18	5
15,000-19,999	– 53	– 102	– 45	14
20,000-24,999	– 65	– 126	– 54	19
25,000-34,999	– 108	– 126	– 95	33
35,000-49,999	– 187	– 221	– 178	79
50,000-99,999	– 614	– 338	– 514	261
More than 100,000	– 2,170	– 674	– 1,730	1,464
Average	– 100	– 121	– 86	39

TABLE 4

TOTAL PROPERTY TAX CHANGES RESULTING FROM PROPOSITION 13

Household Income	Average Total Change in Property Taxes	Average Change in Property Tax Burden	Total Income Tax Offset against Property Tax	Average Change in Property Tax Net of Offset	Average Change in Property Tax Burden Net of Offset
$2,000-3,999	$– 126	– 3.8%	$ 0	$– 126	– 3.8%
4,000-5,999	– 180	– 3.6	0	– 180	– 3.6
6,000-7,999	– 239	– 3.4	1	– 238	– 3.4
8,000-9,999	– 276	– 3.1	4	– 273	– 3.0
10,000-11,999	– 273	– 2.6	7	– 276	– 2.5
12,000-14,999	– 328	– 2.4	11	– 317	– 2.4
15,000-19,999	– 472	– 2.7	37	– 435	– 2.5
20,000-24,999	– 541	– 2.4	66	– 475	– 2.2
25,000-34,999	– 727	– 2.5	122	– 605	– 2.1
35,000-49,999	– 1,055	– 2.6	251	– 804	– 2.0
50,000-99,999	– 2,012	– 3.1	532	– 1,480	– 2.3
More than 100,000	– 5,550	– 3.9	2,139	– 3,411	– 2.4
Average	– 585	– 2.9	97	– 488	– 2.6

while less than 25 percent of all homeowning households have incomes below this level. This tenure pattern across income classes explains the pattern that we observe in the sixth column of Table 2—a constant percentage reduction in residential property taxes for households with incomes below $15,000, and a gradually *increasing* percentage reduction as income rises above $15,000.

The above results ignore the deductibility of property taxes from federal and state income taxes. Deductibility implies that a decrease in property tax rates will be partially offset by an increase in federal and state income tax liabilities. These income tax offsets will be greater than zero only for owners who itemize their deductions, and it will increase as the marginal tax rate increases. Therefore the percentage of the tax recaptured by the federal and state governments should be a positive function of income. Our simulation shows an increase in federal income tax liabilities for homeowners of $401 million, which is approximately 20 percent of the total net tax reduction received by homeowners as a result of Proposition 13. This amount implies an average marginal tax rate of 34 percent for the 41 percent of the filing units that itemized their deductions. In addition, state income tax liabilities of homeowners were increased by $94 million. As demonstrated by data presented in table 2, the income tax offset is heavily weighted toward high-income households. This implies that once we offset the lower property taxes by higher income taxes, the net tax cuts become more neutral across income classes. As the data in the last column of table 2 demonstrate, net residential property tax reductions vary only slightly across income classes.

FIGURE 1

The Suits Index of Tax Progressivity

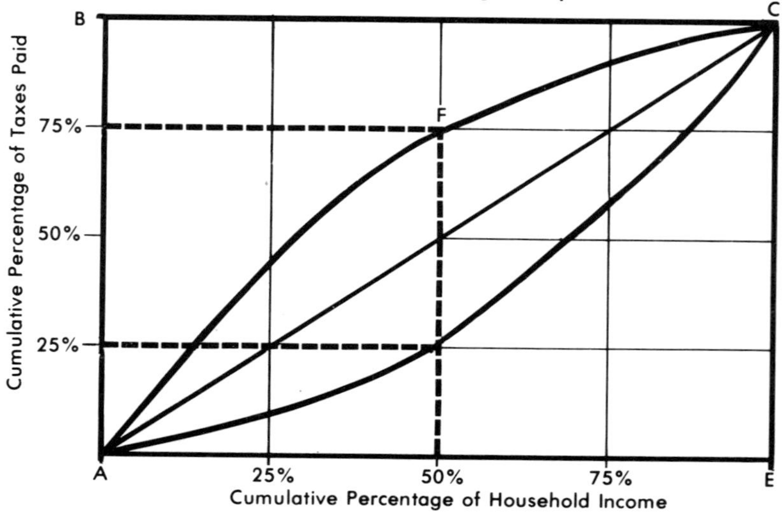

Table 3 displays our simulation results of the impact of Proposition 13 on households in their capacity as owners of rental property and business, and as consumers of products whose prices are affected by the reduction in nonresidential property taxes. Nonresidential tax cuts are shown in columns 1 and 2 of table 3, while the impact on landlords is shown in column 3. The table indicates that increases in both capital income and rental incomes flow primarily to high-income households. In fact, 61 percent of the total nonresidential tax reductions allocated to the owners of business went to households with incomes greater than $30,000 and 79 percent went to households with incomes of $25,000. Likewise, 62 percent of the total tax reductions going to California landlords went to households with income in excess of $30,000, and 80 percent went to households with incomes greater than $25,000. This pro-rich pattern is at least partially offset by an increase in federal taxes on the extra income realized by California capitalists and landlords. This offset is shown in column 4 of table 3.

The overall impact of Proposition 13 can be determined by adding the component tax changes. This is accomplished in Column 1 of table 4. To interpret these total changes it is useful to divide them by household income, which is done in the second column of table 4. These numbers can be interpreted as changes in tax burdens. Proposition 13 has resulted in an average reduction in tax burden of 2.9 percentage points. A U-shaped pattern emerges. Reductions in property tax burdens are largest for both low-income and high-income households, and smallest for households with incomes between $12,000 and $25,000. It is perhaps ironic that the smallest declines in property tax burden went to the strongest champions of Proposition 13, the middle-income households.[26]

In calculating the net impact of Proposition 13 it is necessary not only to account for higher income taxes because of lower residental property tax deductions, but also higher income taxes because of the higher business and landlord incomes generated directly by Proposition 13. The last column of table 4 displays the changes in property tax burdens net of this total income tax offset. The pattern is still U-shaped, but the smallest declines in burden are extended up the income distribution, and now include households with incomes between $20,000 and $50,000.

The data in the previous tables show how different income classes are treated under Proposition 13, but they do not provide a good summary measure of its impact. It is possible to summarize the overall impact of Proposition 13 as pro-poor or pro-rich? Several statistics do exist that allow us to summarize distributional impacts. One measure of the incidence of a given level of taxation is the

Suits Index of Tax Progressivity developed by Daniel Suits (1977). The Suits index is similar to the well-known Gini coefficient, except that it compares a cumulative probability distribution of tax liabilities with a similar distribution of household income. In figure 1, the curves ADC and AFC, known as Lorenz curves, show the cumulative percent of taxes paid for a given cumulative percent of income. Curve AFC represents a more regressive tax than ADC. For example, for the tax represented by AFC, 75 percent of the tax is paid by households with the lowest 50 percent of income, while for curve ADC this group pays only 25 percent of the tax. The Suits Index is equal to the area between the Lorenz curve and the diagonal, divided by the area of the triangle AEC. If the Lorenz curve coincides with the diagonal, then the Suits Index is zero, indicating a proportional tax. If the Lorenz curve is above the diagonal, the Suits Index takes on negative values, and the tax is regressive. The index has a range from –1 to +1 with positive numbers indicating progressivity.

We have calculated a Suits Index for *residential* property taxes both pre- and post-Proposition 13, and with and without the income tax offset. These indices will allow us to summarize the collective impact on homeowners, tenants, and landlords of the Proposition 13 residential property tax cut. The Suits Index without the property tax offset falls from –.170 to –.307, implying that the poor end up paying a greater share of the remaining residential property tax as a result of Proposition 13. This result occurs because homeowners receive much greater tax reductions than do renters, and homeowners are concentrated in the income classes above \$20,000. The tax reduction on rental property also favors the rich because 80 percent of the decrease is distributed to landlords, who are heavily concentrated in the upper income classes. Taking into account the income tax offsets against residential property taxes, the Suits Index falls to –.226 as a result of Proposition 13. This still implies a movement toward greater regressivity of the residential property tax. However, since the income tax offsets have only a trivial impact on households with incomes below \$15,000, and large impacts on high-income households, the post-Proposition 13 property tax is less regressive than it would be in the absence of the state and federal income tax offsets.

The previous discussion refers solely to the pre- and post-Proposition 13 distribution of tax burdens of the residential property tax. In order to summarize the impact of changes in total property tax liabilities, we have constructed an index of the Distribution of Change (DOC), which addresses the question of how a reduction in taxes is distributed to different income groups. It compares the cumulative probability distribution of the total *changes* in property taxes (residential plus business) with a cumulative probability distribution of income. As with the Suites Index, the range of the DOC index is from –1 to +1. However, because the overall change in taxes was negative, negative values indicate that, relative to their share of total income, the poor realize a greater proportion of the tax reduction than the rich.[27]

The value of the DOC index when we do not consider income tax offsets is .006, implying that Proposition 13, under our incidence assumptions, has distributed total property tax reductions close to proportionately across income classes. This value represents the sum of several components of the tax cut, each with a different incidence pattern. By decomposing the DOC we can determine the distribution of each portion of the tax cut. The DOC of the portion of the residential tax cut realized by owners and renters is equal to –.168, indicating that the poor realize a greater proportion of the tax cut than the rich. However, when we add the landlord benefit the DOC becomes –.056. If the portion of the nonresidential property tax reduction distributed to owners of business is included, the DOC becomes .022, while inclusion of the price reduction to consumers changes the DOC to .006. This decomposition reveals that the portion of the tax cut realized by consumers of both housing and other consumption products tends to benefit the poor, while that realized by owners of capital and landlords is heavily weighted toward the rich. These offsetting factors produce a value for the final index marginally above zero, indicating that the tax cuts are slightly more beneficial to the rich.

Finally, we can calculate the DOC index after accounting for offsets in state and federal income taxes resulting from lower itemized property tax reductions and the higher levels of landlord and capital income generated by Proposition 13. The value of the index with full income tax offsets is –.066, implying that relative to their incomes, the net impact of Proposition 13 gives the poor a slightly greater share of the net tax reduction than the rich.

We can summarize our simulation results as indicating that the imposition of Proposition 13 as compared with a world where no tax limitations occurred results in a property tax system (without income tax offsets) that is substantially more regressive. This is the case even though the distribution of the property tax reduction is proportional to income. The poor benefit from a reduced reliance on a regressive tax. However, the reductions are made in such a way that the poor's share of the remaining property tax goes up rather than down. Many of the very wealthy receive large benefits from Proposition 13, while the middle class receive the smallest benefits relative to their income of any group.

It is important to ask how sensitive these results are to the incidence and tax-shifting assumption outlined in previous sections. To answer this question, we have simulated the impact of Proposition 13 under alternative assumptions about the extent to which the residential tax cut is rebated to renters, and the business tax is shifted forward to consumers. As an alternative assumption, we have chosen 75 percent as the proportion of the Proposition 13 induced property tax cut that is passed back to tenants. This is equal to the prereform percentage of property tax borne by renters, and may best be thought of as the long-run equilibrium situation after Proposition 13. We have also assumed that the proportion of nonresidential property tax cuts shifted to consumers in the form of lower prices increases from 37 percent to 64 percent. Again this is consistent with a longer-run, more competitive situation.

The results of a simulation of Proposition 13 under these long-run assumptions reverse the previous results. Ignoring income tax offsets, the changes in tax burdens induced by Proposition 13 now favor the poor, and the residential property tax becomes *less* regressive. Under these long-run assumptions, the Suits Index declines from –.170 to –.126, implying a movement in the direction of progressivity of residential property taxes. The DOC index moves from .006 under our basic assumptions, to –.132, indicating that in the very long run the poor will share proportionately more in the overall tax reductions resulting from Proposition 13.

Extra caution must be taken in interpreting these long-run results. Over time Proposition 13 will have a growing impact on mobility. As long as housing price inflation exceeds 2 percent per year, a household's effective property tax rate declines with each passing year. This has two consequences; first, it provides an incentive not to move and, second, it greatly increases the horizontal inequities between frequent and infrequent movers. The latter implies that two otherwise equal households will face dramatically different effective property tax rates, if one household is a frequent mover.

As a preliminary test of the sensitivity of our distributional results to the rate of population mobility, we have reduced the average rate of residential mobility by 50 percent. This alternative mobility assumption increases the initial reduction in residential property taxes by $225 million, an amount that is 7 percent greater than the tax reduction implied by our standard mobility assumptions. Although reducing everyone's housing turnover has a substantial negative impact on property tax revenue, this reduced mobility will not by itself be detrimental to the poor. However, if the poor homeowner moves more frequently than the average household, over time the impact of Proposition 13 will be to substantially increase both the average effective tax rate faced by the poor, and the proposition of total property taxes levied on them. No firm evidence currently exists on the impact of Proposition 13 on mobility rates by income class. However, evidence does exist that business properties change hands much less frequently than residential properties. This implies that over time, a much larger share of total property taxes will come from residential taxes. This shift in the source of property tax revenues will tend to benefit higher-income residents. The general issue of the long-run impact of Proposition 13 on mobility patterns will be addressed in future simulation work with this model. (See Chernick and Reschovsky, 1982).

PROPOSITION 13 COMPARED TO AN ALTERNATIVE TAX CUT

Although it is enlightening to compare Proposition 13 with a situation characterized by the absence of tax cuts, our understanding of Proposition 13 can be considerably enhanced by comparing it with an alternative tax cut of an equal magnitude. Our alternative tax cut consists of gross cuts of $1.5 billion in residential property taxes, $1.9 billion in sales and excise taxes, $1 billion in corporate income taxes, and $2.5 billion in personal income taxes, for a total of $6.9 billion. Because a larger share of the Proposition 13 tax cut is exported out of state, the tax reduction directly benefiting California residents is approximately $650 million larger under the alternative tax cut than under Proposition 13. Table 5 summarizes the impact of the alternative tax cut and compares it with the impact of Proposition 13.

Column 1 of table 5 shows the average tax reduction by income class under the alternative tax cut. Column 2 displays these tax reductions as a proportion of household income. Except for the lowest income classes, households with incomes below $15,000 experience average tax cuts equal to slightly over 2 percent of their income. Tax reductions as a proportion of income increase mildly for those with incomes from $15,000 to $25,000, and increase quite dramatically for households with incomes greater than $25,000. This pattern can be understood by looking at the distribution of the tax reductions of the individual taxes that make up our alternative tax cut package. Although the reductions in both residential property taxes and sales and excise taxes decline as a proportion of income as income rises, this is more than offset by

TABLE 5

PROPOSITION 13 TAX REDUCTIONS COMPARED WITH ALTERNATIVE TAX CUT

Household Income	Alternative Tax Cut		Differences between Proposition 13 and Alternative		
	Average Total Change in Taxes	Average Change in Tax Burden (% points)	Absolute Differences in Tax Cuts	Differences As a Percentage of Proposition 13 Cut	Absolute Differences As a Percentage of Income
$2,000-3,999	$– 89	– 2.64%	$ 37	29%	1.16%
4,000-5,999	– 104	– 2.07	76	42	1.57
6,000-7,999	– 152	– 2.18	87	36	1.25
8,000-9,999	– 186	– 2.06	90	– 33	1.00
10,000-11,999	– 223	– 2.04	60	– 21	.55
12,000-14,999	– 279	– 2.07	47	– 14	.36
15,000-19,999	– 412	– 2.36	54	– 11	.32
20,000-24,999	– 537	– 2.41	– 9	– 2	– .04
25,000-34,999	– 832	– 2.81	– 130	– 18	– .41
35,000-49,999	– 1,381	– 3.35	– 380	– 36	– .90
50,000-99,999	– 3,125	– 4.81	– 1,211	– 60	– 1.87
More than 100,000	– 7,291	– 5.42	– 2,057	– 37	– 1.75
Average	– 666	– 2.56	– 99	– 17	– .13

the reductions in corporate and personal income taxes, where the reductions are progressive with respect to income. For example, for all households with incomes below $20,000, personal income tax cuts average less than $100. However, above $20,000 the size of the average tax reduction increases rapidly; the average income tax reduction for households with incomes between $35,000 and $50,000 is $725, while for those with incomes above $50,000 the average tax reduction is well in excess of $2,000.[28]

The last three columns of table 5 compare the tax cuts resulting from Proposition 13 with the tax cuts resulting from the alternative tax cuts. Positive numbers imply that the Proposition 13 cuts are greater than the alternative cuts, while negative numbers imply that the Proposition 13 cuts are smaller. A clear pattern emerges. Proposition 13 generates larger tax cuts for low-income households, but smaller cuts for high-income households when compared with the alternative tax cut package. In fact, the breakeven income—the income level where both tax limitations yield equal cuts—is higher than may be apparent from a first look at the data. Because of a smaller degree of tax exporting under the alternative tax cuts, the average household receives a $167 larger tax reduction under the alternative. This implies that, on average, households with incomes below $25,000 would benefit more from Proposition 13 than under the alternative tax cut. That households with incomes as high as $20,000 receive larger absolute reductions under Proposition 13 emphasizes the substantially different income class incidence of the two types of tax cuts. It should also be noted that households with higher incomes, especially those with incomes over $35,000, receive substantially greater benefit from the alternative tax cut.

We thus conclude that relative to an alternative tax cut that may well have been instituted in California had Proposition 13 not passed, Proposition 13 appears quite favorable to lower-income households. The importance one places on this result obviously depends on the reader's judgment as to the likelihood of our alternative tax cut occurring had Proposition 13 not been approved. Other tax cuts, relying less heavily on income tax reductions, would reduce the pro-poor bias of Proposition 13 demonstrated in our results.

Conclusions

In this paper we have used a detailed microsimulation model of the property tax system and the state and federal income tax systems to study the income distributional consequences of Proposition 13. Our model allows us to mimic accurately the complexities and the interactions that characterize these tax systems. Primarily because state revenues largely replaced lost property tax revenues, public services cuts in California have been relatively small. The major impact of Proposition 13 has thus taken the form of reduced property tax burdens. When compared with a situation of no tax limitations, the overall impact of Proposition 13 has slightly favored high-income households in California. Both the residential and non-residential portions of the property tax provide somewhat higher benefits to high-income households. However, because property taxes are deductible from state and federal income taxes, and income tax liabilities rise as landlord and business incomes grow, the property tax cuts are partially offset by higher income taxes. As these offsets rise with income, the net impact of Proposition 13 slightly favored lower-income households.

When Proposition 13 is compared with an equal sized alternative tax cut that includes cuts in sales and excise taxes, in both corporate and personal income taxes, and a small cut in residential property taxes, the Proposition 13 cuts are shown to be considerably more pro-poor, providing larger tax cuts than does the alternative tax cut for households with incomes below $25,000. This differential incidence result underlines the role of Proposition 13 in changing the overall incidence of the California tax system. Though in isolation Proposition 13 appears to favor the rich, the reduction in the importance of the property tax, relative to more broad-based state taxes, is highly favorable to the poorest citizens of California.

These results are all based on the assumption that mobility decisions and housing markets react with considerable sluggishness to a tax change. Over a long period of time, however, as markets respond more fully, it is likely that the impacts of Proposition 13 will come to favor the poor more strongly. This result, however, must be treated with caution, as no account is made for the long-run impact of Proposition 13 on mobility patterns.

What conclusions can be drawn from California's experience with Proposition 13 that may be relevant to other states that have imposed or are considering tax limitations? We have seen that the incidence of Proposition 13 depends on the interaction of a large number of factors. The reduction in tax liabilities depends on household's housing consumption, its housing tenure, the tax rate it faces, its eligibility for various property tax exemptions, and the manner in which its housing unit is assessed. The incidence of a tax cut will obviously depend on the joint distribution of these factors across income classes. For example, a concentration of low-income homeowners in high tax rate communities will tend to make a Proposition 13 type tax cut more pro-poor.

One factor that varies tremendously across states is the degree of interjurisdictional variation in effective tax rates. For example, in the six largest metropolitan areas in California, center city effective tax rates averaged 17 percent higher than the average suburban rate. These intrametropolitan tax rate differences are small relative to those in many of the older metropolitan areas in the Northeast and Midwest. In order to determine the impact of interjurisdictional tax differences, we simulated a uniform effective property tax rate across California that generated the same total amount of revenue as was generated in 1978 prior to Proposition 13. With a uniform tax rate the Suits Index is reduced from –.170 to –.116, a 31 percent decrease in the regressivity of the residential property tax. As renters lived in communities with higher than average tax rates, on average, moving to a uniform rate results in an average 33 percent decrease in the effective tax rate faced by renters, and an average 11 percent increase for owners.

We then simulated the impact of moving from an equal revenue, uniform tax rate situation to the imposition of Proposition 13. The Suits Index moves from –.116 with uniform taxes to –.290 with Proposition 13, implying a larger *increase* in the regressivity of the residential property tax than occurred under our initial simulation. This increase in regressivity stems from homeowners being the largest beneficiaries of the reductions in residential property taxes generated by Proposition 13, and as on average they face higher tax rates under an equal revenue, uniform tax scheme, they thus receive larger tax reductions as the result of Proposition 13.

This result suggests that we should find a pro-poor impact of a Proposition 13 type tax limitation that is imposed in a state with larger interjurisdictional tax rate differences and where lower-income residents live in high tax rate jurisdictions. However, this does not necessarily mean that the effect of Proposition 13, if enacted in states meeting these conditions, will benefit the poor. We must recall that California was able to reimburse its local governments for lost property tax revenues out of a large state government surplus, and can continue to bail out local governments by drawing on revenues from a reasonably progressive state tax system.

In the final analysis, the assessment of the distributional impacts of any tax limitation measure requires the careful study of a large number of factors, many of them highly specific to an individual state and to the exact nature of the tax limitation. Although our study emphasizes that property tax reductions are more beneficial to the poor than many other types of tax reductions that states might consider, our study also points out the sensitivity of results and conclusions to a large number of elements that make up the property tax system, and to assumptions concerning its incidence.

Notes

1. During the past several years, property tax limitations have been enacted in several states. In the November 1980 elections, proposals to limit the property tax passed in Massachusetts and Nevada but failed in Ohio and Michigan.

2. In addition to the other papers in this volume, several excellent papers appear in the proceedings of a conference on tax and expenditure limitations, published as a supplement to the *National Tax Journal,* June 1979.

3. An exception is a paper by Case (1979).

4. These estimates were made by Oakland (1979).

5. See Haveman and Hollenbeck (1980) for a collection of papers that employ microsimulation analysis.

6. Studies by Netzer (1966), Slavet, Bradbury, and Moss (1975), and Phares (1980) used aggregate data. The well-known Pechman and Okner study (1974) relied on micro data, but assumed away inter- and intrajurisdictional tax rate differences.

7. Excellent discussions of propety tax incidence can be found in Aaron (1975), McLure (1977) and Ladd (1973).

8. Not all economists will agree with our assumptions concerning the incidence of Proposition 13. Several authors, for example, Aaron (1975) and De Tray (1980), have argued that interjurisdictional property tax differentials will be fully capitalized in the value of housing. This argument implies that the commonly found pattern of the poor concentrated in high tax-price communities (i.e., high tax rates relative to public services provided), while the rich live in low tax-price towns, will have no impact on the incidence of the property tax, because the poor who face high tax-prices will be fully compensated by lower housing prices, while the rich will have to pay housing premiums to live in low tax communities. Full capitalization implies that the long-run incidence of the property tax is more progressive than would be the case if tax differentials were borne by the consumers of housing. We argue that full capitalization requires a highly competitive theory of migration. However, such factors as fiscal zoning and racial discimination restrict the options of many poor people, forcing them to choose among a much smaller group of communities than are available to wealthier households. The result is a relatively inelastic demand for these communities, which prevents typically higher tax rates in the available communities from being fully capitalized into housing prices.

However, it should be stressed that, for both owners and renters, the degree of capitalization of property tax differentials prior to Proposition 13 has no effect on the dollar value of the reduction received under Proposition 13, or on the income class incidence of the reduction. Given the ability under our model to simulate pre-reform tax liabilities, the reduction is simply equal to the change in tax rates times the value of the property prior to Proposition 13. For renters, the reduction is equal to the percentage of the property tax reduction rebated to renters through lower rents. The relevance of capitalization to the incidence of Proposition 13 lies in the comparison between the income class incidence of the reduction and the pre-Proposition 13 income class incidence of the property tax. Our assumption of incomplete capitalization implies a more regressive property tax incidence than would be the case under full capitalization. Hence, we argue that reduced reliance on the property tax relative to broader based state taxes such as the income tax tends to make the overall tax system in California more progressive.

9. Since Proposition 13 will have a relatively minor impact on the national average property tax rate, its primary impact will be on the consumers of housing. In the long run, the small change in the national average property tax rate will result in a higher rate of return to the nation's owners of capital. This implies that some portion of homeowners' benefits from Proposition 13 will be exported to non-California owners of capital. However, during the "transition period" discussed in this paper, the entire benefit of homeowners' reduced tax liabilities resulting from Proposition 13 will flow to homeowners themselves rather than to the owners of capital. The impact of Proposition 13 on the rate of return on capital throughout the nation requires a significant degree of capital mobility. We assume that adjustments to capital stock will occur only over a period of several years.

10. A doubling of house values was not at all uncommon in California between 1975 and 1978.

11. Proposition 13 provides households with an incentive not to move. By moving, a household forgoes its reduced assessed value. The longer a household does not move, the greater the "tax penalty" to moving. The consensus among housing market experts in California is that Proposition 13 has not yet reduced turnover rates, but over time its effect on mobility will become noticeable. See Balderston, Heyman, and Smith (1979). Chernick and Reschovsky (1982) predict that by 1985 the tax penalty will average over 8 percent of household income for low income families, but average 2 percent of income for high income households.

12. The "new view" of property tax incidence, which assigns the entire burden of the average rate of taxation to the owners of capital, is not applicable to these tax rate differentials because, in the long run, capital is mobile between states. McLure (1977) provides a concise discussion of the property tax incidence assumptions that are relevant in response to nationwide and to local tax changes.

13. There are widespread reports that the absence of rent reductions after the implementation of Proposition 13 spurred the passage of rent control ordinances throughout the state. The short-run impact of these ordinances is to increase the pass-back of rent reductions to current renters. However, to the extent that rent controls reduce the supply of additional rental units, the ultimate burden may rest largely on future renters.

14. If labor and capital were perfectly mobile and all markets competitive, the reduction in business property taxes would increase returns to California landlords and the return to capital throughout the nation. The initially higher return to capital within California because of the lowered property tax liability will induce capital to flow into the state, lowering the higher California rate

while slightly increasing the rate of return to capital in the rest of the nation.

15. In some industries market power is constrained by regulations. For example, utility rates are generally set by state agencies on the basis of a "normal" rate of return. It is therefore likely that the state rate-setting commission will pass some of the reduced propety tax liability of utility companies back to consumers in the form of lower utility rates.

16. The U.S. Department of Commerce (1979) estimated that Proposition 13 resulted in a $1.9 billion increase in pretax corporate profits in 1978, and this resulted in a $700 million increase in federal corporate income tax liabilities.

17. In a recent study Phares (1980) constructed estimates of interstate tax exporting by updating McLure's earlier work.

18. In brief, the procedure we employed involves the allocation of real property, and hence the tax reduction, to: (1) industrial production for local markets; (2) industrial production for national markets not dominated by California firms; (3) industrial production for national markets deominated by California firms; (4) agricultural production; (5) commerce and services; and (6) vacant land. For the portion of the tax reduction shifted to consumers, several different exporting assumptions are made. For industrial production for national markets, the share exported equals one minus California's proportion of retail sales in the nation. For commercial activity, and industrial production for local markets, we follow McLure's assumption that 6 percent is exported to reflect tourism in California. Finally, we assume that 75 percent of agricultural production is exported.

In order to determine the proportion of business profits exported to non-Californians, we must first distinguish between the two types of business ownership—corporate and noncorporate. Following a procedure used by Slavet, Bradbury and Moss (1975) that relies on IRS *Statistics on Income,* we determine the division between corporate and noncorporate ownership for our six types of property. Corporate profits are allocated to California residents in proportion to their share of total dividends received. Various assumptions are made about the exporting of noncorporate profits for each type of property. In general, only a small portion of noncorporate profits is exported from California.

19. Although the average effective rate—taxes as a proportion of the market value of real property—is not particularly high in California, the rapid rise in property values during the mid-1970s implies that the average tax burden in California—taxes as a proportion of income—was considerably above the national average.

20. In 1978 homeowners over the age of 62 with incomes below $12,000 were eligible for a property tax rebate payment. The allowable rebate equals a specified percentage of the total tax liability on the first $7,500 of assessed value of a house. The rebate percentage is calculated on a sliding scale that varies from 96 percent for those with incomes below $3,000 to 4 percent for those households with incomes between $11,500 and $12,000. In 1978 approximately 50 percent of the eligible households applied for and received rebates.

Elderly renters with an income below $5,000 were also eligible for a rebate payment in 1978. The rebates were equal to a specified percentage of a fixed amount—$220, where again the percentage is inversely proportional to household income. Only 40 percent of eligible households actually received rebate payments.

21. Nominal 1975 property tax rates for California were assembled. These data included rates for center cities, composite property tax rates for each incorporated municipality within the suburban rings of the six largest SMSAs, and SMSA average tax rates for the remaining small SMSAs. The rates used are weighted averages of the municipal, school district, county, and special district rates applicable to each area. Each household was then assigned a property tax rate, using a combination of exact and probabilistic information. Center city households were simply assigned the nominal tax rate for their jurisdictions, except for those SMSAs with multiple center-cities. In the latter case, households were randomly assigned to center cities, based on the demographic characteristics of each center city. To reproduce suburban variations in tax rates, population proportions for each incorporated area and the remaining unincorporated areas were converted to a cumulative frequency, ordered by tax rates. Based on this cumulative frequency, suburban households were randomly assigned tax rates, so as to mirror the actual distribution of tax rates in the suburban ring. In the smaller SMSAs, the appropriate SMSA average tax rate was assigned to each household. Thus, an accurate characterization of variations in property tax rates was introduced into the sample.

22. Based on evidence in Peterson (1973), we have assumed that the gross rent multiplier increases by 3 percent for each 10 percent increase in rents.

23. We have employed for this purpose the state and federal income tax modules of the Transfer Income Model (TRIM). The TRIM income tax modules are highly detailed models of the federal and state income tax systems. Using the SIE sample they determine each person's filing status and the type of return filed (e.g., single, joint, married filing separatly). Adjustments are made to the Census income definitions used by SIE in order to determine Adjusted Gross Income (AGI); this includes estimating capital gains income, and excluding transfer income. Taxable income is calculated by subtracting exemptions and estimated itemized deductions from AGI whenever itemized deductions exceed the appropriate standard deduction. We modify both the federal and state income tax modules by combining our simulated property tax liabilities of homeowners with data from the Internal Revenue Service on the average size of other itemized deductions for each of over 1,700 demographic-income classes. This allows us to determine the impact of changing property tax liabilities on changes in itemizing/nonitemizing status, in total itemized deductions, and in total income tax liabilities. In determining final income tax liabilities, credits (e.g., for earned income, for child care expenses), are subtracted where appropriate. Recent changes in the California tax code have also been built into the model. These include the replacement of the personal exemption with a personal credit.

24. See Balderston, Heyman, and Smith (1979). A study by the county appraiser in Santa Clara County found a 14 percent turnover rate (implying a move every 7.15 years) for single-family houses in the county in 1977. It should be noted, though, that Santa Clara includes "Silicon Valley" with its high-paying, rapidly expanding electronics industry, and thus its turnover rate is probably significantly higher than the rate in much of the rest of the state. In fact, the turnover rate in neighboring San Mateo County has averaged slightly under 10 percent over the past few years.

25. The income measure used is census money income. Incidence results for the lowest class, \$0-\$2,000, are not discussed because the large transitory

component of income in this class makes the estimates highly unreliable.

26. See Citrin (1979) for an analysis of voter preferences with regard to Proposition 13.

27. Depending on the initial distribution of tax burdens, the DOC may indicate a different pattern of incidence than the Suits Index. For example, in the case of a regressive tax, a tax cut which is distributed in proportion to income would imply a DOC equal to zero, while the Suits Indices of pre- and post-tax-cut incidence would show greater regressivity of tax burdens. Because the poor were paying a higher percentage of their income before the tax cut, a tax reduction that is proportional to income would leave the poor paying a greater share of the remaining tax.

28. The distributional impact of the alternative tax cut can be summarized by the DOC index. We have calculated the value of the DOC index as .169, implying that the alternative tax cut results in a significant pro-rich tax change.

Bibliography

Aaron, Henry J. *Who Pays the Property Tax: A New View?,* Washington, D.C.: The Brookings Institution, 1975.

Balderston, Frederick, I. Michael Heyman, and Wallace F. Smith. "Proposition 13, Property Transfers, and the Real Estate Markets," Research Report 79-1, Institute of Governmental Studies, University of California, Berkeley, March 1979.

Berkeley Planning Associates, "Case Study of the Impact of Proposition 13 on Human Services Financing," Draft Report, July 1980.

Case, Karl E., "Proposition 13 and the Distribution of Income," Paper presented at a Conference of the Committee on Taxation, Resources, and Economic Development, Cambridge, Mass., September 1979.

Chernick, Howard and Andrew Reschovsky, "The Consequences of Limitations of Growth in the Property Tax Base," in John M. Quigley, ed., *Perspectives on Local Public Finance and Public Policy,* vol. 1, Greenwich, Conn.: JAI Press, Inc., 1982.

Citrin, Jack, "Do People Want Something for Nothing: Public Opinion on Taxes and Government Spending," Supplment, *National Tax Journal,* June 1979.

DeTray, Dennis, "The Incidence of State and Local Taxes Under Fiscal Changes: Methodology," Working Draft, Santa Monica: Rand Corporation, May 1980.

Haveman, Robert H. and Kevin Hollenbeck, eds. *Microeconomic Simulation Models for Public Policy Analysis,* New York: Academic Press, 1980.

Ladd, Helen F., "The Role of the Property Tax: A Reassessment," in *Broad-Based Taxes: New Options and Sources,* edited by Richard A. Musgrave, Baltimore: Johns Hopkins Press, 1973.

Levy, Frank, "On Understanding Proposition 13," *The Public Interest,* Summer 1979.

McLure, Charles E., Jr., "The Interstate Exporting of State and Local Taxes Estimates for 1962," *National Tax Journal,* March 1967.

———, "The 'New View' of the Property Tax: A Caveat," *National Tax Journal,* March 1977.

Mieszkowski, Peter M., "On the Theory of Tax Incidence," *Journal of Political Economy,* June 1967.

———, "The Property Tax: An Excise Tax or a Profits Tax?," *Journal of Public Economics,* April 1972.

Milsczynski, Dean J., "Land Use and Proposition 13: The California Experience," Tax Policy Roundtable Publications, No. 6, Lincoln Institute of Land Policy, Cambridge, Mass., 1981.

Netzer, Dick, *Economic of the Property Tax,* Washington, D.C.: Brookings *Institution,* 1966.

Oakland, William H., "Proposition 13—Genesis and Consequences," Supplement, *National Tax Journal,* June 1979.

Pechman, Joseph A. and Benjamin A. Okner, *Who Bears the Tax Burden?* Washington, D.C.: Brookings Institution, 1974.

Peterson, George E., "The 'Regressivity' of the Residential Property Tax," mimeo, Washington, The Urban Institute, 1972.

———, A. Solomon, et al., *Property Taxes, Housing the Cities,* Lexington, Mass.: D.C. Heath & Co., 1973.

Phares, Donald, *Who Pays State and Local Taxes?* Cambridge, Mass.: Oelgeschlager, Gunn, and Hain, 1980.

Rosen, Kenneth T., "The Impact of Proposition 13 on House Prices in Northern California: A Test of the Interjurisdictional Capitalization Hypothesis," Working Paper, Center for Real Estate and Urban Economics, University of California, Berkeley, June 1980.

Shapiro, Perry, David Puryear and John Ross, "Tax and Expenditure Limitations in Retrospectand Prospect," Supplement, *National Tax Journal,* June 1979.

Slavet, Joseph S., Katharine L. Bradbury, and Philip I. Moss, *Financing State-Local Services,* Lexington, Mass.: D.C. Heath & Co., 1975.

Suits, Daniel B., "The Measurement of Tax Progressivity," *American Economic Review,* September 1977.

U.S. Bureau of the Census, *1977 Annual Housing Survey. Housing Characteristics of Recent Movers,* Washington, 1979.

———, *1977 Census of Governments: Taxable Property Values and Assessment/Sales Ratios,* Washington, 1978.

U.S. Department of Commerce, *Survey of Current Business,* Washington, 1979.

13

Policy Consequences *

HAROLD WOLMAN
GEORGE PETERSON

How do local governments respond to the need for fiscal constraint? Surprisingly, relatively little is known about this question, despite a growing recognition that many local governments do indeed face a fiscally constrained environment.[1] The lack of knowledge is, to a large extent, a consequence of the fact that most previous research on municipal fiscal behavior has taken place in or assumed an environment of expanding budgetary resources.

The Urban Institute has undertaken a series of studies designed, in part, to provide an understanding of local fiscal behavior and its consequences under greater budgetary restrictiveness.[2] In this article we will draw upon this work, most of which is still in progress, to set forth a series of preliminary findings about local government policy responses to fiscal constraint. These findings should not be interpreted as our conception of the invariable behavior of local governments facing fiscal constraint; rather they should be viewed as an initial effort to describe the most common behavior of fiscally constrained local governments under most circumstances.

Mr. Wolman is a senior research associate in the Public Finance Program at the Urban Institute. Mr. Peterson is director of the Public Finance Program at the Urban Institute.

Fiscal Constraint

Local governments might face budgetary restrictions for a variety of reasons: a tax base which has not grown as fast as inflation; a reduction in intergovernmental assistance; a formal fiscal limitation on local revenues or expenditures (such as Proposition 13 in California or the New Jersey cap law which limits municipalities to a 5 percent annual increase in expenditures); greater resistance on the part of citizens to local tax increases; and mismanagement that results in unplanned deficits in the operating budget.

Governments facing fiscal constraint have three broad policy choices or combinations of choices, depending on the specific cause of constraint. They might increase intergovernmental revenues, increase own-source revenues, or reduce expenditures. Within this context our research supports the following preliminary findings concerning local government responses to fiscal pressure.

Increasing Intergovernmental Revenues

Local governments faced with fiscal constraint will first attempt to increase intergovernmental revenues. If such an effort is successful, the local unit can sustain expenditures without the need for local tax increases.

When possible, local governments will simply substitute intergovernmental assistance for local funds. In some cases—general revenue sharing and Anti-Recession Fiscal Assistance—there are no legal problems involved in this. Trenton, for example, uses its entire general revenue sharing payment to support its fire department, thus substituting for what otherwise would have required locally raised revenue. In other cases federal or state program requirements prohibit or make direct substitution difficult. Nonetheless it is virtually certain that some such substitution occurs, particularly in programs such as CETA. Trenton, for example, reduced its municipally funded payroll by 247 positions between 1970-1979; in the latter year it had 254 CETA employees. Buffalo reduced its locally funded payroll by 24 percent between 1975-1979. In 1979, CETA accounted for approximately 25 percent of Buffalo's workforce.

When substitution is not possible, our studies indicate that local governments faced with the prospect of cutback will re-arrange program emphasis to maintain total spending and government employment levels, even if this requires shifting from the locally preferred program mix. In Mercer County, New Jersey, a 34 percent decrease in Federal Title XX Social Services revenues (Title XX is essentially a block grant for social services) prompted a search for ways to shift programs to categorical grants. When the opportunities for direct funding replacement were exhausted, county officials created new programs and trimmed old ones in ways that would generate federal funding for the same social services staff. Thus they were able to retain existing employees and maintain the previous total funding level without new taxes, although the mix of social services provided was substantially different. Successful application of this strategy presumes the existence of untapped federal aid opportunities, something which will be harder to discover as fiscal constraints move into their second or third year.

Increasing Own-Source Revenues

Governments faced with fiscal constraint and unable to increase intergovernmental assistance will likely choose some combination of expenditure reduction and an increase in local revenues rather than rely solely on one or the other.

It is widely believed that in the existing Proposition 13 tax revolt environment, governments facing fiscal constraints will cut expenditures or moderate expenditure increases rather than increase tax rates or add new taxes. However, while it is likely that the propensity to raise taxes or reduce expenditures has shifted in favor of the latter, local governments have not totally forsaken tax increases as a response to fiscal constraint. Trenton, New Jersey, facing a stagnating tax base, has increased property tax rates in three of the past four years—a cumulative increase of 20.5 percent—and has reduced real expenditures at the same time by more than 8 percent. Erie County, New York, when faced with a fiscal crisis in 1976, increased its tax rate by 36 percent and cut expenditures by 15 percent. Cleveland raised its local income tax rate by 50 percent in 1979 and faces the prospect of a proposal for further increases as the city attempts to recover from default.

In some cases tax increases may not be possible. Formal limitations on tax rates or revenue growth, in fact, often foreclose local flexibility in deciding what mix of expenditure restrictions and tax increases should be used to close a budget gap. While increases in user charges and fees are frequently employed by local governments facing fiscal constraint, they are particularly important for local governments—such as those in California—facing strict formal limitations on tax revenue growth.

Expenditure Reduction Strategies

If a decision is made to decrease expenditures from local sources what strategies might be pursued?[3] Our listing of these strategies implies a loose preference ordering for local governments. The strategies, however, are not mutually exclusive, and in reality, local governments are likely to engage in several simultaneously rather than proceed through the list in seriatim.

PROGRAM EFFICIENCY

Local officials will attempt first to reduce expenditures through reducing waste and improving efficiency. The rhetoric of expenditure reduction frequently implies that governments can absorb substantial cuts in spending without any real effect on the level of service provided, simply by cutting waste and achieving greater efficiency. Indeed, public officials faced with the need to reduce spending do seek out areas where greater efficiencies can be achieved—frequently with some success. Many of the governments we are examining, for example, are making greater use of automatic data processing systems in an effort to increase productivity; Trenton has switched to a system of self-insurance. There also appears to be increasing resort to contracting with private firms for the provision of services as an explicit means of reducing costs.

It appears that there is some slack in government operations, and that governments will reduce this slack before engaging in real service reductions. However, real expenditure reductions of the magnitude now being absorbed by many cities cannot be achieved through efficiency gains alone. In these cities, management changes to increase productivity are as much a preparatory sign of serious intent in budget cutting as a source of expenditure savings in themselves.

SPENDING SHIFTS

Governments will attempt to shift expenditure burdens to other levels of government. Just as local governments react to budgetary pressure by trying to generate new aid from higher levels of government, so one of their first reactions is to try to shift spending responsibilities. An extreme (but not infrequent) case would be the total shift of responsibility for providing and financing a service to another level of government or to the private sector. A few examples provide a better sense of this shifting of activity. Cincinnati reacted to the fiscal pressure of the mid-seventies by persuading the state of Ohio to take over responsibility for operating the University of Cincinnati. Other cities have followed suit by transferring city universities and municipal hospitals to other levels of government. On a smaller scale, Trenton has convinced Mercer County to take over two main roads which run through the city and which previously had been the city's responsibility to maintain. In the Buffalo, Erie County area, the county has assumed responsibility for a variety of central police functions and for many cultural activities from the fiscally pressed city. In addition, the city has given its zoo to the Buffalo Zoological Society, a private non-profit organization, and is now responsible for assuming only a small portion of the zoo's operating deficit (the county provides most of the required subsidy).

PAYROLL COSTS

Local officials will attempt to secure tacit settlements with public employee organizations on how the personnel budget will be reduced. Since upwards of 70 percent of local operating costs consist of expenditures on personnel, municipal payroll costs are an almost unavoidable target for expenditure reduction. Reductions in total payroll costs can be accomplished either by decreasing the total number of municipal employees or by decreasing (in real terms) the average salary per employee. Though both choices initially will be resisted by public employee groups, once they are convinced of the need for expenditure reductions, they frequently will have a preference for bearing the brunt of the reduction through workforce reductions or wage restraint. City governments will try to make public employee groups partners in this aspect of the budget decision, so as to defuse employee resistance as far as possible. For example, New York City police and fire unions accepted severe wage restrictions as the price of avoiding further layoffs of personnel. In contrast, Detroit police and fire unions insisted on steep pay increases, which they ultimately received through binding arbitration, even though this necessitated large-scale layoffs in the uniformed forces. Local union politics will explain much of the preference of union leaders for different strategies.

SUPPORT FUNCTIONS

When expenditure reductions are made, services will be maintained to the extent possible, at the expense of ancillary and support functions. Administrators first will attempt to reduce spending for purchase of equipment, travel, overtime, and administrative and record-keeping functions. As much as possible, reductions will be made in ways which do not visibly reduce services. When Trenton's state health aid dropped, for example, the health department did not reduce personnel but made cuts in supplies and travel.

The above four preliminary findings represent preferred retrenchment techniques, for they result in reduced local expenditures without corresponding reductions in the level of services received by citizens and with the least antagonism of public employee groups. However, significant reductions in the level of services provided may not be avoidable.

LOCALLY FUNDED SERVICES

Expenditure reduction will occur disproportionately in programs funded wholly from local sources compared to programs funded partially through intergovernmental assistance. This finding suggests that local governments will cut spending first from services which are entirely locally funded, even if these are higher priority services, because of the much greater loss in revenues, and total spending incurred by reducing participation in federally funded programs. (A dollar reduction for a 75 percent matching grant would result in the local government losing three additional federal dollars, while a dollar reduction in a locally funded program merely results in that dollar loss alone.)

A plausible case has also been made for the contrary proposition, namely that local governments, when faced with fiscal pressure, will reduce local spending in federal programs because these programs are, from local government's point of view, the lowest-priority services they provide. This proposition implies that federally supported services rank so low in local priorities that, even with federal leveraging, local dollars buy less valuable outputs than when spent on items of local choice.

Empirically our studies indicate that programs that are totally locally funded are much more suspectible to expenditure and service reductions. In Trenton, public works and public safety have borne the brunt of expenditure reductions. Trenton's budget direction commented:

> In general, intergovernmental expenditures are not cut . . . . Social services have been insulated from the city's budget cuts because they are federally funded. Trenton's cuts have all been in the delivery of essential, but locally funded services.

Buffalo has pursued the same strategy. It has suffered major cuts in public works, streets, and sanitation. In Mercer County, New Jersey, the program areas growing most slowly or declining in real terms have been those that are almost completely dependent on local funds (parks, general government), while the areas experiencing the fastest expenditure growth have been those most heavily funded through intergovernmental revenue (human services).

MINORITY PROGRAMS

Expenditure reductions are not focused disproportionately on programs designed primarily to serve low-income or minority groups. It is frequently argued that expenditures will be reduced first in programs with the weakest constituencies (either in terms of a weak political organization or low public support). This is generally interpreted to mean that the human service programs—programs designed primarily for the poor—would be the most likely to be cut because they have the least political support at the local level. However, it appears that the tendency to reduce expenditures at the weakest political point is strongly mitigated by two factors. First, the human services programs are also the most heavily federally funded programs—and thus, as suggested by the last proposition, the ones least likely to suffer reductions. Second, most human services programs are the responsibility of the county or state rather than municipal government; most cities simply do not have the opportunity to reduce local spending for human services programs vary substantially. County governments—which do have the opportunity—are generally in better fiscal condition than their central cities and thus not as driven to make massive expenditure reductions.

Local recipients of some human services in fiscally constrained cities may nonetheless find benefits reduced through actions taken at the state level. The state determines benefit levels for AFDC and other income support programs, and in New Jersey these levels have increased by only 7.6 percent for AFDC since 1976 and not at all for general assistance—indicating a local of political strength among these groups.

Overall, however, it appears that budget reductions do not occur systematically in programs targeted to poor and minority groups. This does not necessarily imply that the poor do not bear a disproportionate portion of the burden. If they do, it is likely to be through a different mechanism than cutting programs aimed at the poor. It is possible, for example, that reductions in the more traditional locally-funded programs are disproportionately focused on poor and minority neighborhoods. However, we have not obtained evidence to test this possibility.

BUREAUCRATIC MAINTENANCE

Expenditure reduction decisions will be made according to internal bureaucratic dynamics. This proposition suggests that in times of fiscal restraint budget decisions will be determined by the need to maintain the bureaucracy as a functioning social system. More specifically, expenditure reductions will be made by across-the-board cuts among departments and functions; and expenditure cuts will be made within departments in a manner which minimizes the loss of employment for existing employees.

Thus, in order to minimize strife and to achieve what is perceived to be an equitable distribution of burdens, governments will respond to the need to reduce expenditures with across-the-board percentage cuts among departments and functions, leaving department heads to determine the specific allocation of cuts among programs. This procedure is likely to satisfy external political needs as well.

Trenton, for example, has undergone a series of real expenditure reductions. The mayor's professional budget staff has favored targeted and selected cuts and has presented him with suggested options. However, the mayor has decided upon more or less across-the-board cuts among discretionary items. Buffalo's normal budgetary process involves across-the-board spending cuts from current service-level expenditures for three different priority levels of service: police and fire, which take the smallest percentage reductions; a second group which has suffered severe reductions in previous years and which will receive a moderate rate in the present year; and a third remaining group will receive the heaviest reduction. When Erie County, New York, experienced a major fiscal crisis in 1976-77, it cut police and fire allocations by 7.5 percent and all other departments by 15 percent. This strategy reduces differential treatment to cases that can be specifically justified before the public.

Expenditure cuts will also be made within departments in a manner that minimizes the loss of employment for existing employees. Thus layoffs are avoided if at all possible; personnel levels drop due to attrition and to hiring freezes. The result, of course, might be a substantial distortion in government priorities due to differential turnover rates. Mercer County's reaction to a 34 percent cut in Title XX funds in 1977 was particuarly instructive; the resulting adjustments were arranged so that no one lost their job as a consequence of the cut.

LOW-VISIBILITY SERVICES

Expenditure reductions will be made in spending areas of least public visibility or whose consequences can be deferred to the future. Expenditure reductions will come first in areas such as maintenance and capital outlays where the consequences of cutbacks are not immediately visible. Our interviews suggest that this hypothesis is substantially accurate; maintenance particularly seems to suffer in situations of fiscal pressure. Trenton, Buffalo, Cleveland, New York, and other cities suffering severe pressure all have cut back substantially on maintenance, particularly of streets and parks.

This strategy of cutting in the *least* visible areas must be distinguished from the gamesmanship which frequently accompanies the initial debate about how to react to fiscal stress. In an effort to create the climate for an unpopular action such as increasing taxes or extracting additional resources from other units of government, local officials may first threaten cuts in the *most* visible areas, particularly police and fire protection. The purpose is to demonstrate what terrible consequences might occur if additional revenue is not forthcoming or the situation is not taken seriously. However, the reductions actually made are seldom in such visible and politically threatening areas.

Nonetheless the effects of these cuts, even in relatively invisible areas, cannot be totally hidden. Over time, the citizenry begins to perceive the consequences. When asked whether Trenton's populace had perceived the effects of the cuts (as evidenced by complaints to city hall), the budget director observed,

> Parks are not being maintained and grass is not being trimmed. People are noticing that. Also streets are not being cleaned as frequently and this is being noticed. In the police area we have had to cut back on walking patrols and people have complained about this.

Specialized organizations have sprung up in many cities to call attention to the less obvious or long-run consequences of spending reductions. Preservation of capital facilities and adequate pension funding have become favorite topics of business-oriented groups and civil organizations concerned about the next generation of taxpayers and service recipients. The bond market, too, has served as a restraint on cities' abilities to push costs into the future, as bond buyers have become increasingly wary of buying debt issues from governments that are accumulating hidden liabilities for the future.

GOVERNMENT INACTION

Expenditure reduction will be made, where possible, through inaction. This has given great significance to the automatic indexing of spending levels. The most obvious way to achieve invisible expenditure reduction is to let inflation take its toll by increasing benefit levels or program funding at a rate less than inflation. Thus New Jersey's benefit levels for AFDC payments increased by only 7.6 percent between 1976-79, despite a 27.2 percent increase in the consumer price index; benefit levels for general assistance did not increase at all. In New York State the basic welfare grant has not been increased since 1973. One consequence of this was to hold down the number of eligible AFDC recipients as well. Inflation thus accomplished what would have been extremely difficult to achieve through the political process, and perhaps regarded as inequitable if spelled out as an explicit choice. In contrast, California welfare grant levels have kept pace with inflation through automatic indexing with the cost of living, despite efforts by the governor to cut back. California courts have ruled that the statutory requirement of indexing cannot be overridden by the regular budget process. Throughout the state and local sector, programs that have received statutory constitutional indexing have fared far better than programs where raising benefit or spending levels requires explicit action.

PRIORITY SETTING

Expenditure reductions usually are not made on the basis of explicit priority-setting procedures designed to determine the relative costs and benefits of various programs. Other than the ad hoc division of services into frills and essentials, fixed costs (for example debt service) and flexible costs, and federally-supported versus locally supported expenditures, little effort seems to be made at the central level to set priorities on an objective basis. Certainly the arsenal of analytic tools that economists and other social scientists have developed as aids to decision-making are conspicuously absent from budget decisions. Furthermore, it is not simply that formal and systematic analysis does not occur; the officials that we interviewed—who generally impressed us as intelligent and reasonable people—simply did not approach the problems of expenditure reduction in terms of prioritizing expenditures and cutting in areas where benefits were lowest in relation to costs. Where the concept of priorities did occur—usually, though infrequently, at the intradepartmental level—it was either in terms of the "need" of a specific recipient group (the poor have a greater need for services) or in terms of a dichotomy between frills and essential services.

Conclusion

The above discussion suggests that public officials employ a variety of means to hide and mitigate the effects of expenditure reductions. As indicated, however, it would be a serious mistake to imply that reductions of the magnitude we have have observed can be expected to be absorbed without an adverse impact on service recipients. Several of the strategies we have identified cannot be followed after the first year. Therefore, it remains to be seen whether as fiscal constraints become a more nearly permanent reality, local governments react to more formal priority setting to determine future budget levels.

Notes

1. For useful existing work see Meltsner (1971); Advisory Committee on Intergovernmental Relations (ACIR, 1973); Levine (1978; 1979); Peterson (1978); and Pascal et al. (1979).
2. These include studies of "State and Local Expenditure Changes in an Era of Fiscal Constraint" (funded by HEW); "Municipal Strategies to Cope with Fiscal Stress" (Kettering Foundation); "Municipal Public Employee Compensation" (the City of New York and the Revson Foundation); "Fiscal Issues of State and Local Pensions" (funded by serveral federal agencies); and "Urban Fiscal Monitoring," including short case studies of several cities facing fiscal difficulties (funded by HUD).
3. It is important to keep in mind the distinction between strategies utilized to determine where and how reductions should be made *among* departments or functional areas and strategies for making reductions *within* departments, functional areas, or programs.

References

Advisory Commission on Intergovernmental Relations (ACIR), *City Financial Emergencies: The Intergovernmental Dimension,* Washington, D.C.: U.S. Government Printing Office, 1973.

Levine, C., "More on cutback management: hard questions for hard times," *Public Administration Review* 39 (March/April 1979): 179-83.

Levine, C., "Organizational decline and cutback management," *Public Administration Review* 38 (July/August 1978): 316-325.

Meltsner, A., *The Politics of City Revenue.* Berkeley: University of California Press, 1971.

Pascal, A. et al., *Fiscal Containment of Local and State Government,* Santa Monica: The Rand Corporation, 1979.

Peterson, G., *Urban Fiscal Monitoring.* Washington, D.C.: The Urban Institute (draft), 1978.

14

Effect on Planners and the Planning Process

EDITH NETTER

I would like first to elaborate on the term "cutback" planning. In 1975 Herbert Gans wrote an article on planning for declining and poor cities.[1] In it he coined the phrase "cutback" planning, which meant planning for reduced and declining capital and operating expenditures.

In the past, cities had to plan for growth, Gans said. Now they must plan for stability and decline. They must identify who must bear the costs, financial and otherwise, of the consequences of stasis and decline. Planners must determine how much redistribution is possible in a declining city and, in so doing, they must balance the interests of individual citizens and the urban populace.

We now live in a time of general austerity. Because of statewide tax and expenditure limitations, many local governments, whether urban or rural, municipal or county, must engage in cutback planning. In the context of planning and land use regulation, there are two ways to define cutback planning—the first, cutbacks on local planning staffs; the second, cutbacks on development and public services.

Ms. Netter is an attorney with Robinson, Robinson & Cole, Hartford, Ct. She would like to express her appreciation to Damon Dunn, a student at the Kent College of Law, Chicago, for his assistance in the preparation of this article.

Planning has a reputation for being a luxury: desirable when the economy is strong, but expendable when monies are scarce.[2] Planning is not tangible, like a new school or fire station. Nor does it have an immediate quantifiable impact on the public health, safety, or welfare, like a new police station or hospital. But done properly, planning can provide the mechanism for an efficient and equitable allocation of resources. Thus, planning should become even more important in times of high unemployment, housing and energy shortages, and industrial decline.

California's Proposition 13 illustrates the impact of TELS on local planning. Preliminary surveys by the California Office of Planning and Research reflect no substantial decreases in the number of planners employed.[3] California cities and counties report staff reductions of 4 to 5 percent.[4] These decreases usually have occurred because of attrition.

However, the final impact of Proposition 13 has yet to be felt, since the state still has a budget surplus with which it has been subsidizing local governments.[5] Staff cuts have occurred in some agencies—probably a forewarning of things to come. For instance, the Association of Bay Area Governments did not share in the surplus and was forced to reduce its staff considerably.[6]

Budget restrictions also have made the hiring of in-house specialists and outside consultants impractical.[7] This trend is sure to have an affect on the quality of work done by local planning staffs.

Long-range planning is the most vulnerable of all planning services. For instance, long-range planners working in the Los Angeles planning department have been reassigned to implementation divisions.[8] Other cities have followed suit. Decreases in the size of long-range planning staffs have been most notable in small- to medium-sized cities.[9]

To date, reductions in the size of long-range planning staffs have not prohibited local governments in California from adopting state-mandated plans.[10] However, no study has been made to determine whether the quality of those plans has suffered because of budget cutbacks.

To avoid making substantial cutbacks, many agencies are charging higher fees, such as fees for plan and zoning amendments, to offset costs of current planning. According to an article in the *Cal-Tax Research Bulletin,* over 30 percent of all California Cities,[11] and over half of all counties,[12] have increased planning and development fees.

Some agencies are seeking more than 100 percent fee recovery to pay for the costs of long-range planning. Cities have raised zoning amendment fees by as much as 200 percent.[13] One issue that will arise in states with TELS is: Can fees be used to offset the costs of long-range planning? If the courts or the state legislatures say "no," then it is possible that planning agencies will try to combine plans and implementing regulations into single ordinances. This would make it difficult to put separate price tags on the planning and the implementing portions of the ordinance. Thus, planners would argue that costs for both portions could be recovered by fees. In California, the costs of specific plans, which are planning and regulatory devices, can be offset by fees.

The Impact of TELS on Development

Because of TELS and the general push for belt tightening, the movement for regulatory simplication has reached new proportions. Developers have always maintained that land use regulations drive up housing costs. Now there is a second reason for streamlining regulations—local government administrators are finding they must develop means of staying within their own budgets.[14]

Complicated regulatory procedures mean delay and, therefore, increased costs for the developers. Developers in markets where the demand for housing is high will be more likely to pass on costs.[15] The opposite is true of developers where the market is "soft."[16] The American Planning Association study on regulatory simplification concludes that additional costs are almost always passed on to consumers in the form of increased housing prices.[17] A recent study of the housing industry in the Houston area, for example, points out that a five and one-half month increase in processing time costs the homebuyer a minimum of $560 to $840 per lot.[18]

Linked to delay, and often even more of a problem, is uncertainty. Like all private investors, the developer makes a "go/no-go" decision based on a projection of a minimum acceptable return.[19] In a recent editorial written on behalf of homebuilders, the writer stated that "traditionally the rewards have been adequate to justify the risk." But when a builder has his front money at risk not for nine or ten months but for two or three years, the traditional rewards simply do not compensate . . . ."[20]

Developers also point out that the regulatory process may, in some cases, have an anticompetitive effect. In some particularly restrictive areas, developers say they are competing for permits, not homebuyers. Once they have obtained official approvals, there is relatively little competition for the consumers' dollars.[21] Further, the difficulty of mastering the ins and outs of the local system may discourage entry by new firms.[22] Finally, some smaller firms claim they are being driven out of the market, since they simply cannot compete with larger firms. The larger firms have—to put it colloquially—"patient money" (which are reserves that can be tied up in long-term land inventories).[23] Moreover, they can wait out two-year approval periods and they can afford expensive, topnotch consultants and attorneys.

The exact cost of regulatory procedures is not known. But it is commonly agreed that complicated regulations are among the many factors that drive up housing costs. As a result, planning agencies around the country are devising ways to simplify their regulations without sacrificing the quality of development.

One way to make the regulatory process more efficient is to clarify the groundrules for decision making. For example, comprehensive plans can be drafted to provide practical guidelines for development. Opponents of planning say that plans and the requirement that regulations be consistent with them are just one more step in an already complicated process of land use regulation and development.[24]

However, the planning process can reduce uncertainty and delay. If the plan is drafted with specificity and implemented accordingly, developers and citizens alike will be able to predict where development will occur. Moreover, additional delay need not result. In states where regulations must be consistent with plans, a developer who obtains a plan amendment will usually then be granted a zoning amendment. Thus, although two hearings are required (one for a plan amendment and one for a zoning amendment), the major battle will be fought at the front end.[25]

How essential is planning to effective and efficient regulation? To what degree are bottlenecks in the review process symptomatic of poor planning? It is safe to state that, although a solid comprehensive plan is no guarantee of a smooth review process, the absence of an up-to-date plan can be an invitation to even worse problems.

Planning for TELS and Public Service Austerity

Local governments, when faced with TELS, may cut back on public services. Those municipalities that attempt to save money by limiting services in poor and minority neighborhoods may find themselves in court. Local governments have a constitutional obligation to provide comparable services throughout their jurisdiction. That duty extends not only to the provision of new services, but also to the remedying of past discriminatory practices.

To date, plaintiffs have won several reported equalization of services suits.[26] Because we live in times of austerity, this type of litigation will become more prevalent. In a suit recently filed against the Chicago Park District, the plaintiffs alleged that the Park District discriminates on the basis of race when it allocates facilities, personnel, and programs among city parks.[27] And, in Goldsboro, North Carolina, a group of black residents also has filed suit during the last year. The group alleges that the city, its mayor, and councilpersons have not provided equal services. The services under consideration are street paving and lighting, sewage and drainage facilities, fire protection, and parks.[28]

Equalization of service suits have been brought under the Civil Rights Act of 1871 (42 U.S.C. Sec. 1983), the equal protection clause of the Fourteenth Amendment, and Title VI of the Civil Rights Acts of 1964. The principal argument usually is that the city and its officials denied black residents their right to equal protection. The theory used is that qualitative and quantitative inequality in the provision of municipal services is a manifestation of racial discrimination. The suits generally have been class actions, brought in federal district court. The defenses offered by the city may include special geographic or topographic problems that allegedly exist in the blighted area, special traffic patterns, and long-range planning considerations. (For example, some city planners hav adopted triage programs, whereby certain neighborhoods will be denied new services because it is not cost-efficient to preserve those areas).[29] Where improvements are funded by special assessment, cities also have argued that only persons who can afford to pay must be provided with services.

In *Hawkins v. Shaw*[30] disadvantaged black citizens brought a class action arguing that the town mayor and five aldermen provided certain services in a racially discriminatory manner. The services to be provided included street paving and lighting, sanitary sewers, surface water drainage, water mains, and fire hydrants. The services were financed by ad valorem taxes and the sale of water and electricity to town residents.

The plaintiffs brought the suit under Sec. 1983. Since they were requesting injunctive relief, not damages, the suit could be brought against the city as well as its officials. (Only recently has the Supreme Court ruled that a Sec. 1983 action for damages can be brought against local governments.)[31] Basically, the plaintiffs argued that there was a history of disparity in the services the town provided to white and black neighborhoods.

First, the plaintiffs argued that the housing was segregated along racial lines. Second, they claimed that the quality and quantity of services the town provided to black and white residents was grossly disproportionate.

The plaintiffs carefully documented their case. They showed that blacks occupied 97 percent of all housing facing unpaved streets. Whites occupied the remaining 3 percent. The city, however, did not dispute the statistical evidence. Unbelievably enough, the city maintained that the residents historically had little or no interest in modern improvements. The city argued that, when it did provide services, it has exercised its best business judgment regarding location.

The trial court agreed with the city.[32] The court applied a traditional standard of review and found there was no *de facto* racial discrimination. But the Fifth Circuit reversed, stating that the evidence showed a "substantial qualitative and quantitative inequity in the level and nature of services accorded white and black neighborhoods."[33]

The appellate court applied a more stringent standard of review, requiring the city to show a compelling interest. However, the city was unable to do so. The city argued that traffic usage, need, and width constituted a compelling state interest sufficient to overcome a charge of race discrimination in the paving of streets. But the court did not buy these arguments, since the city had not applied these criteria equally in black and white areas.

The city also pointed out that it had extended sanitary sewers to new areas in a nondiscriminatory manner. But this was not constitutionally sufficient, the court said, since the effect of such a policy was to "freeze in" the results of past discrimination.

Because this case was handed down four years before the Supreme Court's decision in *Washington v. Davis,*[34] the plaintiffs did not have to prove motive. Instead, they only had to show that the city's actions had a disparate impact on black and white citizens.

When the court fashioned a remedy, it took into account what it considered to be the appropriate balance between federal and state relations. The town had to submit a plan, outlining an equalization of services program. The trial court would use, as its yardstick for review, the quality and quantity of services in the white section of town. A comparison would then be made between services in the black and white neighborhoods. On rehearing, the Fifth Circuit affirmed its order.[35]

Plaintiffs are now using Title VI as a fall-back position, the reason they are doing this is that a showing of motive must be made in equal protection cases. Under Title VI, on the other hand, there is some authority for the proposition that a showing of motive is not required.[36] However, the U.S. Supreme Court's Decision in *Bakke*[37] makes this authority open to question. Of course, Title VI also requires that the entity involved is receiving federal financial assistance.

The plaintiffs in *Johnson v. City of Arcadia*[38] were the first to successfully bring an equalization of services suit after *Washington v. Davis* (the discriminatory motive case). The suit was brought under Section 1983 (and equal protection), Title VI, and the Federal Revenue Sharing Act. Black citizens brought a class action. They argued that Arcadia had systematically discriminated against black citizens in the provision of services and facilities. The services involved were street paving, parks, recreation, and water facilities. The plaintiffs substantiated their claim with official city minute books, a consultant's study that had been commissioned by the city, and testimony made by an author and a photographer concerning an eight-month investigation they had conducted.

The pattern of proof in a case such as this is critical. Numerous statistics were entered into the record. With respect to street paving, the plaintiffs offered comparative statistics concerning the number of feet of paved streets and the number of households fronting paved streets. Parks and recreational facilities were evaluated in light of quality and access. The underground water system in black and white neighborhoods was looked at in terms of the quality of the system—that is, the ability of the distribution system to deliver at each fire hydrant a specified number of gallons per minute.

The court applied the substantive standards established in *Hawkins v. Shaw*. Basically, the court held that once a municipality elects to provide services, it must provide equal services to the minority community. First, a showing must be made that racially identifiable neighborhoods exist in the municipality. Then, the services in the minority community will be compared with those in the white neighborhoods.

The plaintiffs, the court ruled, met the intent test by showing a statistical pattern of unequal service distribution and a history of discrimination. The court upheld the plaintiffs' claim and ordered the parties to design an equalization of services plan. The court then enjoined the city from initiating any major service or improvement program in the white community until court-ordered services for the black community were completed. Moreover, the city had to adhere to the construction, maintenance, and finance schedules approved by the court. Federal revenue-sharing funds were to be paid out according to a schedule developed by the parties and approved by the court. The city was also required to place in an escrow account some federal revenue-sharing money to guarantee construction of the facilities and performance of the services outlined in the order.

What lessons can be learned from the early case–*Hawkins v. Shaw* and the later, motive case–*Johnson v. City of Arcadia?* At least three points should be made. First, comparable services must be provided to black and white communities. Second, equalization of service suits can be brought successfully. And third, equal protection is the preferable theory for relief. I make this point, even though discriminatory motive must be shown. Title VI is less advantageous for several reasons. The scope of relief is more narrow and the method of proof is more difficult. Furthermore, the principle reason for bringing a Title VI action may no longer be applicable. Because of *Bakke,* a showing of discriminatory motive may now be required.

To sum up: TELS will probably have an adverse effect on planning staffs and on public services. Perhaps there will be at least one positive result–maybe the push for regulatory simplification will improve the development process.

Notes

1. Gans, "Planning for Declining and Poor Cities," 41 *Journal of the American Institute of Planners* 305 (1975).
2. See, *e.g.*, Healy, R. and J. Rosenberg, *Land Use and the States,* 1979, 2d Ed.
3. Del Pero and Detwiler, "California's Local Planning Departments Still Strong After Proposition 13," Local Government Unit, Governor's Office of Planning and Research (unpublished paper).
4. *Id.*, p. 3, table II.
5. "How Planners are Coping," *Planning,* September 1978, p. 14.
6. *Id.*, p. 15.
7. *Id.*, p. 16.
8. *Id.*, p. 14.
9. Del Pero and Detwiler, *supra.,* note 3.
10. *Id.*, p. 5.
11. *Cal-Tax Research Bulletin,* Local Government Profile, Nov. 1978.
12. *Id.*
13. "Building Fees Hiked Following Prop. 13" *Los Angeles Times,* July 23, 1978, pt. VIII, p. 23.
14. See draft, APA Study, "Simplifying Development Regulation: A Guidebook for local Governments," March, 1980, HUD Grant No. H-2996.
15. Gruen, Gruen and Associates, *Effects of Regulation on Housing: Two Case Studies,* Urban Land Institute, 1977.

16. *Id.*
17. Draft, APA Study, *Simplifying Development Regulation: A Guidebook for Local Governments,* pp. 8-9.
18. *Id.*
19. *Id.*
20. *Id.*
21. Eury, "Technical Report: The Delay Costs of Government Regulations in Houston Housing Market." Rice Center for Community Design and Research, May, 1978.
22. Draft, APA study, *supra.,* p. 10.
23. *Id.*
24. Netter and Vraniole, *Linking Plans and Regulations: Local Responses to Consistency Laws in California and Florida,* Planning Advisory Service, Report No. 363, American Planning Association, 1981.
25. *Id.*
26. See, *e.g.*, Hawkins v. Town of Shaw, 437 F.2d 1280 (5th Cir. 1971), *aff'd on rehearing en banc,* 461 F.2d 1171 (5th Cir. 1972); Johnson v. City of Arcadia, 450 F. Suppl. 1363 (N.D. Fla. 1978).
27. *Midwest Community Council v. Chicago Park District,* amended complaint in the United States District Court for the Northern District of Illinois, Eastern Division, No. 79C 3187.
28. *Jones v. City of Goldsboro,* complaint in the United States District Court for the Eastern District of North Carolina, No. 79-14G-CIV-8.
29. Gans, b. 307.
30. 437 F.2d 1280 (5th Cir. 1971) *aff'd on rehearing en banc,* 461 F.2d 1171 (5th Cir. 1972).
31. *Monell v. Dept. of Social Services,* 436 U.S. 658 (1978).
32. 303 F. Supp. 1162 (N.D. Miss. 1969).
33. 437 F.2d at 1288.
34. 426 U.S. 229 (1976).
35. 461 F.2d 1171 (5th Cir. 1972).
36. *Lau v. Nichols,* 414 U.S. 563, 568 (1974).
37. *Regents of the University of California v. Bakke,* 438 U.S. 265 (1978).
38. 450 F. Supp. 1363 (N.D. Fla. 1978).